This book is to be returned on
or before the date stamped below

The completion of the European Community's single market programme will stimulate the European economy and affect the rest of the world principally through its effects on trade among EC member states and on the Community's external trade. Although there has been much discussion of the effects of '1992' on economic welfare, there has been relatively little detailed analysis of the trade issues involved. This volume offers a major reappraisal of the effect of completing the EC's single market programme on trade among EC member states and also on the Community's external trade. Individual chapters assess the effects of '1992' on EC and world trade and welfare, and analyse its effects on competition if transport costs and taste differences remain after completing the internal market. Detailed case studies show that integration has complex effects on trade flows and prices and stress the importance of devising a satisfactory international trade policy for the completed market. Other chapters estimate the elasticities of demand for imports within the EC and examine the effects of industrial policy.

Trade flows and trade policy after '1992'

Centre for Economic Policy Research

Executive Committee

Chairman
Anthony Loehnis

Vice-Chairman
Adam Ridley

Giorgio Basevi
Honor Chapman
Guillermo de la Dehesa
Sheila Drew Smith
Jacob A. Frenkel
Sarah Hogg

Otmar Issing
Mervyn King
Peter Middleton
Mario Sarcinelli
Alasdair Smith

Officers

Director
Richard Portes

Deputy Director
Stephen Yeo

Director of Finance and Research Administration
Wendy Thompson

19 May 1992

Trade flows and trade policy after '1992'

Edited by

L. ALAN WINTERS

Published by the Press Syndicate of the University of Cambridge
The Pitt Building, Trumpington Street, Cambridge CB2 1RP
40 West 20th Street, New York, NY 10011-4211, USA
10 Stamford Road, Oakleigh, Victoria 3166, Australia

First published 1992

Printed in Great Britain by Bell and Bain Ltd., Glasgow

A catalogue record for this book is available from the British Library

Library of Congress cataloguing in publication data

Trade flows and trade policy after '1992' / edited by L. Alan Winters.
     p.   cm.
Includes index.
ISBN 0 521 44020 3 (hc)
1. European Economic Community countries – Commercial policy – Congresses.
2. European Economic Community countries – Commercial policy – Econometric
models – Congresses.
3. Europe 1992 – Congresses.
I. Winters, L. Alan.
HF1532.5.T73   1992
382'.3'094 – dc20   92–27968   CIP

ISBN 0 521 44020 3   hardback

CE

Contents

Figures

Tables

xiv

Preface

This volume contains the proceedings of the Conference 'Trade Flows and Trade Policy After "1992"' held at the Institut National de la Statistique et des Etudes Economiques (INSEE), Paris, on 16–18 January 1992.

The conference represented the final output of the CEPR research programme 'Completing the European Internal Market: The Consequences of "1992" for International Trade', which was supported by the Commission of the European Communities' Stimulation Programme in Economic Science, the UK Department of Trade and Industry and the Foreign and Commonwealth Office. Individual projects on the programme also received support from the Alfred P. Sloan Foundation, the British Council, the Norwegian Research Councils for Applied Social Science Research (NORAS), Science and Humanities (NAVF) and Science and Technology (NTNF), the School for Accounting, Banking and Economics at The University of Wales, Bangor, the School of Social Science at Birmingham University, the Southampton University Management School, the UK Department of Trade and Industry and the UK ESRC (grants no. R000231763 and R00023 1932). CEPR is grateful to all these organisations.

The timely production of the volume has been possible only with the unstinting support of David Guthrie and Kate Millward of the CEPR and Barbara Docherty as Production Editor. I should like to record my pleasure at working with them. I am also grateful to Jennifer Jones of CEPR for her help in organising the conference and to Michel Glaude of INSEE for the latter's excellent hospitality. Paul Brenton and Cillian Ryan acted as rapporteurs at the conference and, with Michael Gasiorek, at the preceding research workshops. I am grateful to them for their hard work, which has made editing the volume so much easier. Finally I am grateful to the participants of the conference and its precursor meetings, whose stimulating comments and contributions have generated so much interesting work.

The programme behind this volume has run for two and a half years. I should like to pay tribute to the support I have received as director from the staff at CEPR, especially Richard Portes, Stephen Yeo, Wendy Thompson and Peter Johns, from my colleagues in Bangor and Birmingham, especially Sue James and Maureen Hyde, from my family, and finally from the researchers on the programme.

At the conception of this project in 1988 most economists felt some doubt about whether '1992' would actually be fully and successfully implemented, but were confident of their own ability to analyse and understand it. In the event, the majority of the policies entailed in '1992' have been put into place in one form or another, but the economics profession has uncovered ever more subtleties and caveats in the analysis of economic integration. Hence while there remains a continuing need for policy analysis and discussion of the efficient implementation of existing legislation, there has also emerged a new academic agenda in these areas. This spreads beyond '1992' to issues such as the enlargement of the European Communities; relations with, and the prospective recovery in, Eastern Europe; and proposals for regional integration schemes throughout the world. CEPR's International Trade programme will remain at the forefront of research in these areas, and is pleased to offer the present volume as a contribution to the continuing debate.

L. Alan Winters   May 1992
University of Birmingham and CEPR

List of conference participants

Kym Anderson *GATT and CEPR*
Richard Baldwin *Institut Universitaire des Hautes Etudes Internationales, Genève, and CEPR*
Claude Bismut *Commissariat Géneral du Plan*
Anton Brender *Centre d'Etudes Prospectives et d'Informations Internationales, Paris*
Paul Brenton *University of Birmingham*
Jean-Michel Charpin *Banque Nationale de Paris*
Jacques le Cacheux *Observatoire Français des Conjonctures Economiques, Paris*
Neil Chrimes *Foreign and Commonwealth Office, London*
Cristina Corado *Universidade Nova de Lisboa*
Olivier Cortes *Centre d'Etudes Prospectives et d'Informations Internationales, Paris*
Henry Ergas *OECD*
Riccardo Faini *Università degli Studi di Brescia and CEPR*
Harry Flam *Institute for International Economic Studies, Stockholm*
Michael Gasiorek *University of Sussex*
Konstantine Gatsios *Fitzwilliam College, Cambridge, and CEPR*
Michel Glaude *INSEE*
Ian Goldin *OECD Development Centre*
Jan Haaland *Norwegian School of Economics and Business Administration, Bergen*
Peter Johns *CEPR*
Pierre Joly *INSEE*
Larry Karp *University of Southampton and CEPR*
Jacob Kol *Erasmus Universeit Rotterdam*
Elizabeth Kremp *Centre d'Etudes Prospectives et d'Informations Internationales, Paris*

Gernot Klepper *Institut für Weltwirtschaft, Kiel, and CEPR*
Philippe Lefournier *L'Expansion*
Edmond Lisle *Conseil National de la Recherche Scientifique, Paris*
Christopher Moir *UK Department of Trade and Industry*
Damien Neven *Université de Liège and CEPR*
Joaquim Oliveira-Martins *OECD*
Sébastian Paris-Horvitz *Centre d'Etudes Prospectives et d'Informations Internationales, Paris*
Jeffrey Perloff *University of California at Berkeley*
Richard Portes *CEPR and Birkbeck College, London*
Salvano Presa *Commission of the European Communities*
Patrick Rey *ENSAE, Paris, and CEPR*
Lars-Hendrik Röller *INSEAD*
Cillian Ryan *University of Birmingham*
Joël Toujas-Bernate *INSEE*
Anthony J. Venables *University of Southampton and CEPR*
L. Alan Winters *University of Birmingham and CEPR*
Ian Wooton *University of Western Ontario*

Part One
Introduction

1 European trade and welfare after '1992'

L. ALAN WINTERS

1 Introduction

International commerce is the medium through which completing the European internal market ('1992' is a convenient shorthand) will have its main effects. The principal stimulus towards efficiency within the European Communities (EC) is the increased competition induced by freer intra-EC trade, while the principal effects on third countries operate through extra-EC trade or its closely related cousin international factor mobility.

This volume presents some of the results of a major research programme undertaken by Research Fellows and Affiliates of the Centre for Economic Policy Research during the period 1989–92. Its aim was to quantify and assess the effects of '1992' on international trade and economic welfare.[1] Welfare has attracted huge amounts of comment and analysis, but trade has not, to date, received very thorough treatment. It is, however, the defining characteristic of this volume: every chapter is concerned either with Europe's post-'1992' international trade – both in the EC and between the EC and other countries – or with its trade policy. This introductory chapter places the research in its context and summarises the contributions that follow below. It is not a full survey of the literature on '1992', but is rather a selective sketch of the development of the quantitative analysis of the effects of '1992' on international trade and their welfare consequences.

The major contribution to estimating the effects of '1992' was the EC's own study, CEC (1988a). This huge undertaking, which combined many separate sectoral and subject studies, was a great feat of applied economics in terms of its coverage and innovative applications; it was, however, undertaken very rapidly and by a wide range of academic researchers and consultancy companies, and perhaps as a result left a number of issues unresolved. Much of the subsequent literature has

3

sought either to comment on or to extend the CEC benchmark results, but recently new academic work tackling fundamental issues from scratch has begun to appear – not least in this volume and its predecessor, Winters and Venables (1991). This chapter reflects this intellectual history: it starts with a discussion of CEC (1988a), notes some of the work of its commentators, explores some more recent themes, and finally offers a brief summary of the policy conclusions of the research.

2   The 'official' estimates

CEC (1988a) and its associated 16 volumes of research reports – *Research on The Cost of Non-Europe: Basic Findings* – provided a hugely detailed study of economic integration. The study was strictly designed to assess the economic costs imposed by the incompleteness of integration within the EC rather than to predict the effects of the '1992' programme *per se*; hence it ignored any failures of implementation in the latter. In fact its results may be treated as conditional predictions, a convention that we follow both here and in the chapters below, where we generally assume that '1992' takes the form of perfect integration and harmonisation.

2.1   Price effects

It would be superfluous to describe the '1992' process in a volume such as this – see, for example, Pelkmans and Winters (1988) or Owen and Dynes (1990) – but for analytical purposes we need to identify two broad sets of measures.

The first component of '1992' is intended to remove the barriers to trade between member states of the EC (intra-EC trade). These barriers have been enumerated elsewhere – e.g. CEC (1988a) and Pelkmans and Winters (1988) – but for our purposes three dimensions are important. First, whether the current barriers are revenue-raising (e.g. tariffs and quantitative restrictions, which create rents) or resource-using (e.g. queueing or completing paperwork): the returns to abolishing the latter are potentially much greater. Second, we should distinguish between barriers that operate on prices or costs (e.g. excessive product testing requirements) and those that operate on quantities (e.g. national import restrictions or public purchasing restrictions): these require different analytical approaches, especially if there is uncertainty about the parameters of economic behaviour (see p. 279 below). Finally, we need to know whether the removal/reduction of barriers is restricted primarily to intra-EC trade or affects all EC imports nearly equally. Examples of the former group include the simplification of documentation on intra-EC trade, the elimination of customs' formalities on internal borders and the extension of public purchasing to all EC firms. Such reforms increase the competitiveness of EC countries' imports from their partners relative to both domestic supplies and non-partner imports. Thus they potentially generate both trade creation (the replacement of domestic output by cheaper partner suppliers) and trade diversion (the replacement of extra-EC imports by dearer intra-EC ones). Reductions in barriers common to imports from all sources, such as the harmonisation of standards and testing procedures, on the other hand, benefit imports from all sources relative to domestic supplies and result only in trade creation. Unfortunately, even now, the relative importance of these two sets of barriers is unclear.

The second component of '1992' is a series of internal measures designed to improve the competitiveness of EC firms – e.g. labour and capital mobility, a more vigorous competition policy and the stimulation of R&D. Since these benefit EC firms relative to non-EC firms, they potentially cause both trade diversion and trade suppression (the elimination of imports by domestic supplies). Again, however, it has proved hard to quantify these effects relative to those of the previous paragraph. Hence the overall impact of '1992' on the relative prices of domestic supplies, intra-EC imports and extra-EC imports remains somewhat uncertain. It represents an important area for detailed future research.

Once one has obtained an estimate of the changes in relative price that '1992' causes, the traditional tools of customs union theory – Viner's (1950) concepts of trade creation and trade diversion – may be applied. These assume perfectly competitive markets and, implicitly because they consider only one market at a time, internationally segmented markets. The former assumption ensures that price equals marginal costs, so that the competitiveness of imports can change only by the extent that barriers are reduced, while the latter implies that there are virtually no spillovers from one EC market to another. For most commodities the barriers to intra-EC trade are low – perhaps 2 per cent of the gross value of trade – so the traditional analysis would suggest only a slight reorientation of EC trade in response to '1992'. This is particularly true of trade diversion, given that the homogeneous primary commodities such as agricultural products or coal, for which one might expect the highest elasticities of substitution between suppliers and hence the greatest diversion, will continue to be subject to policies which restrict competition between EC and non-EC producers. Thus the reduction of waiting times at internal borders will add little to the existing trade diversion induced by the Common Agricultural Policy.

One case in which intra-EC trade restrictions are important is public procurement. This is strongly biased in favour of national firms despite the existence of both EC directives and a GATT Code requiring some openness. The competitive model is not appropriate for many such industries, but the evident degree of distortion is such that even this approach would predict significant changes in trade patterns.[2] However, unless the Uruguay Round induces a major global liberalisation, '1992' will result in little additional trade diversion, simply because there is almost no third-country trade to divert. On the other hand '1992' appears to have stimulated foreign direct investment inflows in public procurement industries. Several motives might exist for such inflows but prominent among them, especially for heavy engineering firms, is the desire for a local presence in order to qualify for public contracts.

The modesty of the traditional effects, even allowing for public procurement, is clear from the first of CEC's (1988a) four stages of quantification. These are presented in detail for 65 industries in Cawley and Davenport (1988). Although Cawley and Davenport allow the costs of extra-EC, as well as intra-EC, imports to fall, they find trade diversion for every good. The total, however, is equivalent to only about 2.5 per cent of final goods' imports, or ECU 8 billion at 1985 prices and quantities; the associated trade creation is around 4 per cent, or ECU 8 billion,[3] and the net effect on EC welfare is also around ECU 8 billion. In fact, given Smith and Venables' (1991) analysis of trade shares in imperfectly competitive industries, and the preliminary results reported by Brenton and Winters in Chapter 10 below, I suspect that even CEC's modest trade diversion effects may be over-estimated.

CEC's stage 2 – also described in Cawley and Davenport (1988) – considers the effects of eliminating EC internal cost-increasing restrictions – e.g. excessive regulation and fragmented standards. The main effects are felt through changes in the efficiency of the financial and other services' sectors, but significant gains also originate in industrial sectors. In addition to the direct resource savings from improved efficiency in these sectors, important indirect effects arise from the reductions in costs in the industries they supply. The net effect on welfare is estimated by CEC (1988a) to be between ECU 57 billion and 71 billion, while in terms of international trade, extra-EC imports fall by approximately a further 7.5 per cent.[4]

CEC assumes that the efficiency improvements in stage 2 are both restricted to EC suppliers and uniformly distributed across them, for they consider neither reductions in third-country costs of supply, nor any resulting trade creation or suppression within the EC. This is clearly over-simplified, for as their own research shows, and as confirmed by Ryan in Chapter 4 below, the implied changes in the costs of banking services, for instance, vary strongly across member states. This suggests – and may require for its beneficial effects – a substantial reorientation of banking trade within the EC. Moreover, because there is currently such a high degree of home market bias in the supply of such services – regulation, transactions and control costs are all lower when banks are operating in their home markets – different changes in banking costs will lead to different changes in the costs and/or profit margins of downstream producers. These in turn will generate a new round of relative price changes and hence of 'indirect' trade effects throughout the EC economy.

The estimated benefits and trade effects of regulatory reform are considerably greater than those of removing trade barriers. This is mainly because, while trade barriers directly affect only the 14 per cent of total output that is traded within the EC, production regulations affect all output within the relevant sectors.

The combination of CEC's stages 1 and 2 implies reductions in extra-EC imports of approximately 10 per cent, and CEC suggests that this will turn the terms of trade against extra-EC suppliers by perhaps half of 1 per cent. This reflects their assumption that in most markets the EC is a small purchaser facing almost constant import prices. If this is the case, the traditional competitive model would predict that the costs to the rest of the world of any '1992'-induced trade diversion would be very low: a nearly horizontal supply curve implies that the factors of production released by the fall in exports to the EC can be switched to other markets or other activities with almost no loss of productivity.

2.2 Imperfect competition

While the traditional competitive/segmented markets approach may suggest significant effects in particular sectors, and while eliminating cost-increasing restrictions might bring significant welfare benefits as the costs of intra-marginal trade are reduced, they would hardly justify the high hopes that were expressed for '1992'. To do that one needs a broader paradigm.

Intellectually the most interesting element of the CEC (1988a) study is the estimation of the effects of increased competition and market integration in imperfectly competitive markets, based on work by Smith and Venables (1988a, 1988b). Working with a combination of Brander and Krugman's (1983) reciprocal dumping model of international trade and the demand for variety models of Krugman (1979), Smith and Venables implement a model in which reducing intra-EC trade barriers increases competition in EC markets; this, in turn, reduces profit margins, increases intra-EC market shares and, because there are fixed costs, reduces EC average costs. If they do not also benefit significantly from the reduction in barriers, extra-EC suppliers will find their market shares eroded – i.e. there will be something akin to trade diversion – and they might also face increased competition elsewhere in the world as the EC's costs fall.

Smith and Venables study each of 10 industries in partial equilibrium, calibrating their model of multi-country imperfect competition to 1982 data. They recognise not only the endogeneity of prices, but also that of the numbers of firms and of varieties produced by each firm. They conduct exercises variously with fixed or variable numbers of firms and with Cournot or Bertrand competition. If EC markets remain segmented after '1992' – i.e. if firms can continue to price independently in each EC market – the extra competition entailed in reducing trade costs within the EC increases intra-EC trade and EC exports and reduces extra EC-imports. Details vary according to industry structure, but representative of Smith and Venables' 10 sample industries is office machinery: with Cournot oligopoly and fixed industry size, a reduction in barriers equivalent to 2.5 per cent of the gross value of trade generates changes of 45 per cent, 6 per cent and − 25 per cent in intra-EC imports, EC exports and extra-EC imports respectively. The authors correctly caution against paying regard to the precise magnitudes, but the trade effects here are plainly large.

In a second set of exercises Smith and Venables examine 'complete market integration', in which producers are obliged to charge the same factory gate prices to all EC buyers. Such integration is a clearly implied objective of '1992' with its attempts to break down market segmentation by policies such as the effective abolition of Article 115 (which prevents the free movement of *third-country* goods between EC member states), and using competition policy to attack observed price differentials between markets.

Product differentiation means that firms have varying degrees of market power in each of their markets and in simple models of oligopoly these are related to their market shares. Firms tend to command large shares of their home markets, either because of trade barriers or because taste biases favour them, and smaller shares of exports markets; hence their returns (factory-gate prices) are higher for home sales than for exports. This is the reciprocal dumping aspect of the model. Full integration prevents such price discrimination, with the result (in this model, but see p. 19 below) that domestic prices fall, domestic sales increase, export prices rise within the EC, and both intra-EC and extra-EC imports fall. The net effect is beneficial to consumers and serves further to improve EC relative to non-EC competitiveness. In fact in Smith and Venables' Cournot integrated market experiment with variable industry size, extra-EC imports fall by more than one-third in half the cases.

CEC (1988a) extrapolates from Smith and Venables' 10 industries to the whole EC economy by calculating the ratios of the welfare gains from their full integration runs to those of the static ('direct' – stages 1 and 2) exercise above.[5] These ratios vary from unity for unconcentrated industries with few economies of scale to 6 for concentrated scale-intensive industries. Then, classifying all industries according to scale and concentration, CEC applies the appropriate multiplier to the static welfare estimates. This generates welfare benefits to '1992' of over ECU 60 billion, but its consequences for international trade are unreported. They must, however, be significant: the unweighted average of the ratio of Smith and Venables' change in extra-EC imports to the corresponding static effects in Cawley and Davenport (1988) is approximately 3 in the integrated markets scenario.

CEC also attempts to disaggregate these 'indirect' effects into competitive and economies of scale components. The former, which stem from the effects of '1992' on profit margins and firm numbers, are calculated from the differences between Smith and Venables' integrated/variable-industry-size runs and their segmented/fixed-industry-size runs. Since the latter generate only small effects, the bulk of Smith and Venables' welfare gains are attributed to increased competition. CEC then adds to these a separate, much larger, and conceptually quite different estimate of the economies of scale effects based on Schwalbach (1988). This adds further welfare gains to the overall estimate, raising them to around ECU 180 billion or 6 per cent of GDP. Again the trade effects of this modification are unreported, but if the effects are additional to Smith and Venables' we should expect further induced changes in trade patterns.

No reliance can be placed on the precise sizes of the trade effects in this exercise, especially those of changes in extra-EC imports and EC exports because, in addition to all the usual problems with calibrated models, the Rest of the World is not modelled explicitly. Nevertheless, one cannot avoid concluding that the changes in these trade flows have been underestimated by CEC (1988a). Pure trade diversion may have been overstated in stage 1, but the implications of the remainder of their exercise for third-countries' trade must make the final effects larger than those reported by CEC.

3   Refining the estimates

3.1   Third-country effects

CEC (1988a) provides a valuable benchmark for much subsequent research and comment, not least because its information base is so much greater than that available to other studies. Hence other researchers have sought both to refine and to extend elements of the CEC study – for instance, to look more closely at particular third-country effects or at the distribution of gains among member states. In most cases these studies have adopted one part or other of the CEC methodology and broadly speaking they have tended to confirm the magnitudes suggested by CEC. Thus, for example, Norman (1989) considers the effects of '1992' on the EFTA pharmaceuticals' and motor vehicles' sectors. He finds significant losses of sales for Norway and Sweden if '1992' entails full integration – respectively 9 per cent and 6 per cent in pharmaceuticals and 0 per cent and 9 per cent in vehicles. The last increases to 12 per cent if increased efficiency reduces EC costs by just 1 per cent.

Similarly Smith's (1989) estimates for vehicles are 'in line with' Smith and Venables' and suggest modest reductions in EC imports, the Japanese market share falling from 9.2 per cent to 8.8 per cent. In this market, however, the critical issue is not barriers to intra-EC trade, but the treatment of restrictions against Japan after '1992'. If the current national VERs were abolished Japan would double or treble its market share (depending on its investment response). If national restrictions were replaced by an EC-wide VER fixed at the initial market share, neither trade nor EC welfare would change much, but Japan would still gain because she could redirect exports to the high-priced French and Italian markets. Actual policy for vehicles has now been decided, and is intended to evolve from continued, if somewhat looser, national restrictions in 1993 to free trade by 1999.

Davenport and Page (1991) consider the effects of '1992' on developing countries. In addition to a number of sectoral studies they provide a broad look at trade patterns based largely on Cawley and Davenport's (1988) traditional partial equilibrium modelling. To this they add an additional stimulus to trade based on the growth that '1992' will generate for the EC economy – see p. 13 below. They conclude that developing countries have neither much to fear nor much to gain from '1992' provided that the EC's trade policy regime is not affected: total exports from developing countries might increase by around 3 per cent.

Norman (1989, 1991) considers the effects of the Scandinavian EFTA countries in general. He suggests that they are likely to be quite significant because the EC is such an important trading partner. In particular, '1992' will tend to shift Scandinavian 'comparative advantage' within the goods' sector back towards simple forest and metal products; this is because the improvements in EC efficiency in more sophisticated goods cannot be matched in EFTA since, with relatively open borders in these sectors, they are already relatively efficient. He notes, however, strong benefits to

Scandinavian countries' membership of the EC, because in services and agriculture they have small, protected and concentrated industry structures. He also predicts some efficiency gains in Scandinavian industry as a result of joining – presumably because of the reduction in the real costs of trade with EC members. Finally, Norman observes that the pressures for Norway and Finland to seek membership of the EC will depend strongly on whether Sweden, their other major trading partner, does so.

Hufbauer (1990) provides an overview of the effects on the USA, built up from sectoral studies and consideration of the external implications of CEC (1988a). He concludes that in the absence of a policy shift towards protection the USA will be a mild gainer from '1992'.

3.2   Distributional effects

The geographical distribution of the gains from '1992' within the EC is clearly of great interest to individual member states, but was held to lie outside the brief of the original CEC (1988a) analysis. This was undoubtedly wise from a political point of view – for the matter is potentially very divisive – but the issue could not be evaded indefinitely. CEC (1990) offers a partial analysis based on the identification of sectors that are 'sensitive' to '1992' followed by national analyses of competitiveness in these sectors. The definition of 'sensitivity' is based on the concepts of CEC (1988a), industries being held to be sensitive if they face significant intra-EC trade barriers, have large intra-EC price dispersions, and offer large scope for economies of scale. However, the final analysis was not very satisfactory, for it was based on trade patterns and behaviour up to the late 1980s, and could take account of neither the additional flexibility that '1992' was hoped to induce nor the interactions between sectors.

A broader-brush, but more satisfying, approach to internal distributional issues was that of Neven (1990). By analysing labour costs across the EC, Neven concludes that there is little currently unexploited comparative advantage between the Northern EC members but plenty of scope for increased labour-intensive exports from the Southern members. If he is correct and comparative advantage is the relevant determinant of intra-EC commerce, then Smith and Venables' results are exaggerated because the scope for increased intra-EC-North trade will be less than they suppose. Such a view also implies that '1992' will have a relatively smaller effect on third-country producers of sophisticated goods – e.g. Japan and the USA – and a relatively greater one on exporters of labour-intensive goods – developing countries. The analytical distinction between Neven and Smith and Venables is stark – see Norman (1991); but in truth we have so little feel for the relative importance of factor endowments and imperfect competition in EC trade, or their interactions, that it is currently impossible to arbitrate properly between the two approaches.

A third approach to the geographical dimension of '1992' – ripe for further research – is Krugman's (1991) economic geography. Krugman and Venables (1990) show that variations in the relative importance of factor prices, economies of scale in one production location, and the costs of selling in distant markets (transportation, etc.) can lead industry variously to concentrate in either richer (high-cost) locations, or poorer (low-cost) ones, or not to concentrate at all. Krugman and Venables consider only horizontal product differentiation, but Motta (1990) asks similar questions in the context of vertical differentiation. If the marginal costs of high- and low-quality products are similar – for instance, because quality depends on fixed costs such as R&D – the integrated market can support only a finite number of varieties, and integration will lead to the elimination of some varieties and, probably, firms. The casualties are likely to be low-quality firms, with the result that, although poor country consumers benefit from being able to obtain high-quality goods more cheaply than previously, the loss of profits as those countries' firms fail may be more than their consumer gains.[6]

3.3   The magnitude of the gains

A number of commentators have argued that the CEC (1988a) results are misleading because they ignore or overstate particular economic arguments. Thus Geroski (1989), for example, argues that far too much faith is put in economies of scale as the engine of welfare improvements. EC firms are not, he argues, particularly small relative to the EC market (according to CEC data, most industries would support 20 or more firms at around minimum efficient scale), and taste diversity within the EC would preclude huge production runs even within a fully integrated single market. He has also observed that for managerial reasons, large EC firms do not appear to be particularly efficient – Geroski and Jacquemin (1986). Pelkmans and Winters (1988) and Winters (1988a) also caution against too great an optimism with regard to economies of scale.

Peck (1989) also scorns the CEC estimate of 6 per cent welfare gains on the grounds that CEC (1988a) is overly optimistic in its assumptions and selective in the use of its own detailed studies. He notes that three alternative calculations of the overall gains – summing CEC's sectoral study results, using the business survey results, and plotting the effects of price convergence – all generate smaller estimates. He concedes, however, that all three alternatives have less complete coverage than the modelling exercise, and that dynamic gains may also generate integration, so it is not clear what weight he puts on this observation. Peck also doubts the ability of the EC to handle the political strains of '1992' as the dramatic industrial reorganisations predicted by the models start to occur on the ground. This problem was assumed away by CEC (1988a), but is of immense policy significance. So far the record is satisfactory in this respect, but there is a great need to ensure that neither implicit support for ailing sectors or national champions, nor defensive mergers or tacit collusion among EC firms undermines the pro-competitive effects of '1992'. Competition policy clearly has a key role to play in implementing '1992', see Winters (1988a) and pp. 26–8 below. Peck's own (back of a very small envelope) estimate is that '1992' may generate twice the gains associated with the original creation of the EEC – about 2 per cent of GDP overall.

In a completely different analysis Baldwin (1989 and 1992) argues that because CEC (1988a) ignores the effects of integration on the returns to investment in physical and human capital, it dramatically under-states the welfare effects of '1992'. Recent models of endogenous growth stress the external increasing returns to scale to investment and the dynamic processes of innovation; hence they can adduce benefits additional to the traditional '1992' effects as the latter increase Europe's overall scale and/or innovativeness. There is no consensus about such theory yet, but Baldwin shows that several models could produce substantially higher growth estimates than CEC's. In many models these benefits would spread to the rest of the world in the form of increased European demand and technological spillovers, but in some cases Europe's success would be at the expense of other countries.

These interesting avenues have not yet been much explored, but two studies in the earlier volume from this programme suggest that it would be premature to take the dynamic effects for granted. Ulph (1991) shows that when R&D is modelled explicitly, the changes in EC research policy associated with '1992' – specifically encouraging pre-competitive research joint ventures – could reduce EC innovation and technological competitiveness. Caballero and Lyons (1991) – on whose earlier work Baldwin draws – suggest that while external economies of scale seem to exist, internal economies may well have been over-estimated by CEC and that there is little evidence for inter-country externalities within the EC.

4   Recent advances – a summary of the volume

4.1   General equilibrium analysis

An obvious problem with the CEC (1988a) analysis was its fundamentally partial equilibrium nature. This was addressed elliptically in CEC's macroeconomic exercise which used estimates of certain sectoral effects as productivity shocks in a macroeconomic model. The macro and resource allocation approaches to economic modelling are so disparate, however, that the status of their union must be very suspect. Hence the formal general equilibrium analysis of the resource allocation effects of '1992' was a natural and pressing extension to the early work.

The first and most obvious step is to feed the overall income effect of '1992' back onto the individual components from which it has been derived. Thus, for example, the trade-diverting effects of the preferential removal of trade barriers identified above will be at least partly offset by the import-expanding effects of economic growth. Thus if we accept CEC's estimate of a GDP gain of around 5 per cent and allow an average income elasticity of demand for extra-EC imports of 2, a further 10 per cent of demand is generated, which would just offset the reductions in extra-EC imports identified in CEC's stages 1 and 2.

This sort of argument has been made by Davenport (1990) and Matthews and McAleese (1990), who use it to estimate the effects of '1992' on the developing countries, and by Hufbauer (1990) who applies it to the USA. Matthews and McAleese consider primary products and find that growth is the dominant effect of '1992' on the relevant exporters; Davenport, on the other hand, finds that growth does not offset the diversion of manufactured exports implied by the combination of all stages of the CEC exercise. Hufbauer compares the growth effect only with 'stage 1' diversion and predicts a comfortable net increase in US exports from '1992'. Positively speaking, Davenport's is the relevant comparison, for all stages of the CEC analysis will affect international trade, but in terms of policy Hufbauer's is: the losses of US exports resulting from EC internal regulatory changes and increases in internal competition are not, strictly speaking, trade diversion at all, and hence need not be addressed by compensatory policy.

The more important general equilibrium question is to recognise that factors of production and material inputs are not available to all industries at fixed prices. hence the tendency in partial equilibrium analysis for all industries to expand as a result of '1992' is likely to be mitigated by increases in factor prices. With a fixed endowment of factors one industry's expansion (in terms of inputs) will be another's contraction. This means that '1992' is likely to have more complex effects on international trade flows than partial equilibrium analysis would suggest. If, for example, it favours one set of industries – say, those with economies of scale and imperfect competition – it will stimulate EC net exports in those industries and curtail them in others, and this in turn will affect pattern of specialisation elsewhere in the world.

Two early attempts at general equilibrium modelling of '1992' were Stoeckel, Pearce and Banks (1990) and Haaland (1990). Both papers use traditional competitive general equilibrium models of world trade and shock them with cost and productivity changes derived from CEC (1988a).[7] Haaland assumes productivity improvements of 7 per cent in EC 'hi-tech' industry and 2 per cent in other EC sectors as a result of '1992'. This reduces world hi-tech prices by 4 per cent relative to labour-intensive goods and by 3 per cent relative to capital-intensive goods. It also increases hi-tech output in the EC by 30 per cent, and reduces it by 5–12 per cent in other industrial countries. Absolutely the biggest effects are on Japan whose 'comparative advantage' is switched significantly back towards capital-intensive goods by the boost to the EC hi-tech sectors.[8] EFTA is proportionately the largest loser of hi-tech activity, however, but can avoid these losses by accession to the EC.

Haaland (1990) presents many interesting results beyond those detailed above, but comments that if, in the end, we believe that much of EC industry is imperfectly competitive, we should incorporate that feature directly into our general equilibrium models. This is no mean task, either conceptually or practically, but it has now been achieved. Previews were offered by Norman (1989) and by Gasiorek, Smith and Venables (1991), and full analyses are now available in Part II in Chapters 2 and 3 below.

In Chapter 2 Michael Gasiorek, Alasdair Smith and Tony Venables describe a computable general equilibrium model with 8 country blocks – France, Germany, Italy, the UK, Iberia, EC North, Greece plus Ireland, and the Rest of the World. Each country contains 15 industries – a large perfectly competitive (numéraire) sector plus 14 imperfectly competitive sectors – and 5 factors of production – 4 types of labour (differentiated by skill level) and capital. They use this model to repeat the two earlier exercises conducted for CEC (1988a): a 2.5 per cent reduction in trade costs, and a 2.5 per cent cost reduction accompanied by full market integration.

The results show that '1992' expands EC output in all the imperfectly competitive industries and raises wages in all countries. This is possible because it gives firms access to larger markets, thus reducing their unit costs through economies of scale, and because the reduction in trade costs releases real resources which then produce additional output. The increases in output are relatively small, however, except in Iberia, Greece and Ireland where they are of the order of about 5 per cent. In general skilled workers gain more than unskilled workers because the imperfectly competitive sectors on which '1992' has greatest effects are typically the most intensive users of skilled labour. '1992' brings welfare gains to all economies, the largest being in economies in which labour is relatively cheap and initial industrial concentration relatively high. Hence Iberia, Greece and Ireland achieve gains of around 2 per cent of GDP.

The imperfectly competitive sectors cover only about one-third of the economy and the model does not explicitly add in the regulatory gains of CEC's stage 2. Hence the figures quoted are clearly under-estimates of the total gains to '1992'. On the other hand, they do arise from the goods' industries that are most susceptible to integration gains, so it seems likely that they would not gross up to the full 6 per cent foreseen in CEC. Hence while the general equilibrium results broadly confirm Smith and Venables' previous partial equilibrium analysis, they do not entirely support the 'official' estimates based upon them. On the other hand, all these exercises are subject to wide margins of error, so not much should be made of small percentage differences.

Gasiorek, Smith and Venables also offer two interesting decompositions of the sources of welfare gains. These suggest that while the direct benefits of reduced trade costs are relatively important in the short run, the expansion of existing firms in the imperfectly competitive sectors becomes more so in the longer run and when markets are fully integrated. The welfare effects of firm entry and exit are relatively small, less than 10 per cent of the total welfare gain in most cases, as generally are those of trade diversion. Two noteworthy exceptions to the latter observation, however, are food products and textiles, in which trade diversion nearly offsets the other gains in some exercises.

The effect of '1992' on extra-EC trade is most pronounced in industries where EC output grows the most. Thus EC exports rise (and imports fall) most strongly in metal products, non-metallic mineral products, transport equipment, and food products. The effect is greatest in the long-run, integrated markets simulation, in which EC exports in these sectors rise by between 25 per cent and 35 per cent and imports fall by 15–40 per cent.

In Chapter 3 a similar model is employed by Jan Haaland and Victor Norman to analyse the global production and trade effects of '1992' and of the creation of the European Economic Area (EEA) between the EC and EFTA. Using the same broad theoretical structure as Chapter 2, they develop a model with 5 world regions – the EC, EFTA, USA, Japan and the Rest of the World, 13 sectors and 3 (non-tradeable) primary factors – capital and two types of labour.

Haaland and Norman explore the same set of trade-cost reductions and integration experiments as Gasiorek, Smith and Venables. Their first conclusion is that European integration is important for the European partners, but that the effects on non-European regions are small. Second, both the gains and the sectoral consequences for EFTA depend crucially upon whether or not it integrates with the EC. For example, participation in the internal market through the EEA yields a gain equivalent to 3.7 per cent of their expenditure on traded goods – almost twice the gain that the EC is expected to enjoy from the internal market (1.9 per cent). The strongest effects are felt in engineering and other skill-intensive industries. These sectors experience a significant negative impact if EFTA stands aloof from European integration, because '1992' boosts EC competitiveness in these areas, but experience strong growth in the EEA scenario. In the latter case, EFTA's output of transport equipment rises by 23 per cent and that of machinery by 18 per cent relative to the '1992' case. Haaland and Norman also suggest that the real wages of skilled labour will rise by proportionally more than those of other factors.

The insight that general equilibrium analysis gives to the quantification of the effects of '1992' is important, especially for international trade, which cannot be satisfactorily handled in any other way. Hence, although the most interesting analytical issues remaining for '1992' scholars concern the behaviour by particular firms or in particular markets, and hence need first to be considered in a partial equilibrium context, having once developed general equilibrium models, the marginal costs of introducing industry-level refinements into them are not high. Moreover, even if industries behave in surprising ways, international economic integration will clearly have general equilibrium effects that must be allowed for in any satisfactory overall quantification.

The third general equilibrium model in this volume is Cillian Ryan's analysis in Chapter 4 of the impact of integration on the intertemporal component of financial services. Information on financial services is not readily available – it is too valuable to market participants for that – and so CEC (1988a) was forced to rely on relatively crude means of assessing the effects of integration. Ryan provides an alternative set of measures by developing a general equilibrium model which focuses on the markets for short- and long-run borrowing and lending within the EC. Following CEC (1988a) Ryan assumes that '1992' will cause the convergence of the costs of providing banking services towards their lowest, best-practice, values. He considers both full and partial (as in CEC, 1988a) convergence, but is not able to distinguish whether it occurs via competitive pressure reducing costs in locally-owned institutions, via mergers between strong and weak institutions (in which case convergence might be towards mean rather than best practice), or via the displacement of local firms by imports from the most efficient EC suppliers. In the latter case a substantial increase in intra-EC trade in banking services will result. In addition to the convergence of costs, Ryan plots the benefits of further financial market integration in the EC: these arise because larger markets allow a better matching of borrowers to lenders than smaller markets.

Ryan's data – which were carefully constructed for this exercise – suggest that banking firms in France, Italy, the UK and the Netherlands are considerably less efficient in providing intertemporal banking services than their Belgian and German counterparts. Thus when markets are opened up it is these countries which enjoy the bulk of the gains from trade. These gains appear to be considerably greater than those predicted by CEC (1988a), even though intertemporal services represent only about 65 per cent of the financial intermediation output considered by the latter. This is because Ryan models the gains that accrue to depositors as well as to borrowers, and because the factor reallocation from the services' to the goods' sector consequent upon the efficiency gains in banking yield further gains. It is notable that, contrary to the common perception, the increase in the demand for banking services as their prices fall is insufficient to compensate for the reductions in inputs induced by the increases in efficiency. Thus job losses are likely in this sector unless the demand for other financial services rises significantly.

A two-sector model is probably too crude to permit the accurate quantification of the effects of '1992', but Ryan's results do highlight some important policy issues. For example, efficiency in intermediation services such as banking is important both in its own right and as a means to efficient transactions in the rest of the economy. Increased efficiency may well entail the flow of resources out of rather than into the sector. The integration of intertemporal financial service markets may induce substantial and long-lived changes in member states' net foreign borrowing behaviour which, in turn, will show up in correspondingly large current account imbalances. But because the latter will derive from agents' voluntary optimising behaviour they will present no financing problem nor need any remedial policy.

4.2   Modelling market integration – partial equilibrium

Part III of the book moves from general equilibrium analysis of the whole economy to partial equilibrium studies of particular markets. This allows researchers to focus more closely on the particular features of those markets and, in the chapters included here, to reassess two pieces of conventional wisdom about the effects of market integration.

In Chapter 5 Jan Haaland and Ian Wooton challenge the view that the full integration of imperfectly competitive markets, such as is often assumed in models of '1992', will necessarily lead to lower home market prices and hence to gains for domestic consumers and losses for domestic producers. The conventional view arises because, in the underlying model, price–cost margins are directly related to market shares, and integration is modelled as a move from segmented to integrated markets. Thus, prior to integration firms can price discriminate between EC markets, and because domestic firms generally have larger shares of their home markets they can charge higher prices there – see p. 8 above. After '1992', however, with a genuinely single European market, it is their shares of the EC market as a whole which will determine market power. Since these will be below their initial shares of their home markets firms will lose market power and their domestic price–cost margins will decline. Since each market is typically dominated by domestic firms, this effect will outweigh the fact that exporters now charge higher prices (EC-wide shares exceed their previous export shares), and so average prices in each market will fall. Haaland and Wooton show, however, that life is not so simple.

Using a simple model of international trade in an oligopolistic industry, Haaland and Wooton show that if intra-EC trade costs remain positive after integration, or if there is bias in consumer preferences towards home-produced goods, then market integration may reduce competition and lead to losses for consumers. This is because the pre-'1992' segmented markets permit 'reciprocal dumping', whereby firms supply goods to foreign markets at relatively low prices, which has beneficial pro-competitive effects. When markets become integrated this practice is no longer possible. As a result firms find it more expensive to maintain their market shares abroad because any reduction in price in an EC export market must simultaneously be applied in the home market. This in turn reduces the incentive to export and thus, in each home market, reduces the competitive pressure from imports. If the reduction in competitive import pressure allows domestic firms to raise their home prices, the prices of all EC supplies in a market will have risen, and the welfare implications will be opposite to those of the 'conventional wisdom': consumers lose and producers gain. Even in the normal case in which integration reduces domestic prices, the welfare consequences for consumers are not clear, since import prices will have increased.

The empirical work to establish the relevance of this argument to EC integration is currently lacking – it requires, *inter alia*, the accurate measurement of consumer taste biases and intra-EC trading costs, and so is a formidable task. Nonetheless Haaland and Wooton use a simple simulation model to establish that their result is more than a theoretical curiosum. They show that a number of factors increase the probability of welfare losses from integration: greater substitutability between home and foreign goods – because it enhances the disciplinary effects of dumping in the initial segmented market case; a less competitive home industry – because it is better able to exploit the subsequent absence of dumping; higher trade costs between markets – because they segment markets even under integration; and greater consumer bias towards home goods – which also segments markets but less potently than trade costs.

Haaland and Wooton's analysis docs not undermine Gasiorek, Smith and Venables' results, for the effects it identifies are already present in the latter's model. It does, however, explain more clearly what is going on and highlights the need for future research to distinguish between consumer biases and trade costs as causes of home-market bias. It also highlights the need for strong intra-EC competition post-'1992' – see p. 26 below.

In Chapter 6 Gernot Klepper identifies another potential surprise in market integration, arising from the presence of arbitrageurs who ship goods from high- to low-price markets. Klepper analyses the pharmaceutical market – one of the most segmented and regulated of markets in the EC. This market is characterised by national certification procedures, patents and, in Southern countries, price controls; all these policies tend to reduce competition and encourage price discrimination between markets. The Commission's recent directives on the transparency of price controls and on the authorisation of medicinal products will make it more difficult for firms to disguise price discrimination and offer the possibility of European-wide certification; they thus seem likely to represent a modest move towards an integrated market.

Klepper considers a model of a price discriminating monopoly or a duopoly selling to one price-controlled and one price-uncontrolled market and facing a competitive fringe of firms which arbitrage drugs between the high- and low-price markets. He finds that a relaxation of price controls in the low-price market can have ambiguous effects on prices in the uncontrolled market. The usual expectation is that prices in both markets will rise, because arbitrage will be discouraged by the higher price in the previously controlled market. However, if the arbitrageurs' costs rise at a sufficiently increasing rate with the level of arbitrage, and if their activity is sufficiently sensitive to the size of the price differential, the residual demand curves facing drug producers in the uncontrolled market may be such that it is more profitable for them to lower prices and increase sales. Harmonising certification procedures between EC markets would also reduce price discrimination and have similarly ambiguous effects on prices in the uncontrolled market.

Klepper suggests that the '1992'-related directives on licensing drugs and the transparency of price controls will put pressure on governments to reduce discriminatory price controls rather than affecting the impediments to arbitrage, which largely arise from the behaviour of supplying companies. Given some casual information on arbitrageurs' cost structures he speculates that, in response to these directives, prices in the Southern European countries will rise, whereas those in the uncontrolled markets of the North will change little. We can thus expect producer profits to rise at the expense of consumer surplus in the South, while consumer surplus in countries like Belgium, the Netherlands, Germany and the UK will not significantly change.

4.3   Trade and industrial policy

Part IV of the volume is concerned with trade and industrial policy in the completed internal market. In Chapter 7 L. Alan Winters presents a computable model of the EC footwear market and uses it to explore various issues of EC trade policy. He shows that Spanish and Portuguese accession to the EC led to trade creation in footwear, and hence to enhanced consumer welfare, both in the original EC countries and in the new members; however, within the original membership this effect was offset by trade diversion as the new preferences granted to Spain reduced imports from more efficient producers from developing countries. Among producers, those in the new member states gained strongly, but their counterparts in the original EC suffered some loss of profits from the trade creation. Hence although consumers in the original EC gained from enlargement, if one gives consumer surplus, profits and tariff revenue equal weight in the national objective function, those countries' net welfare was slightly reduced. One cannot generalise this result to other sectors, however, for with its high tariffs, footwear was particularly prone to trade diversion.

Winters next considers the bilateral quotas and VERs imposed on Korean and Taiwanese footwear in 1988 by France and Italy. These reduced welfare not only in the restricted markets (losses of 2.1 per cent of expenditure on footwear in France and 0.7 per cent in Italy), but also elsewhere in the EC because the import restrictions reduced competitive pressures on other producers (particularly in Italy) and so led them to increase prices elsewhere.

'1992' will make the maintenance of such national quantitative import restrictions largely impossible, since in the absence of border controls between member states it will be impossible to prevent trade deflection. That is, '1992' will render inoperative Article 115 of the Treaty of Rome which permits the segmentation of the EC market for third-country goods. In footwear, however, '1992' was anticipated, for in 1990 the French and Italian restrictions were replaced by EC-wide VERs on Korea and Taiwan. These were not materially more restrictive than their predecessors but led to a significant redistribution of the costs of protection. In particular, the costs of supporting French and Italian producers now fell heavily on consumers elsewhere in the EC. Italian producers, with strong sales elsewhere in the EC, suffered virtually no loss of profits because their gains in the newly protected markets of the UK and Germany offset their losses as their home market was liberalised. French producers, on the other hand, did suffer, since their sales are concentrated on the domestic market, so that the switch from a French to an EC-wide quota removed much of their protection. Taiwan and Korea also gained from the policy change since they now earned scarcity rents on sales throughout the EC rather than just in France and Italy, and so did other producers, for their sales and prices were increased by trade diversion. There was thus a strong coalition of producer interests in favour of the broadening of protection.

Winters' analysis of the combination of national quantitative restrictions differs from previous analyses of the abolition of Article 115. Chapter 7 assumes that footwear is differentiated by type, supplier and market, whereas Winters (1988b) assumed that exporters supplied identical goods to each EC market, while Hamilton (1991) assumed the homogeneity of all supplies, both foreign and domestic. In the last case both Article 115 *and* barriers to internal trade are necessary to segment EC markets because flows of EC-produced goods are sufficient to equalise the prices between markets even if third-country supplies cannot flow freely. Hence the abolition of the internal barriers under '1992' will render Article 115 nugatory without any further action.

Winters' final policy exercise is the removal of tariffs and quantitative restrictions on imports from Eastern Europe as is planned under the EC's 'Europe Agreements' with Czecho-Slovakia, Hungary and Poland. Imports could nearly double if these countries can overcome some of their supply constraints, increasing their share of EC markets from 3.4 per cent to 5.7 per cent; this will confer considerable benefits on EC consumers – possibly ECU 200 million per annum – while leading to relatively mild losses for producers. The losses will fall most heavily on Italian producers, who are major suppliers of leather footwear to Germany and the UK, the principal markets for Eastern Europe. Winters observes that although the gains from liberalisation will be reduced for Eastern Europe by the loss of their initial quota rents and for the EC by the loss of tariff revenues, the net effect will be strongly positive for both parties. Hence, he argues, liberalisation represents an obvious way to encourage development in Eastern Europe.

In Chapter 8 Larry Karp and Jeffrey Perloff examine the long-run value of inflexibility, and reconsider the conventional wisdom relating to the possible use of strategic trade and domestic adjustment policies by the EC. They employ a duopoly model in a dynamic environment, representing adjustment policies by taxes or subsidies to firms' gross investment. They contrast the relative merits of non-linear adjustment subsidies or taxes – for example, where the tax depends on the value of the firm's investment or disinvestment – with linear policies proportional to the quantity of investment. They show that the optimal linear adjustment policy is an investment subsidy, which improves a firm's strategic power by raising the level of domestic investment and discouraging investment by its rival. This is the common strategic subsidy argument generalised to a dynamic environment.

An *ad valorem* policy, on the other hand, affects both the level and the curvature of the investment schedule; for example, if the costs of investment were related to the square of the level of investment – because, say, of increasing management or disruption costs – an *ad valorem* tax on the value (cost) of investment would make costs rise more rapidly as the level of investment increased. Similarly, a tax on disinvestment would penalise downsizing a firm. Since the strategic incentive to investment depends on a firm's power to influence its rival, raising the domestic firm's adjustment costs by taxing investment or disinvestment commits it more firmly to its current level of output, and hence discourages pre-emptive investment by rival firms. Thus a non-linear tax will have two opposing effects: a linear part, raising the cost of investment and thus keeping the domestic firm small, and a non-linear part, discouraging rivals from pre-emptive investment and thus encouraging the firm to grow and *to stay* larger. Karp and Perloff show that the latter effect could dominate. Moreover, they also show that by altering the cost of changing in size, a non-linear policy will probably require a lower level of government transfers to achieve the same outcome as a linear policy which can influence only the level of investment.

Karp and Perloff argue that most EC member countries have non-linear adjustment policies – for example, investment grants proportional to the cost of investment, notification requirements for plant closures, and adjustment assistance for declining firms. They also note that the Social Chapter of the draft Treaty of Maastricht entails restrictions to adjustment – the very grounds on which the British government objected to it. Their results suggest, however, that such inflexibility may in fact be profit-enhancing quite apart from any social benefits it may confer. Karp and Perloff's results might also explain the relative success of German firms in EC markets compared with, say, British ones. A German firm's entry to a market is a credible long-term commitment, because German social legislation makes it costly for it to withdraw: wise rivals will not try to dislodge it.

4.4   Empirical evidence

The predominant mode of quantitative analysis of '1992' has been simulation studies, and although many researchers have devoted considerable effort to establishing data sets for calibrating their models, relatively little attention has been paid to estimating the parameters of economic behaviour. Part V of this volume contains two studies intended to redress this balance. In Chapter 9 Joaquim Oliveira-Martins and Joël Toujas-Bernate discuss how the effects of product differentiation at the level of the firm may be incorporated into aggregate import demand equations. Recent models of international trade with imperfect competition and product differentiation show that the ratio of the aggregate market shares of producers from two countries is determined by relative prices and the number of firms (or varieties) in each country. Oliveira-Martins and Toujas-Bernate argue that the representative number of firms or products for each supplier can be proxied by an index of national industrial activity in the sectors concerned. This approach, which like Gasiorek, Smith and Venables in Chapter 2 treats firms as the units of differentiation, contrasts with the normal 'Armington' assumption in which products are differentiated only by place of production. It may, however, be modelled as a simple extension of the Armington equation.

Oliveira-Martins and Toujas-Bernate start by highlighting the need for a new approach to import functions by showing the general absence of stable long-run empirical relationships between relative prices and import shares. This result rejects the use of trade models based solely on relative price effects and suggests the need to include non-price factors. They then estimate demand systems for 3 industries (textiles, chemicals, electrical machinery), in each of the 4 main EC markets, identifying 3 suppliers – domestic, EC, and the Rest of the World. They construct a composite price index to capture the effects of both the price and non-price (product differentiation) effects and find that the explanation of market shares is substantially improved by the latter component. Their parameter estimates suggest that the effects of changes in non-price factors may be quite large whilst changes in pure prices have a relatively moderate impact on market shares. They do not, however, overturn the common finding among empirical researchers that the price elasticities of demand facing exporters are relatively low.

In the final Chapter 10 Paul Brenton and L. Alan Winters present the results of estimating disaggregate bilateral import demand functions and consider the implications of the low price elasticities they derive for the modelling of the effects of '1992'. In previous work Brenton and Winters (1992) have used a theoretically desirable model, the Almost Ideal Demand System, to model the allocation of expenditure on a good across both domestic sources and different suppliers of imports. Using data for the German market for 70 manufacturing industries their principal results suggested that price elasticities were rather low – the majority were close to unity – and that the expenditure elasticity for domestic supplies exceeded unity whilst those for most import suppliers were less than 1.

In Chapter 10 Brenton and Winters explore, first, whether these results are confirmed by data for another market and, second, whether the conclusion of relatively low price elasticities is sensitive to change in the functional form of the demand equations. Applying the Almost Ideal Demand System to data for the Italian market for a sample of 15 manufacturing industries confirms the basic results, as does the application of a simple 'Armingtonian' constant elasticity of substitution (CES) demand system to both German and Italian data. Moreover, neither of two alternative estimations – one using instrumental variables to allow for simultaneity and/or errors-in-variables and the other using a first difference transformation of the CES model to allow for autocorrelation – leads to any significant change in the magnitude of the elasticities.

Neither Chapter 9 nor 10 has resolved all the empirical problems of estimating trade elasticities, and in neither are the estimates as precise as one would wish. However, some attempt to link theoretical models to empirical realities is required, and the regularity with which researchers find very low price elasticities of demand must prompt us to ask how the analysis of '1992' would be affected if, in the end, such estimates were vindicated. In posing this question Brenton and Winters note that the effects of the current barriers to trade and competition in the EC are generally defined in terms of the higher prices they cause. If the sensitivity of demand to changes in prices is as low as is suggested by their results, then the effects of barrier removal in '1992' will not be as great as many have forecast. However, where the barriers work to constrain quantities directly, as for example with import quotas or public procurement biases, very large effects on prices and rents will be felt, and liberalisation will be accompanied by larger changes in these dimensions than previously anticipated. If this is the case then more attention needs to be directed towards issues such as the price effects of VERs and the distribution of rents emanating from quantitative restrictions.

5   Some policy conclusions

The CEPR study of '1992', the main results of which appear here and in Winters and Venables (1991), has generated a number of important policy conclusions. The prime one is, perhaps, that '1992' is likely to be economically beneficial within Europe – especially if, as seems likely, it is extended to EFTA countries – and not of great significance – either positive or negative – elsewhere. Certainly there is presently no sign that '1992' has spawned a Fortress Europe in terms either of policies or of outcomes. On the other hand, while '1992' has generated a fair degree of liberalisation internally, it has not led to much external liberalisation, and as the EC economy slips into recession it remains an important policy requirement that there be no backsliding in this respect. Indeed, in terms of operationalising '1992', the most important policy conclusion is that competition, and especially external competition, must be preserved.

The importance of domestic competition was stressed by the Commission in CEC (1988a) and by early commentators such as Winters (1988a), Kay (1989) and Geroski (1989). More recently Ulph (1991) has shown that reducing competition at the 'pre-competitive' stage of R&D is far from certain to improve EC research performance, and Haaland and Wooton in Chapter 5 below have shown the need for competition to constrain the exploitation of the reduction in intra-EC imports following full integration. Similarly, Klepper's analysis in Chapter 6 shows the potential for a competitive arbitrage sector to undermine the distortions created and exploited by imperfectly competitive pharmaceutical companies.

External competition is even more important. Jacquemin and Sapir (1991) show the importance of extra-EC imports in constraining EC profit margins in a fashion that intra-EC trade apparently cannot. I interpret this as reflecting the greater ease with which tacit, maybe even unconscious, collusion can grow up between EC producers than between EC and non-EC producers. Micossi and Viesti's (1991) catalogue of the benefits deriving from inflows of Japanese investment to some parts of the EC, and the fears that it arouses among existing producers in other parts, is consistent with such a view. Similarly, Norman (1991) shows the great benefits of breaking down local airline monopolies, and if the European Commission cannot achieve that, external competition should be used instead. In terms of the present volume, extra-EC competition is likely to be more potent than domestic competition in constraining monopoly power in Haaland and Wooton's model (Chapter 5), and also in the simulation models of Gasiorek, Smith and Venables and of Haaland and Norman (Chapters 2 and 3). More directly, Winters in Chapter 7 illustrates the benefits of liberal trade with the rest of the world.

A related conclusion illustrated in Chapter 7 and implicit in Chapter 2 is that different member states have different interests in particular trade policies. Trade policy tends to have greater distributive than aggregate effects – i.e. an individual country's or factor's interests are frequently opposed to the overall interest – and EC decision-making has a strong national dimension, because the Council of Members and the various EC committees are based on national representation. This conjunction makes the institutional framework for policy-making very important. '1992' makes trade policy 'more common', because it undermines national restrictions and constrains the use of many other means of meeting national protectionist pressures; hence it throws a greater weight on these EC institutions. The need to build multi-member coalitions to change policy may make it more difficult to introduce protective measures, but conversely it may enhance the role of administered protection and the effectiveness of Brussels-based lobbying, and will almost certainly make it more difficult to agree the dismantling of what protection does exist. The examples of the EC's other common policies – agriculture and transport – are hardly encouraging, and while the EC has been moderately liberal over international trade during the last few years, the need for both for vigilance in policy-making and for research on the institutional structure of EC trade policy remains.

Chapters 5 by Haaland and Wooton and 6 by Klepper suggest that the effects of full market integration depend on subtle and, to date, largely unquantified aspects of the markets concerned. Similarly Karp and Perloff in Chapter 8 suggest that apparently minor differences between policy instruments can have important implications for the size or even the sign of their effects. This might be taken as suggesting the need for careful case-by-case policy-making – integrating here, allowing dumping there, and so on. In fact, it should rather be interpreted as illustrating the nearly impossible informational demands that such an approach would impose, and the desirability of adopting simple and robust policy stances such as free trade.

For understandable political reasons quantifying the external impact of '1992' has been left to academic rather than official researchers. The effects on developing countries seem likely to be generally benign: primary exporters will benefit from increased growth; EC comparative advantage in manufactures will shift away from the goods produced by most developing countries (Haaland, 1990); and the replacement of national by EC-wide trade policy will, unless it becomes materially more restrictive, allow exporters to reap higher profits – see Chapter 7 below. Even where EC imports fall – for example, textiles and food processing in Chapter 2 below – the consequences are not catastrophic for suppliers because the rents in these industries are not high and the terms of trade are little affected. Finally, developing countries will benefit from the reductions in EC export prices that '1992' induces.

Turning to industrial countries, the competitive effects of '1992' are somewhat greater. The '1992' efficiency gains for EC firms will increase their shares of all markets, and for industries in which rents are significant this will reduce foreign firms' profits. On the other hand, those producers will benefit from the additional EC growth and overseas consumers will benefit from lower EC export prices. Moreover, although Gasiorek, Smith and Venables confirm that EC imports will fall significantly (relative to the *anti-monde*, not necessarily actually through time) in certain sectors, these sectors are only part of the EC economy and the EC accounts for only a small share of partners' production. Hence the overall impact of '1992' on industrial countries' welfare is proportionately small even if negative: Haaland and Norman suggests losses of four-tenths of 1 per cent of expenditure on tradeable goods for EFTA and well below one-tenth of 1 per cent for Japan and the USA.

What can and should be done about these losses? For EFTA they are avoidable and may be turned into significant gains by joining the EC or the EEA. For Japan and the USA such an option is not available, but a similar competitive stimulus to that of '1992' might be generated by opening up their trade unilaterally or by seeking improved access to EC markets via multilateral negotiations. Certainly, as I have noted above, because the principal effects of '1992' arise from EC internal measures such as regulatory reform and increased competition, they should not be the subject of discussion in trade fora such as the GATT. Regulatory reform is open to other countries, and no trading nation would wish to argue that its partners should continue with inefficient internal practices just in order that it maintains its shares of their markets.

Taken as a whole the results reported in this volume suggest that there remains much uncertainty about the economic effects of '1992'. Critical parameters are not well estimated, subtle and unmeasured issues such as the extent of consumers' biases towards home goods determine the effects of integration, the presence of arbitrage may increase prices after liberalisation, inflexibility can confer welfare gains, and general equilibrium feedbacks are important. These results do not undermine previous estimates of the effects of '1992', but they do suggest the need for work of a thoroughness and sophistication not often found in this debate before serious conclusions can be drawn.

NOTES

1 'The International Trade Consequences of "1992"', was supported by the Commission of the European Communities' Stimulation Programme in Economic Science, the UK Department of Trade and Industry and the UK Foreign and Commonwealth Office. My own contributions have also been partly supported by the Economic and Social Research Council (grant no. R00023 1932). Section 2 draws on Winters (1991, 1992). I am grateful to Paul Brenton for comments on this chapter, to him and Cillian Ryan who acted as rapporteurs at the conference on which the volume is based, and to Tina Attwell and Maureen Hyde for typing.
2 In fact '1992' will probably not eliminate public procurement biasses entirely because monitoring is so difficult and because the enforcement mechanism is flawed; see, for example, Winters (1988a).
3 The absolute figures refer only to a sub-set of member countries accounting for around 88 per cent of EC GDP.
4 Stage 2 also includes some minor effects from economies of scale in the production of intermediates – based essentially on Corden's (1972) analytical model and Pratten's (1988) engineering estimates of scale effects.
5 It is at least arguable that the denominator should be just stage 1 effects, since Smith and Venables have no factor explicitly equivalent to stage 2.
6 More formal analysis of this interesting model is given in Motta (1992).
7 The 'hybriding' of general equilibrium models and the CEC estimates is subject to some conceptual problems, but fewer than those attending the union of CEC and macro models.
8 'Comparative advantage' is measured here by sectors' shares of the total value added and is defined to include the effects of scale, policy and other distortions.

REFERENCES

Baldwin, R.A. (1989) 'On the growth effect of 1992', *Economic Policy*, **9**, pp. 3–54.
—— (1992) 'Measurable dynamic gains from trade', *Journal of Political Economy*, **100**, pp. 162–74.
Bliss, C. and J. Braga de Macedo (1990) *Unity with Diversity in the European Economy*, London: Cambridge University Press.
Brander, J.A. and P.R. Krugman (1983) 'A reciprocal dumping model of international trade', *Journal of International Economics*, **15**, pp. 313–21.
Brenton, P. and L.A. Winters (1992) 'Estimating the international trade effects of "1992": West Germany', *Journal of Common Market Studies*, **30(2)** (June).
Caballero, R.J. and R.K. Lyons (1991) 'External effects and Europe's integration', Chapter 3 in Winters and Venables (1991) pp. 34–50.
Cawley, R. and M. Davenport (1988) 'Partial equilibrium calculations of the impact of internal market barriers in the European Community', *Economic Paper*, **73**, Brussels: European Commission.
Centre for Business Strategy (1989) *1992: Myths and Realities*, London: Centre for Business Strategy.
Commission of the European Communities (CEC) (1988a) 'The economics of 1992', *The European Economy*, **35** (March), Brussels, European Commission.

(1988b) *Research on the Cost of Non-Europe: Basic Findings*, 16 vols, Brussels: European Commission.

(1990) 'The impact of the internal market by industrial sector: the challenge for the Member States', *The European Economy – Social Europe, Special Edition*, Brussels: European Commission.

Corden, W.M. (1972) 'Economics of scale and customs union theory', *Journal of Political Economy*, **80**, pp. 465–75.

Davenport, M. (1990) 'The external policy of the Community and its effects upon the manufactured goods of developing countries', *Journal of Common Market Studies*, **29**, pp. 181–200.

Davenport, M. and S. Page (1991) *Europe: 1992 and the Developing World*, London: Overseas Development Institute.

Gasiorek, M., A. Smith and A.J. Venables (1991) 'Completing the internal market in the EC: factor demands and comparative advantage', Chapter 2 in Winters and Venables (1991) pp. 9–30.

Geroski, P.A. (1989) 'The choice between diversity and scale', Chapter 2 in Centre for Business Strategy (1989) pp. 29–45.

Geroski, P. and A. Jacquemin (1986) 'Industrial change, barriers to mobility, and European industrial policy', *Economic Policy*, **1**, pp. 169–205.

Haaland, J. (1990) 'Assessing the effects of EC integration on EFTA countries: the position of Norway and Sweden', *Journal of Common Market Studies*, **28**, pp. 379–400.

Hamilton, C.B. (1991) 'European Community external protection and 1992: voluntary export restraints applied to Pacific Asia', *European Economic Review*, **35**, pp. 377–87.

Hamilton, C.B. and L.A. Winters (1992) 'Opening up trade in Eastern Europe', *Economic Policy*, **14**, pp. 78–116.

Hufbauer, G.C. (1990) *Europe 1992: An American Perspective*, Washington, D.C.: Brookings Institution.

Jacquemin, A. and A. Sapir (1988) 'International trade and integration of the European Community: an econometric analysis', *European Economic Review*, **32**, pp. 1439–50.

(1991) 'Competition and imports in the European market', Chapter 5 in Winters and Venables (1991) pp. 82–91.

Kay, J.A. (1989) 'Myths and Realities', Chapter 1 in Centre for Business Strategy (1989) pp. 1–28.

Krugman, P.R. (1979) 'Increasing returns, monopolistic competition, and international trade', *Journal of International Economics*, **9**, pp. 469–79.

(1991) *Economics and Geography*, Cambridge, Mass.: MIT Press.

Krugman, P.R. and A.J. Venables (1990) 'Integration and the competitiveness of peripheral industry', Chapter 3 in Bliss and Braga de Macedo (1990) pp. 56–75.

Markusen, J.R. and A.J. Venables (1988) 'Trade policy with increasing returns to scale and imperfect competition: contradictory results from competing assumptions', *Journal of International Economics*, **24**, pp. 299–316.

Matthews, A. and D. McAleese (1990), 'LDC primary exports to the EC: prospects post-1992', *Journal of Common Market Studies*, **29**, pp. 157–80.

Micossi, S. and G. Viesti (1991) 'Japanese direct manufacturing investment in Europe', Chapter 10 in Winters and Venables (1991) pp. 200–30.

Motta, M. (1990) 'Recent models of international trade and distributional gains from integration', *Rivista Internationale di Science Economiche e Commerciale*, **37**, pp. 713–36.

(1992) 'Sunk costs and trade liberalisation', *Economic Journal*, **102**, pp. 578–87.

Neven, D.J. (1990) 'EC integration towards 1992: some distributional aspects', *Economic Policy*, **10**, pp. 13–62.

Norman, V.D. (1989) 'EFTA and the internal European market', *Economic Policy*, **9**, pp. 423–66.

(1990) 'Comment', *Economic Policy*, **10**, pp. 49–52.

(1991) '1992 and EFTA', Chapter 7 in Winters and Venables (1991).

Owen, R. and M. Dynes (1990) *The Times Guide to 1992*, London: Times Books, pp. 120–39.

Peck, M.J. (1989) 'Industrial organisation and the gains from Europe 1992', *Brookings Papers in Economic Activity*, **2**, pp. 277–300.

Pelkmans, J. and L.A. Winters (1988) '*Europe's Domestic Market*', Chatham House Paper, **43**, London: Royal Institute for International Affairs.

Pratten, C. (1988) 'A survey of the economies of scale', Chapter 1 in CEC (1988b), vol. 2, pp. 11–165.

Schwalbach, J. (1988) 'Economies of scale and intra-community trade', Chapter 3 in CEC (1988b), vol. 2.

Smith, A. (1989) 'The market for cars in the enlarged European Community', *European Economic Review*, **32**, pp. 1501–25.

Smith, A. and A.J. Venables (1988a) 'Completing the internal market in the European Community: some industry simulations, *European Economic Review*, **32(7)** pp. 1501–25.

(1988b) 'The costs of non-Europe: an assessment based on a formal model of imperfect competition and economies of scale', Chapter 5 in CEC (1988b), vol. 2.

(1991) 'Economic integration and market access', *European Economic Review*, **35**, pp. 388–97.

Stoeckel, A., D. Pearce and G. Banks (1990) *Western Trade Blocks: Game, Set, or Match for the Asia-Pacific and the World Economy?*, Canberra: Centre for International Economics.

Ulph, D.T. (1991) 'Technology policy in the completed European market', Chapter 8 in Winters and Venables (1991) pp. 142–61.

Viner, J. (1950) *The Customs Union Issue*, New York: Carnegie Endowment for International Peace.

Winters, L.A. (1988a) 'Plain speaking about 1992', *University of Wales Economics and Business Review*, **4** (Winter) pp. 49–54.

(1988b) 'Completing the European Internal Market: some notes on trade policy', *European Economic Review*, **32**, pp. 1477–99.

(1991), 'International Trade and "1992": an overview', *European Economic Review*, **35**, pp. 367–77.

(1992) 'The policy and welfare implications of the international trade consequences of "1992"', *American Economic Review, Papers and Proceedings*, **82**, pp. 104–8.

Winters, L.A. and A.J. Venables (1991) *European Integration: Trade and Industry*, London: Cambridge University Press.

Part Two
General equilibrium analyses

2 '1992': trade and welfare – a general equilibrium model

MICHAEL GASIOREK, ALASDAIR SMITH
and ANTHONY J. VENABLES

1 Introduction

The aim of this chapter is to investigate the role of general equilibrium effects in European integration. Smith and Venables (1988) used a partial equilibrium approach to investigate the effects of the '1992' programme on intra-industry trade and competition, and hence on prices, output and welfare. The completion of the internal market was found to be a pro-competitive policy, leading to substantial increases in firm scale, and bringing welfare gains from lower prices and, with increasing returns to scale, lower costs.

A partial equilibrium approach to the study of the completion of the internal market is incomplete, and therefore potentially misleading, for two reasons. First, partial equilibrium analysis assumes that resources drawn into the industry under study are available at prices equal to social opportunity cost. If one imperfectly competitive industry's expansion is – because of overall resource constraints – another's contraction, then this assumption is invalid, and we may over-estimate the welfare gains associated with the policy. Second, partial equilibrium studies assume that input supply curves are horizontal, so that resources are available to the industry at a constant price. If input supply curves to each industry are in fact upward sloping, partial equilibrium studies over-estimate the quantity effects of the policy. Input supply considerations affect not only inputs of primary factors, but also inputs of intermediates, which may themselves be produced by imperfectly competitive industries, so generating 'linkages' between industries.

In an earlier study (Gasiorek, Smith and Venables, 1991), we took a general equilibrium approach to modelling the completion of the internal market. We did not address the welfare implications of the policy, concentrating on modelling inputs to each industry and investigating the effects of completion of the market on factor demands and factor prices.

35

This chapter is based on a richer data set, which allows us to model the country structure of EC markets at a more disaggregated level, and to adopt a slightly more disaggregated treatment of labour markets; and although we report and discuss the implications for factor markets and EC outputs of the policy change, we focus mainly on the welfare effects and on the effects on the Rest of the World (ROW).

We construct a general equilibrium model in which production uses intermediate goods and 5 primary factors of production. The model contains a perfectly competitive composite sector, and a number of imperfectly competitive industries. These industries operate under increasing returns to scale and support an equilibrium with intra-industry trade. We consider two kinds of policy experiments: a reduction in intra-EC trade costs for these industries; and the same intra-EC trade cost reduction but now accompanied by a change in market behaviour, from a 'segmented' market quantity equilibrium, to an 'integrated' market quantity equilibrium.

The chapter is organised as follows. Section 2 sketches the model (with more detail provided in an Appendix on pp. 61–2), and section 3 discusses the data used and the calibration of the model to the base data set. Section 4 describes the effects on EC production and external trade of the two main policy experiments undertaken, and section 5 looks at their implications for factor prices. Section 6 describes the effects of the two policy experiments on welfare. Welfare effects are decomposed into parts attributable to the direct effect of the policy, to interaction with distortions, and to terms of trade changes. Section 7 presents sensitivity analyses, both with respect to an alternative policy experiment in which the reduction in trade costs is not uniform across industries and with respect to the assumptions about market structure used in the calibration of the model.

2   The model

We work with 8 countries. 7 represent the EC: France, Germany, Italy, the UK, Other EC North (Benelux and Denmark), Greece/Ireland, and Iberia (Spain and Portugal). (The anomalous linking of Ireland and Greece reflects our judgement about the quality of the data available on these countries rather than geographical ignorance.) The eighth country, ROW, is a rather simple representation of the Rest of the World. In our 1991 study, we worked with an alternative level of aggregation, in which Iberia, Other EC North and Greece/Ireland are treated as a single country, the Rest of the EC. Aggregation is not a simple matter of presentation, because the assumption of national market segmentation implies that an aggregation of national markets entails a change in firms' pricing behaviour in these markets, and further because the impact of a reduction in intra-EC trade costs depends on the country structure imposed on the EC. The structure we work with is as disaggregated as data allow and while some intra-EC trade is treated as intra-country rather than inter-country trade, less than 15 per cent of trade is so misclassified.

Each country is endowed with 5 primary factors of production: capital (factor 1), and labour disaggregated into 4 skill types. The types of labour are: professional, scientific and related non-manual (factor 2); managerial, clerical and other non-manual (factor 3); skilled manual (factor 4); and unskilled manual (factor 5). We assume that capital is perfectly mobile internationally, and available at a constant price. Other factors are internationally immobile, so their prices adjust to equate demands to endowments. The commodity structure of the model comprises 13 manufacturing industries (listed in Table 2.1, see section 3 below) and 1 financial services' sector, all of which are assumed to be imperfectly competitive, and which are modelled in some detail. The remainder of each economy is aggregated into a single perfectly competitive composite, which is tradeable and which we take as the numéraire.

Each industry contains a number of firms, with n_i^k denoting the number of firms in industry k located in country i. For a particular industry and country all firms are symmetric: for each k and each i, the n_i^k firms have the same production and sales patterns. Each of these firms produces a number of varieties of differentiated product, which we denote m_i^k. The output of each industry is used both in final demand, and as an intermediate.

Consider first final demand. p_{ij}^k and x_{ij}^k denote the price and quantity of a single product variety of industry k produced in country i and used (as a final demand) in country j. (There are $n_i^k m_i^k$ such varieties and, because of symmetry, we do not need to introduce a notation for individual varieties.) Consumer preferences are such that the following aggregation procedure is possible. First, varieties within an industry and country of sale are aggregated into a quantity index X_j^k with associated price index P_j^k. This is done by a constant elasticity of substitution aggregator with elasticity of substitution (common to all countries) denoted ϵ^k. The functional form of this is given in the Appendix. It is important to note that at this level we aggregate over products from all sources of production, so we do not use the Armington assumption of separate nesting of products by geographical source. Second, the quantity and price indices X_j^k, P_j^k are aggregated into utility and expenditure functions. There is a single representative consumer with homothetic preferences in each country. If u_j is utility, E_j is the unit expenditure function, and M_j is income, then the budget constraint is

$$M_j = u_j E_j(\ldots, P_j^k, \ldots) \tag{1}$$

E_j is assumed to be Cobb–Douglas. The functional form is given in the Appendix. Consumer demands both for the aggregate quantity indices and for individual varieties are derived by partial differentiation of the expenditure function.

The quantity of a single product variety of industry k produced in i and used as an intermediate good in j is denoted y_{ij}^k with price q_{ij}^k. Technology is supposed to be such that the following aggregation procedure is possible. First, varieties within an industry and country of sale are aggregated into a quantity index Y_j^k with associated price index Q_j^k. (Once again, they are not separately nested by geographical source.) Second, the quantity and price indices are aggregated into a composite intermediate commodity whose price index in country j is F_j (see the Appendix). This implies that there is a single composite intermediate commodity, so that the proportions in which each industry uses the products of other industries are assumed to be the same.

The costs of a firm in industry k of country i are given by a cost function c_i^k,

$$c_i^k = m_i^k[h^k(z_i^k)G_i^k(F_i, w_i^1, w_i^2, w_i^3, w_i^4, w_i^5)] \tag{2}$$

where

$$z_i^k = \sum_j \{x_{ij}^k + y_{ij}^k\} \tag{3}$$

z_i^k is the total output per variety of a country i firm in industry k. The function h^k describes the returns to scale in industry k. Increasing returns to scale means that $h^k(z_i^k)/z_i^k$ is decreasing in z_i^k, and we employ a functional form for h^k that permits decreasing marginal cost as well as decreasing average cost (see the Appendix). Notice that this function is not country-specific. Furthermore, there are no economies of scope, since c_i^k is linear in m_i^k, and returns to scale are associated with output per variety, z_i^k. The function G_i^k aggregates input prices into cost per unit h. Its arguments are the intermediate price index, F_i, and the prices of the 5 primary factors of production, w_i^l. The functions G_i^k differ by country, but only by a scalar, implying Hicks-neutral technical differences. Input demands, which in equilibrium equal factor supplies, v_i^l, are partial derivatives of these cost functions so we have

$$v_i^l = \sum_k n_i^k m_i^k h^k(z_i^k)\frac{\partial G_i^k(F_i, w_i^1, w_i^2, w_i^3, w_i^4, w_i^5)}{\partial w_i^l} \quad (l = 1, \ldots, 5) \tag{4}$$

The profits of firms are given by

$$\pi_i^k = m_i^k \sum_j \{p_{ij}^k x_{ij}^k + q_{ij}^k y_{ij}^k\}\{1 - \tau_{ij}^k - t_{ij}^k\} - c_i^k \qquad (5)$$

where τ_{ij}^k and t_{ij}^k are respectively the *ad valorem* tariff and transaction costs of shipping a unit of industry k output from economy i to economy j. (The tariff is non-zero only where j is in the EC and i is ROW, when the value of the tariff is the EC's common external tariff, CET). We assume that all external trade barriers are tariffs, not quantity restrictions.

Two alternative assumptions are made about firms' choice of sales quantities for final goods. The first is to assume that firms act as Cournot competitors in segmented markets. Each firm in industry k and country i then chooses sales in market j, x_{ij}^k, taking as constant the sales of all its rivals in each market. Optimisation requires the equation of marginal revenue to marginal cost in each market, where the slope of each firm's perceived demand curve depends on the extent of product differentiation, and on the share of the firm in that market. This will be referred to as the *segmented market* hypothesis. An equation for the equality of marginal revenue to marginal cost is given in the Appendix.

The alternative assumption is that firms choose a total quantity for sale in the 7 EC markets combined, taking as constant total EC sales of rival firms, with the distribution of these aggregate quantities between markets in the EC then determined by arbitrage so as to equate the producer prices of the product, making $p_{ij}^k(1 - t_{ij}^k) = p_{il}^k(1 - t_{il}^k)$ for all countries j, l, in the EC. This second hypothesis will be referred to as the *integrated market* hypothesis. Its force is that the slope of firms' perceived demand curves now depends on product differentiation, and on the firm's share in the EC as a whole, rather than in each separate market. Alternative behavioural hypotheses are possible, some of which are discussed in Venables (1992).

Firms' choice of intermediate sales quantities, y_{ij}^k, is less straightforward. It is possible that purchasers of inputs have some monopsony power, to be combined with the monopoly power of sellers. Further, and perhaps more importantly, even if purchasers of intermediates are input price-takers, the demand for intermediates is a derived demand, and establishing the elasticity of the derived demand curve is not straightforward. For these reasons we assume that the price of a good sold as an intermediate equals the price of the same good sold to final demand, $q_{ij}^k = p_{ij}^k$. Furthermore, the number of varieties of intermediate goods entering the price indices Q_j^k is held constant, so abstracting from any variety effects on the users of intermediate goods.

As has been noted above, each firm produces a number of varieties of product, m_i^k. It is assumed throughout this chapter that these numbers are constant. Furthermore, it is assumed that, at the base, output per variety, z_i^k, is the same for all firms. m_i^k should therefore be thought of as a scaling device, with different firm sizes in the base data set attributed to differences in the number of varieties firms produce, not to differences in output per variety. The effect of this assumption is to ensure that all firms have the same degree of unexploited economies of scale.

All that remains to complete the description of the model is the determination of income. Income accruing to factor l in the economy is $w_i^l v_i^l$. National income is factor income accruing to the 5 factors, plus the profits of firms and CET revenue:

$$M_i = v_i^1 w_i^1 + v_i^2 w_i^2 + v_i^3 w_i^3 + v_i^4 w_i^4 + v_i^5 w_i^5$$

$$+ \sum_k n_i^k \pi_i^k + \sum_k n_8^k m_8^k \tau_{8i}^k \{p_{8i}^k x_{8i}^k + q_{8i} y_{8i}^k\} \tag{6}$$

where country 8 is ROW. Notice that CET revenue is attributed to the importing country, though in reality it accrues to the EC as a whole.

3   Data and calibration

The modelling exercise requires calibrating the model to a particular data set. The principal data requirements are first, trade and domestic sales data broken down by industry and by country; secondly, a range of industry-specific parameters. Numerical specification of the model can then be completed by calculating the values of remaining parameters and endogenous variables such that the base-year observations support an equilibrium. Comprehensive literature reviews were undertaken for a number of the industry-specific parameters required. A complete list of sources is not provided here but is available on request. Key items are referenced in the text.

The overall structure of the model is one of 8 economic areas or 'countries' (listed in section 2), 14 imperfectly competitive industries (listed in Table 2.1), and 1 perfectly competitive sector which comprises the rest of the economy.

The industrial structure used is based on the R25 sub-division of the European Community NACE–CLIO classification scheme. The R25 sub-division distinguishes between 13 manufacturing and 12 non-manufacturing sectors. Here the non-manufacturing sectors are aggregated into 2 sectors – financial services, assumed to be imperfectly competitive, and all of the rest treated as a single perfectly competitive sector; while each of the 13 manufacturing industries is treated as a separate sector.

The base year taken for the calibration is 1985 which is the latest year for which an almost complete set of trade and production data was available.

Where the data were incomplete the data set was supplemented from published Eurostat data and adjusted as appropriate.

3.1   Trade and production

Both trade and production data were obtained from the European Commission: trade data from the VOLIMEX data base, and production data from the BDS data base. These particular data sources were chosen on the grounds of accuracy and reliability. In each case the data base derives from the same source as comparable published Eurostat data, but has been adjusted by the European Commission to improve the degree of compatibility both between different country returns and between the two data bases themselves. Data on international trade in financial services were not available broken down both by country of origin and country of destination, and a matrix of trade data at this level of disaggregation was derived by application of an rAs procedure to the data published in the 1991 Eurostat report *International Trade in Services: EUR12 – From 1979 to 1988.*

Despite the Commission's attempts to reconcile trade and production data, problems of incompatibility remain. There is the fundamental difficulty that trade data are collected on a commodity basis, while production data are collected on an activity basis. Further, the trade data include re-exports, and therefore tend to exaggerate trade flows.

Production statistics for 1985 were not available on the BDS data base for Greece and, in the case of 1 industry, for Portugal. Comparable data were therefore obtained from Eurostat *Structure and Activity of Industry, 1985, Main Results (SAI)*, and scaled as appropriate. For Greece the latest available figures from *SAI* were for 1983, so these were rescaled to account for Greek growth between 1983 and 1985.

3.2   Industrial data

The industry-specific data required include the share of value added in production; the share of each factor in value added; the elasticity of substitution between different factors of production; the share of final demand in the output of each industry; the degree of returns to scale in each industry; and a measure of the number of symmetric firms competing in each industry and each country. Some of the key features of these data are presented in Table 2.1.

The model distinguishes between 5 factors of production – capital (K) and four types of labour: professional, scientific and related non-manual (L1), managerial, clerical and other non-manual (L2), skilled manual

Table 2.1. *Industry data*

Industry	Factor shares in value added (%)				
	K	L1	L2	L3	L4
Metalliferous products	0.424	0.111	0.119	0.086	0.258
Non-metallic mineral products	0.304	0.127	0.153	0.101	0.314
Chemical products	0.322	0.226	0.167	0.072	0.212
Metal products	0.192	0.156	0.158	0.198	0.295
Agric. & ind. machinery	0.161	0.222	0.156	0.268	0.193
Office machy & prec. inst.	0.158	0.330	0.209	0.133	0.170
Electrical goods	0.151	0.253	0.162	0.162	0.271
Transport equipment	0.227	0.166	0.138	0.207	0.260
Food products	0.287	0.149	0.162	0.080	0.321
Textiles, clothing, leather	0.189	0.139	0.162	0.108	0.401
Paper & printing products	0.236	0.183	0.153	0.178	0.249
Rubber & plastic products	0.164	0.156	0.169	0.217	0.295
Timber and other n.e.s	0.231	0.166	0.149	0.079	0.375
Banking and insurance	0.176	0.202	0.621	0.000	0.000
Perfectly competitive sector	0.406	0.094	0.172	0.093	0.233

Industry	Conc-entration	Sub-Industry	IRS	FES	ϵ	ϵ'
Metalliferous products	0.021	1	6	0.09	17.79	17.8
Non-metallic mineral products	0.025	4	8	0.18	14.33	10.7
Chemical products	0.032	3	15	0.28	8.16	7.1
Metal products	0.009	5	7	0.35	16.52	14.7
Agric. & ind. machinery	0.012	5	7	0.64	12.88	12.1
Office machy & prec. inst.	0.078	3	15	0.64	13.42	7.9
Electrical goods	0.037	6	10	0.54	11.15	8.7
Transport equipment	0.057	1	7	0.68	26.12	26.1
Food products	0.008	3	4	0.65	28.50	22.7
Textiles, clothing, leather	0.003	4	3	0.62	31.25	28.4
Paper & printing products	0.005	3	13	0.21	6.94	6.6
Rubber & plastic products	0.005	3	5	0.20	17.47	16.9
Timber and other n.e.s	0.013	2	5	0.54	21.22	18.6
Banking and insurance	0.008	2	5	0.21	21.88	18.8

(L3), and unskilled manual (L4). Both the share of value added in production, and the share of capital in value added were calculated from the BDS data base. The shares of the 4 different types of labour were calculated on the basis of UK earnings data, and the UK Census of Production. UK shares were taken to apply to all countries. The factor shares in value added are listed in Table 2.1. Table 2.1 shows that the most capital-intensive industries are metalliferous products and chemical products, and the least capital-intensive are electrical goods, office machinery and precision instruments, and agricultural and industrial machinery. The industries most intensive in professional and highly skilled workers are the electrical goods industry, office machinery and precision instruments, and financial services (which are assumed to employ no manual labour). The most manual labour-intensive industries are the metal products, rubber and plastic, and textile industries.

The G_i^k component of the cost function is a nested constant elasticity of substitution (CES) function. The capital–labour elasticity of substitution is derived from a review of the available literature and is largely based on the estimate in Piggott and Whalley (1985). In the version of the model presented in this chapter the same measure of elasticity is then also assumed between the different types of labour.

Central to the model is the interaction between the degree of scale returns and the extent of concentration in each industry. We measure the degree of concentration by computing Herfindahl indices. The reciprocal of this index gives the number of equal-sized firms in the industry equivalent to the observed size distribution, and it is this that we use for firm numbers in the model. For most countries, data for the computation of the Herfindahl indices were obtained from Eurostat. The data source here is the same which is used in compiling Eurostat's *Structure and Activity of Industry, 1985, Results by Size Class*, but with a wider size class breakdown. For the remaining countries data were obtained from the respective national statistical offices, except for Portugal where firm numbers were estimated on the basis of firm sizes in Spain. Unfortunately, primarily for reasons of statistical confidentiality, the largest size class for which data were available was rarely greater than 5000 employees, and frequently only 1000 employees. However, where one is interested in establishing the degree of market power firms may have it is precisely in the largest size classes that the most important interactions take place. In order to capture the dispersion of firms in the top size class it was assumed that the size of firms in this class follows a Pareto distribution. The Herfindahl index for each industry and country was then computed on the basis of firms in size classes other than the top class all being of average size for their class, and the size of firms in the top size class following a Pareto distribution.

It is, however, not reasonable to suppose that at this level of aggregation each firm in an industry is competing with all other firms. We have therefore assumed that each industry is divided into sub-industries, with firms competing only at sub-industry level, each firm represented in only 1 sub-industry, and each sub-industry within any industry having the same number of equal-sized firms. The number of sub-industries in each industry was based on a Herfindahl calculation of the number of equal-sized 3-digit industries in each of the 13 manufacturing industries (using output weights from a sample of EC countries), with judgemental modifications for 2 industries (metalliferous products, food products) where the procedure generated an implausible number of sub-industries. The financial services' sector was assumed to consist of 2 sub-industries. The number of sub-industries in each industry is reported in the 'Sub-Ind' column of Table 2.1. When an industry is divided into sub-industries, the relevant measure of concentration is now not the Herfindahl index for the industry, but that for the sub-industry, which is the original index multiplied by the number of sub-industries. Sensitivity analysis with respect to the assumptions about sub-industries is reported in section 7.

The concentration measure reported in the first column of Table 2.1 is the Herfindahl index for sub-industries, adjusted to take account of import penetration. The 6 industries with the highest degree of concentration are (in order) office machinery, transport equipment, electrical goods, chemicals, non-metallic mineral products, and metalliferous products. The 3 industries with the lowest degree of concentration are rubber and plastics, paper, and textiles.

Table 2.1 also lists the degree of assumed returns to scale (IRS). In each case the percentage figure refers to the increase in costs as a result of a 50 per cent reduction in output. These estimates are engineering estimates for which the primary data source was Pratten (1988), supplemented by an extensive literature review.

The 'FES' column of Table 2.1 lists the proportion, obtained from Eurostat, *National Accounts, Input–Output Tables* (1985), of the output of each industry that is devoted to final expenditure as opposed to being used as an intermediate good.

3.3   Demand and calibration

The price elasticity of demand for the industry aggregates, X_j^k and Y_j^k, with respect to the associated price indices, are unity, by the Cobb–Douglas assumption. The price elasticities of demand for individual varieties depend on the elasticities of substitution in the CES aggregators. For intermediate products we assume that this elasticity of substitution is the same for all industries, and equal to 5.

For final products we assume that the base data set represents a long-run equilibrium in which profits are zero. Technology and firm scale imply a relationship between average cost and marginal cost and, with the assumption of long-run equilibrium, this also gives a relationship between price and marginal cost. This price–cost margin is supported at equilibrium by two considerations: product differentiation and market power stemming from the degree of concentration in the industry and the form of interaction between firms. We assume that the base case is a segmented market Cournot equilibrium. The price–cost margin then implies a measure of product differentiation, from which we obtain a value of the elasticity of substitution, ϵ^k. Calibrated values of ϵ^k are reported in Table 2.1. They are to be interpreted as the price elasticity of demand for an individual product variety, holding prices of other varieties and the overall industry price index, P_j^k, constant. These elasticities are very high in food, and textiles, and are relatively low (so products are quite highly differentiated) in industries such as paper and chemicals. This method of calibration does of course depend on the form of the base equilibrium. Sensitivity analysis over equilibrium concepts is undertaken in Venables (1992).

The final stage of calibration involves positioning demand curves (i.e. finding parameters of a_{ij}^k of the aggregators given in the Appendix) such that consumption of products in each country is consistent with the matrix of production and consumption.

4   Quantity changes

In this section we focus on the consequences for trade and production of the reduction in trade barriers arising from the completion of the internal market. We report two sets of results: a 'segmented market' experiment in which there is a reduction in the costs of trade by an amount equal to 2.5 per cent of the value of trade; and an 'integrated market' experiment in which there is the same trade cost reduction plus a switch from segmented market to integrated market equilibrium. Within each of these sets of experiments we consider a short-run case in which firm numbers are held constant and a long-run case in which there is free entry and exit of firms from any of the EC countries. The changes in trade costs and market structure occur only in the 14 imperfectly competitive industries; the perfectly competitive sector is not directly affected by the experiment, but changes in response to changes in other sectors.

4.1   Segmented markets

Table 2.2 shows the changes in total EC output, EC exports to ROW and EC imports from ROW for both the short and the long run. EC output in all the imperfectly competitive industries rises by modest amounts. The distribution of the output changes across industries depends on a number

C

Table 2.2. *Segmented markets – % change in production and external trade*

Industry	EC production		EC exports to ROW		EC imports from ROW	
	SR	LR	SR	LR	SR	LR
Metallif. products	1.9	3.5	1.4	3.3	− 4.2	− 4.4
Non-met. min. products	0.8	2.2	0.5	2.3	− 2.9	− 3.2
Chemical products	1.5	1.4	0.4	0.3	− 4.4	− 4.4
Metal products	0.4	0.6	0.2	0.2	− 2.5	− 2.3
Agric. & ind. mach.	1.6	1.7	0.5	0.5	− 7.1	− 7.0
Office mach.	3.6	3.8	0.3	0.3	− 6.8	− 6.7
Electrical goods	1.8	2.5	0.6	1.3	− 5.0	− 4.9
Transport	5.5	9.7	2.0	8.4	− 19.6	− 20.2
Food products	1.1	2.6	5.6	7.7	− 11.6	− 11.5
Textiles . . .	3.1	3.8	2.2	3.0	− 16.1	− 16.0
Paper & printing	0.6	0.6	0.5	0.2	− 1.4	− 1.1
Timber and other n.e.s	2.2	2.0	1.2	0.9	− 6.5	− 6.4
Rubber & plastic	0.8	2.2	0.5	2.1	− 4.1	− 4.2
Banking and insurance	0.3	0.7	− 0.4	0.1	− 1.0	− 0.8

of factors, including the relative share of intra-EC trade in production of each industry, the degree of economies of scale in the industry, the degree of concentration in the industry, the elasticity of demand for the individual product varieties, and cost changes due to general equilibrium changes in input prices. The higher the share of trade in production the greater the benefits of the reduction in trade costs; the greater the economies of scale in the industry the larger will be the cost reductions arising from increasing output; the more concentrated the industry the greater will be the competitive gains arising from the trade liberalisation; the more elastic is demand in the industry the larger the change in output for a given change in costs (and therefore prices); while the effects of input price changes depend on the factor intensity of the industry. The factors are not all independent as the process of calibrating the model chooses the demand elasticity in order to reconcile the assumption about returns to scale with the information about concentration.

In both the short run and the long run the industries that experience the most expansion in this experiment are office machinery and precision instruments, transport equipment, and textiles, clothing and leather. Office machinery and precision instruments is an industry with large economies of scale, high concentration, and a high proportion of output traded within the EC. The largest output effects are in the two most concentrated industries, in which the pro-competitive effect of intra-EC liberalisation will be greatest. The overall expansion of the imperfectly competitive sector occurs partly due to the release of real resources as trade costs are reduced and as firms exploit the advantages of economies of scale, but also due to the contraction of the perfectly competitive sector. In the short run the perfectly competitive sector contracts by 0.56 per cent and in the long run by 0.82 per cent.

Looking at the external trade of the EC we see a decrease in imports and an increase in exports. As usual there is a trade diversion effect coming from the decrease in the cost of intra-EC trade, and this reduces extra-EC imports. In a perfectly competitive model this effect would be offset by an increase in EC prices, as industries move up supply curves. However, in this framework the reduction in imports is reinforced by falls in EC prices as firms move down marginal cost curves, so generating a relatively large reduction in imports. Similarly in a perfectly competitive economy we would expect to see a decrease in exports; however, because of EC cost reductions, extra-EC exports now increase.

The size of the external trade effects is largest in industries where the production increase is large, and where initial imports are relatively small (so the increase is measured against a small base). Of course, changes in the trade position of the imperfectly competitive industries are mirrored in the trade of the perfectly competitive composite sector, since the balance of payments balances.

No account is taken in the model of quantitative restrictions on trade, though in reality EC imports to some industries, notably transport equipment and textiles, are subject to such restrictions. The declines in demand for imports shown in Table 2.2 as reductions in EC imports from ROW might in reality appear in such cases as reductions in the rents gained by constrained exporters rather than in quantities imported.

Comparing the long run and the short run we see that in most, but not all, industries quantity changes are larger in the long run. These are industries in which exit of firms takes place. Remaining firms operate at larger scale, this giving lower marginal costs and a consequent increase in production and exports.

4.2   Integrated markets

In this section we allow not only for the 2.5 per cent reduction in trade costs but we also assume that EC markets are fully integrated. This means that firms can no longer price discriminate between markets but now compete on an EC-wide basis by setting the same producer price in all

Table 2.3. *Integrated markets – % change in production and external trade*

Industry	EC production		EC exports to ROW		EC imports from ROW	
	SR	LR	SR	LR	SR	LR
Metallif. products	4.9	28.0	3.8	30.5	− 10.7	− 13.9
Non-met. min. products	3.6	29.5	2.0	35.7	− 11.4	− 17.8
Chemical products	4.0	6.9	1.3	2.5	− 9.2	− 7.4
Metal products	1.3	5.3	0.7	2.7	− 7.5	− 5.4
Agric. & ind. mach.	2.6	5.6	1.0	3.0	− 10.4	− 9.4
Office mach.	9.7	10.6	0.9	− 0.2	− 16.9	− 13.9
Electrical goods	6.0	15.9	2.1	11.5	− 15.3	− 15.2
Transport	11.4	25.5	6.7	25.7	− 36.5	− 39.4
Food products	3.8	17.4	12.1	32.7	− 25.2	− 27.5
Textiles . . .	4.8	10.2	5.5	12.0	− 20.9	− 22.1
Paper & printing	1.9	5.8	1.6	5.0	− 4.0	− 3.9
Timber and other n.e.s	3.8	7.3	2.8	5.6	− 9.4	− 9.1
Rubber & plastic	2.3	19.1	1.5	19.7	− 8.1	− 9.7
Banking and insurance	1.5	13.5	− 1.1	9.5	− 6.4	− 3.2

markets. This experiment therefore implies a much greater pro-competitive effect of trade liberalisation as each firm's effective market shares are reduced. Table 2.3 shows the consequences of the same two experiments described previously, but this time with the integrated markets assumption.

As can be seen from the first column of Table 2.3, output changes, even holding the number of firms fixed, are significantly higher than previously – in most cases at least twice as high. As in the segmented market case the distribution of these output changes across industries involves office machinery, electrical goods and transport equipment expanding the most. The pro-competitive effect of this policy reduces profits, so exit of firms occurs in the long run. This greatly increases the output expansion, in particular for metalliferous products, non-metallic mineral products, transport equipment and food products. As before, these changes take place due to the combination of the initial reduction in trade costs and the change in concentration (exit of firms from the industry) which enables remaining firms to take advantage of economies of scale, together with the relatively high elasticities of demand in these industries. The changes in concentration are larger in this experiment as a result of the integrated market assumption which makes the EC market much more competitive than previously. These changes are also accompanied by changes in output in the perfectly competitive sector which now contracts by 1.69 per cent in the short run and by 4.5 per cent in the long run.

EC exporters benefit substantially from the integrated market scenario, with some industries greatly increasing their sales to the rest of the world (food products + 12 per cent; transport equipment + 6.7 per cent). The change in the pattern of external trade flows is much more substantial in the long run. This is particularly true of EC exports to ROW, which rise by large amounts as scale economies induce changes in costs. It is in those EC industries which benefit the most from the pro-competitive effect of the trade liberalisation that the change in EC exports to ROW is the greatest. There is also a very substantial decline in imports of some goods.

5   Factor prices

Tables 2.4 and 2.5 report the implications of the experiments for wages; the price of capital is, by assumption, held constant. Table 2.4 and 2.5 permit comparisons of wage changes across both the 4 types of labour, and across the 7 EC countries.

Looking first across types of labour, it is generally the case that the main beneficiaries are type 1 labour – professional, and scientific and related. This is particularly so in the long-run integrated market experiment. In 6 of the 7 countries the largest wage increase is received by this type of labour. Conversely, unskilled labour is the relative loser. In the long-run integrated market experiment, for 5 of the 7 EC countries, the smallest wage increase is for unskilled manual labour (type 4 labour); and in 4 countries this is a wage reduction (in terms of the numéraire, although not necessarily in real terms). The reasons for the differential impact of

Table 2.4. *Segmented markets – % change in factor prices*

Country	SR (Firm nos fixed)				LR (Firm nos flexible)			
	L1	L2	L3	L4	L1	L2	L3	L4
France	0.57	0.13	0.40	0.24	0.74	0.12	0.47	0.22
Germany	0.34	0.15	0.19	0.11	0.44	0.14	0.31	0.08
Italy	0.59	− 0.02	0.60	0.25	0.70	0.03	0.61	0.23
UK	0.54	0.32	0.28	0.12	0.63	0.33	0.34	0.11
EC North	0.46	0.34	0.21	0.52	0.63	0.30	0.34	0.49
Gr/Ire	1.07	0.74	1.10	0.90	1.60	1.03	0.88	0.77
Iberia	0.92	− 0.05	1.38	0.22	1.00	− 0.08	1.43	0.27

Table 2.5. *Integrated markets – % change in factor prices*

Country	SR (Firm nos fixed)				LR (Firm nos flexible)			
	L1	L2	L3	L4	L1	L2	L3	L4
France	1.80	0.36	1.33	0.59	3.44	0.90	1.41	0.29
Germany	0.78	0.84	0.34	0.37	2.34	2.61	− 0.06	− 0.78
Italy	1.81	0.67	1.41	0.65	3.90	2.60	0.78	− 0.27
UK	2.46	0.89	1.78	0.61	4.36	3.01	0.77	− 0.82
EC North	0.22	0.57	0.42	0.63	1.49	0.83	0.47	0.50
Gr/Ire	2.27	1.32	2.05	1.02	5.28	4.58	0.20	− 0.42
Iberia	1.87	0.91	1.53	1.12	3.43	1.23	1.78	1.40

integration across skill types are clear from Table 2.1. All the imperfectly competitive industries are intensive users of type 1 labour as compared to the perfectly competitive sector; and the industries which are the most intensive users of type 1 labour (office machinery and electrical goods) experience relatively large output increases.

Across countries there is some tendency, albeit small, towards factor price equalisation. The coefficient of variation of the price of the first three kinds of labour across countries shows a slight reduction as a result of the policy experiments, although the coefficient of variation of the wage of the least skilled labour shows a small increase. The tendency towards factor price equalisation, modest though it is, reflects the fact that factor endowment-based comparative advantage is being more fully exploited following the trade liberalisations.

6   The welfare consequences of '1992'

Table 2.6 shows the distribution across EC countries of the changes in welfare as a result of all 4 experiments – segmented and integrated markets in both the short and the long run. Welfare gains are measured by compensating variation, and expressed as a percentage of GDP. Table 2.6 shows that all countries experience a welfare gain from trade liberalisation. However, under the segmented markets hypothesis this welfare gain is comparatively small for most of the EC countries. The welfare gains are highest for Greece/Ireland (+ 1.1 per cent) and the Iberian countries (+ 0.6 per cent). The welfare gains are a little larger in the long run. Significantly larger gains are reported in the integrated market experiment in the long run. Except for France and the Other EC North all countries experience welfare gains in excess of 1 per cent of GDP and for

Table 2.6. *Welfare changes with equal-sized policy experiment*

Country	Segmented CV (ECU million) SR	LR	Change in CV as % GDP SR	LR	Integrated CV (ECU million) SR	LR	Change in CV as % GDP SR	LR
France	2077	2835	0.3	0.4	4316	9651	0.7	1.5
Germany	2030	2423	0.2	0.3	2127	8375	0.2	0.9
Italy	1716	2266	0.3	0.4	3604	9282	0.7	1.8
UK	1652	2372	0.3	0.4	4091	11068	0.7	1.9
EC North	1731	2014	0.4	0.5	1244	3190	0.3	0.8
Gr/Ire	589	726	1.1	1.4	850	1536	1.6	2.9
Iberia	1151	1344	0.6	0.7	1747	4337	0.9	2.2

Greece/Ireland and the Iberian countries the gains exceed 2 per cent of GDP. It is worth noting that the policy experiment directly affects only the 14 industries, which account for approximately 30 per cent of GDP.

In order to gain a greater understanding of the source of these welfare gains we decompose them both by industry and by source of gain, first for the segmented and then for the integrated market experiment.

6.1   Segmented markets

The first column of Table 2.7 gives the welfare gains generated by each industry in the long-run segmented market experiment as a proportion of EC consumption of the industry's product. Two observations can be made. First, the gains are quite small – exceeding 1 per cent of consumption in only 2 industries. Second, the distribution of gains across industry follows quite closely the pattern of output changes previously discussed. In particular, we see that the 2 industries with the largest long-run gains (relative to consumption) are transport equipment and office machinery. Gains are smallest in banking and finance and in metal products. This confirms the fact that the gains are greatest in the more concentrated industries.

The remaining columns of Table 2.7 decompose the gains in each industry into 6 components. The unit is the percentage of the total gain in the industry attributable to each component (and elements may exceed 100 per cent if other components are negative). The first two, *DCSp* and *DCSn*, are changes in consumer surplus. Changes in prices of individual

Table 2.7. *Segmented markets – breakdown of welfare gains (A) as % of total welfare gains in each industry with free entry*

	Total as % of EC cons.	DCSp	DCSn	DIS	DGR	DPR	GE
Metallif. products	0.9	13.5	− 0.9	122.1	− 4.7	0.0	− 30.1
Non-met. min. products	0.6	22.5	− 2.8	96.2	− 1.4	0.0	− 14.4
Chemical products	0.9	35.8	2.0	89.0	− 6.3	0.0	− 20.6
Metal products	0.3	45.1	− 0.7	73.5	− 1.8	0.0	− 16.0
Agric. & ind. mach.	0.9	72.1	− 0.4	37.3	− 6.8	0.0	− 2.3
Office mach.	1.1	78.2	0.3	40.9	− 14.5	0.0	− 4.9
Electrical goods	0.9	63.2	− 5.7	51.0	− 10.0	0.0	1.4
Transport	1.6	91.3	− 15.9	39.5	− 9.4	0.0	− 5.5
Food products	0.4	140.6	− 20.8	64.9	− 27.1	0.0	− 57.8
Textiles ...	0.6	116.0	− 3.7	57.2	− 51.5	0.0	− 17.9
Paper & printing	0.3	27.5	3.4	97.7	− 3.3	0.0	− 25.3
Timber and other n.e.s.	0.6	71.0	3.9	51.8	− 14.9	0.0	− 11.8
Rubber & plastic	0.6	26.1	− 2.5	95.4	− 3.7	0.0	− 15.4
Banking and insurance	0.1	16.3	− 2.0	48.5	0.0	0.0	37.2

products, p_{ij}^k, and the number of products available, n_i^k, change the price indices for each industry in each country P_j^k, and hence the value of the expenditure function and consumers' surplus. The second and third columns give these effects, split into the price effect ($DCSp$, attributable to changes in p_{ij}^k), and the variety effect ($DCSn$, attributable to changes in n_i^k). The latter is positive in industries in which the number of firms has increased and negative if there has been a decrease (and would be zero in a short-run experiment, of course). The fourth column, DIS, gives the analogous effect for intermediates. Changes in intermediate prices, q_{ij}^k, change the intermediate price indices, Q_j^k and F_j, and the value of this change is reported as the change in intermediate surplus produced by each industry which supplies intermediates. The fifth column, DGR, gives the change in external tariff revenue, and the sixth, DPR, the change in profits of firms in the industry. In the long-run experiment shown in Table 2.7, the profit effect is necessarily zero. The seventh column, GE, shows what we call the general equilibrium effect: the change in industry costs due to changes in input prices. The need for this to be accounted for is most easily seen by supposing that wages have fallen. This would raise profits but not, of itself, raise welfare, being simply a redistribution from labour to profits. The change in costs shown in the GE column would in this case be equal and opposite to the effect shown in the *DPR* column. Similarly, if profits rose only because of a fall in intermediate prices, the benefits of this would have been accounted for in *DIS*, and to avoid double counting an equal and opposite cost effect would be recorded in the general equilibrium column. In a partial equilibrium model such general equilibrium effects would of course be absent.

From Table 2.7 it can readily be seen that the greatest gains arise from the change in surpluses arising from the change in prices: the sum of the change in consumer surplus and the change in intermediate surplus. The distribution of these gains between consumer surplus and intermediate surplus follows closely the final expenditure share of each industry (for example, metalliferous products has a very low final expenditure share, and conversely a high intermediate share).

The change in welfare due to the variety effect will depend on whether there is entry or exit in the industry. A large negative change is reported for transport equipment and food products, which are those industries identified earlier as experiencing the greatest declines in firm numbers. The change in government revenue measures trade diversion, and is in all cases negative (it is zero for the banking and finance sector as there is no CET), which reflects the decline in ROW imports to the EC. The pattern of these changes follows closely the pattern of the external trade flows.

Table 2.8. *Segmented markets – breakdown of welfare gains (B) as % of total welfare gains in each industry with free entry*

	Total as % of EC cons.	Direct	Comp.	Diffn.	Div.	Export T of T	Import T of T
Metallif. products	0.8	67.1	48.6	− 0.9	− 4.2	− 11.3	0.7
Non-met. min. products	0.5	51.5	59.4	− 3.0	− 1.2	− 6.7	0.1
Chemical products	0.8	94.9	12.7	2.2	− 5.1	− 5.5	0.8
Metal products	0.2	87.1	17.3	− 0.9	− 1.7	− 1.7	0.0
Agric. & ind. mach.	0.8	90.7	21.5	− 0.6	− 6.2	− 5.8	0.3
Office mach.	1.0	83.9	24.7	− 0.2	− 12.2	− 1.0	4.8
Electrical goods	0.8	73.2	48.0	− 6.2	− 8.3	− 7.7	1.0
Transport	1.5	47.8	89.2	− 16.4	− 8.2	− 14.2	1.9
Food products	0.3	80.9	78.3	− 25.2	− 24.8	− 9.3	0.1
Textiles ...	0.5	124.8	39.6	− 4.9	− 52.7	− 7.2	0.4
Paper & printing	0.3	83.0	18.0	3.8	− 2.6	− 2.2	0.0
Timber and other n.e.s.	0.5	98.1	18.3	4.6	− 14.9	− 6.4	0.3
Rubber & plastic	0.5	66.3	43.6	− 2.7	− 3.1	− 4.2	0.1
Banking and insurance	0.1	59.5	42.5	− 2.3	0.0	0.3	0.0

Table 2.8 presents a different way of decomposing the welfare gains for each industry by looking at the direct cost saving of the policy, at 'distortions' in each industry, and at changes in external terms of trade. The 'distortions' term is relevant because quantity changes have welfare effects if marginal costs differ from marginal social valuations. We identify these effects by first order approximations. This is why the first column of Table 2.8, giving welfare gain generated by each industry as a percentage of consumption, is different from the first column of Table 2.7. Again, the remaining columns in this table give the percentage of the total welfare gain in that industry which is attributable to each component.

The first component of the welfare gain (direct) gives the direct cost saving due to the assumed reduction in the cost of trade. The second, (competition), measures welfare changes associated with the fact that firms set prices above marginal cost. The approximation we use to get this effect is the sum of changes in outputs produced of each good times the price marginal cost margin on that good. Denoting changes by Δ, this is

$$\sum_i n_i^k m_i^k \sum_j \left[\left\{ p_{ij}^k \left(1 - t_{ij}^k \right) - \frac{\partial c_i^k}{\partial z_i^k} \right\} \Delta x_{ij}^k + \left\{ q_{ij}^k \left(1 - t_{ij}^k \right) - \frac{\partial c_i^k}{\partial z_i^k} \right\} \Delta y_{ij}^k \right]$$

It should be noted that since price marginal cost margins are generally higher on home than on export sales, and the policy increases trade volumes, it is quite possible that this effect could be negative.

The next effect (differentiation) gives the value of the distortion associated with the changes in the number of firms. Since firms are unable to capture the entire consumer surplus associated with the introduction of a new product, introducing a product will give a welfare gain. With preferences of the type used here the net welfare gain is $1/(\epsilon - 1)$ times the revenue (and costs) generated by the product. The differentiation effect is therefore:

$$\sum_i m_i^k \sum_j p_{ij}^k x_{ij}^k \frac{\Delta n_i^k}{(\epsilon^k - 1)}$$

The fifth column gives trade diversion: the change in the volume of imports from the rest of the world times the CET. The sixth and seventh columns give the value of changes in external terms of trade. With intra-industry trade these can be reported separately for exports and for imports.

The first thing we learn from Table 2.8 is the high proportion of the welfare gain that is generated by the direct effect of the policy, the assumed reduction in trade costs. In the short run, not shown in Table 2.8, this exceeds 100 per cent of the total gains in 4 industries, implying that the other induced effects are, in total, negative. The proportion of gains attributable to the direct effect is reduced considerably in the long run, though there is still 1 case in which the direct effect exceeds 100 per cent. The competition effect brings a significant share of the gains in most industries, as exit of firms brings increased firm scale. The value of the distortion associated with changes in the number of firms is negative where there is exit from the industry and positive where there is entry. These effects are generally quite small.

Trade diversion creates a welfare cost, and the share of this depends on the size of the increase in imports, the level of the CET, and the overall gain in the industry. The terms of trade changes indicate that, in all industries, there is a fall in both export and import prices. The fall in import prices arises as importers cut price in response to increased competition in the EC. The deterioration of the export terms of trade is a consequence of lower marginal costs of firms in the EC, and is largest in the most concentrated industries, for example office machinery and precision instruments, and transport equipment. It should be noted that ROW gains from the net terms of trade changes reported here. In a perfectly competitive model economic integration would generally improve the terms of trade of the EC, and worsen it for ROW; here, the supply-side improvements in the EC are, in part, exported, so giving welfare gains for ROW.

6.2   Integrated markets

Tables 2.9 and 2.10 provide the same two types of breakdown of the welfare consequences of trade liberalisation but this time for the integrated market scenario. Looking across industries we see much larger gains in this case than in the segmented case (comparing Tables 2.7 and 2.8). However, the relative performance of industries is similar, with transport equipment and office machinery giving the largest gains.

Looking at the decomposition of gains in Table 2.9 we see the pro-competitive nature of the integration experiment leading (through short-run profit changes, not shown in Table 2.9) to a considerable amount of exit, as indicated by the welfare loss associated with the variety effect.

Table 2.10 decomposes the welfare gain by direct effect, distortion, and terms of trade. As would be expected, the proportion of the gain attributable to the direct effect of the policy is now much reduced. Most of the welfare gains are attributable to the competition effect – the expansion of production by firms operating with price in excess of marginal cost. Again, this is partially offset by loss of variety, by trade diversion, and by

Table 2.9. *Integrated markets – breakdown of welfare gains (A) as % of total welfare gains in each industry with free entry*

	Total of % of EC cons.	DCSp	DCSn	DIS	DGR	DPR	GE
Metallif. products	3.2	13.9	− 3.1	129.0	− 4.0	0.0	− 35.9
Non-met. min. products	4.3	21.7	− 6.6	96.3	− 1.1	0.0	− 10.4
Chemical products	2.1	38.9	− 3.4	98.6	− 4.5	0.0	− 29.7
Metal products	0.7	52.8	− 11.1	94.1	− 1.5	0.0	− 34.4
Agric. & ind. mach.	1.4	87.3	− 17.8	46.9	− 5.8	0.0	− 10.6
Office mach.	4.8	76.5	− 1.5	32.7	− 7.1	0.0	− 0.6
Electrical goods	3.5	70.7	− 21.2	57.3	− 7.7	0.0	1.0
Transport	4.5	93.9	− 16.4	40.1	− 6.7	0.0	− 10.9
Food products	1.2	158.7	− 50.7	81.3	− 19.8	0.0	− 69.5
Textiles ...	0.8	159.8	− 19.6	86.4	− 56.5	0.0	− 70.1
Paper & printing	1.3	28.7	− 4.6	103.2	− 2.5	0.0	− 24.8
Timber and other n.e.s	0.9	92.1	− 10.1	72.1	− 13.4	0.0	− 40.7
Rubber & plastic	2.1	26.2	− 7.0	103.8	− 2.2	0.0	− 20.7
Banking and insurance	1.6	9.4	− 7.5	33.6	0.0	0.0	64.5

Table 2.10. *Integrated markets – breakdown of welfare gains (B) as % of total welfare gains in each industry with free entry*

	Total as % of EC cons.	Direct	Comp.	Diffn.	Div.	Export T of T	Import T of T
Metallif. products	3.7	14.0	104.0	− 2.2	− 2.8	− 13.5	0.4
Non-met. min. products	4.9	5.6	107.8	− 5.1	− 0.7	− 7.7	0.1
Chemical products	2.0	36.5	75.3	− 3.4	− 3.3	− 6.2	1.1
Metal products	0.7	25.8	89.2	− 10.9	− 1.2	− 3.0	0.0
Agric. & ind. mach.	1.3	52.5	89.2	− 17.8	− 4.9	− 19.4	0.4
Office mach.	3.0	28.7	79.9	− 3.1	− 8.7	0.0	3.2
Electrical goods	3.6	16.2	119.6	− 17.8	− 5.6	− 13.2	0.8
Transport	4.6	15.6	115.3	− 13.2	− 5.2	− 13.9	1.4
Food products	1.6	14.9	134.6	− 31.6	− 10.9	− 7.1	0.0
Textiles ...	0.8	76.6	100.7	− 16.3	− 44.7	− 16.9	0.5
Paper & printing	1.3	16.5	93.7	− 4.4	− 1.8	− 3.9	0.0
Timber and other n.e.s	0.9	53.3	86.1	− 9.5	− 11.6	− 19.0	0.6
Rubber & plastic	2.3	13.9	98.9	− 5.5	− 1.5	− 5.9	0.1
Banking and insurance	1.7	4.6	102.4	− 6.8	0.0	− 0.3	0.0

deterioration in the export terms of trade as some of the benefits of lower marginal costs are passed to ROW consumers.

The results reported in this section can be compared with the partial equilibrium results of Smith and Venables (1988), where the long-run welfare effects of the segmented market experiment ranged from 0.29 per cent to 1.31 per cent of base consumption (excluding a single good for which the effects were much less), while in the integrated market experiment, the effects ranged from 0.40 per cent to 5.57 per cent of base consumption. The range of numbers reported in the first columns of Tables 2.7 and 2.9 are therefore quite comparable with the earlier partial equilibrium results. The welfare changes by country shown in Table 2.6 seem much smaller, but recall that Table 2.6 shows the welfare change as a fraction of GDP for a policy experiment that is assumed to affect directly approximately 30 per cent of the economy.

7 Alternative experiments and assumptions

The experiments described in the preceding sections all assume that '1992' brings a cost reduction of 2.5 per cent of trade costs uniformly across all 14 industries, but the policy impact of '1992' will surely not be so uniform. The Commission of the European Communities (1989) have attempted to identify goods for which the impact will be greatest, and on the basis of their work, and judgements about the possible impact of '1992' in financial services, we have run an alternative set of policy experiments in which the trade cost reduction is increased to 5 per cent in 4 industries: office machinery, electrical products, transport equipment, and food production, and raised to 10 per cent in banking and finance. So that the overall size of the policy experiment is comparable to that investigated in earlier sections, we have reduced the trade cost reduction in the other 9 industries to 0.566 per cent, a level that ensures that the overall cost reduction on intra-EC trade is the same in both sets of experiments. The aim of this exercise is as much to explore the sensitivity of the model to changes in the size of policy changes as to provide a more accurate model of the inter-sectoral impact of '1992'.

Table 2.11 compares the long-run effect of the two sets of experiments. One striking result is that the aggregate welfare effect of the differential trade cost reduction is considerably greater than that of the uniform trade cost reduction. This is easy to understand in the light of the earlier discussion about the industrial characteristics which lead to large policy effects. The industries in which we are now assuming that the trade cost reduction will be greater include some of the industries with the highest degrees of concentration and economies of scale. Secondly, it should be

Table 2.11. *Distribution of welfare gains by industry in the long run*

	Uniform experiment		Differential experiment	
	Segmented	Integrated	Segmented	Integrated
	ECU million (%)	ECU million (%)	ECU million (%)	ECU million (%)
Metallif. products	1314	9	4963	11	224	1	3931	8
Non-met. min. products	487	4	3575	8	107	1	3062	6
Chemical products	1798	13	4276	9	375	2	2951	6
Metal products	350	3	1020	2	77	0	725	1
Agric. & ind. mach.	1194	9	1879	4	256	1	1007	2
Office mach.	619	4	2638	6	1397	7	3309	6
Electrical goods	1208	9	4777	10	2635	13	5953	11
Transport	2871	21	7864	17	7337	36	11868	23
Food products	1421	10	4637	10	4130	20	6797	13
Textiles ...	948	7	1194	3	120	1	416	1
Paper & printing	397	3	1774	4	107	1	1450	3
Timber and other n.e.s.	421	3	670	1	79	0	336	1
Rubber & plastic	384	3	1468	3	80	0	1140	2
Banking and insurance	479	3	5414	12	3360	17	9264	18
Total	13889	100	46147	100	20283	100	52209	100

noted that the changes in the policy effects are not directly proportional to the changes in policy: as the trade cost reduction is doubled in transport equipment, for example, the welfare gain in that sector more than doubles in the segmented market experiment, and less than doubles in the integrated market case. This is the natural consequence of general equilibrium effects which imply that policy changes originating in one sector have effects that are not confined to that sector alone. The general equilibrium effects seem to be more visible in the integrated market experiment.

The second kind of sensitivity analysis we conduct is with respect to market structure. Evidently, each industry contains many different product types. Our model contains two ways of handling the disaggregation from the industry to the product. One is the division of each industry into sub-industries; the other is by product differentiation within each sub-industry. The results reported so far are based on the division of industries into sub-industries, as reported in Table 2.1, with the corresponding (calibrated) measures of product differentiation, ϵ. How are results changed if we handle the disaggregation differently? The model was recalibrated and the experiments re-run with the assumption that

Table 2.12. *Welfare changes with differential policy experiment and with sub-industries = 1*

	Change in CV as a proportion of GDP							
	Differential experiment				Sub-inds = 1			
	Segmented		Integrated		Segmented		Integrated	
Country	SR	LR	SR	LR	SR	LR	SR	LR
France	0.4	0.6	0.7	1.6	0.3	0.4	0.5	0.9
Germany	0.2	0.4	0.2	1.0	0.2	0.2	0.2	0.6
Italy	0.4	0.7	0.7	2.0	0.3	0.4	0.6	1.1
UK	0.4	0.6	0.8	2.1	0.3	0.4	0.5	1.1
EC North	0.5	0.7	0.4	0.9	0.5	0.5	0.4	0.6
Gr/Ire	1.5	1.9	2.0	3.2	1.2	1.3	1.5	2.1
Iberia	1.2	1.0	1.4	2.8	0.6	0.6	0.8	1.6

each industry consists of a single sub-industry. Making this change means that calibrated elasticities are now lower, as reported in Table 2.1 as ϵ'. Lower ϵ corresponds to a greater degree of product differentiation: as would be expected, not using sub-industries to capture heterogeneity within the industry puts more weight on product differentiation between individual varieties.

This change influences the results in two ways. First, lower demand elasticities mean that quantity changes become somewhat smaller. Second, industries are less concentrated (since firms are not divided between sub-industries), so the pro-competitive effects of policy are smaller. Table 2.12 reports welfare changes in this case. We see that welfare gains in the short-run segmented market experiment are now slightly larger. This is because the increase in trade volumes, with associated trade costs, is slightly less. However, in all other cases gains are reduced. As argued above, gains come from the pro-competitive effects of policy. Shifting competition from the sub-industry to the industry level makes the equilibrium more competitive, reducing the scope for these gains. This appears most significantly in the long-run integrated market experiment, in which gains are reduced by around 40 per cent.

8 Concluding comments

We have modelled '1992' in two ways in this chapter: first as a fairly modest change in intra-EC trade barriers, and second as a change in trade barriers accompanied by a significant change in the behaviour of firms. In both sets of experiments we find large welfare effects from factors associated with imperfect competition. Intra-EC trade liberalisation has pro-competitive effects which make a substantial contribution to the welfare change in the first set and are by far the most important component of the welfare change in the second set of experiments.

By modelling intra-EC trade liberalisation in a general equilibrium model, we can address several important questions that cannot be treated in a partial equilibrium approach. We find modest effects on factor markets as trade liberalisation has differential effects across industries with different factor intensities. General equilibrium effects enter into the accounting of the welfare effects of the policy change, but not with sufficient force to make the order of magnitude of welfare changes different from those that would be derived from a partial equilibrium approach. We also find quite large effects on the EC's external trade, as intra-EC trade liberalisation reduces demand for imports from outside the EC.

Policy simulation in numerically calibrated models should always have health warnings attached. The results are based on a theoretical model that is, at best, a very crude approximation to the real world and on a modest amount of imperfect data. In this exercise there are at least three areas of particular concern.

The first is that ROW is modelled in a fairly rudimentary fashion, so that results on external trade effects should be treated with caution.

Second, it is the effects on competition of trade policy changes that dominate our results, but market structure is probably the area in which the interpretation of our data is most problematic. The analysis we have undertaken of the sensitivity of our results to changing the modelling of competition within the industry shows that while the general shape of the results is broadly unchanged the size of welfare effects of policy is fairly sensitive to the modelling of competition.

Third, there is a considerable degree of uncertainty about what '1992' will actually mean. We have addressed this uncertainty first by undertaking two kinds of policy experiment: a segmented market experiment in which firms' behaviour remains unchanged, and an integrated market experiment in which firms' behaviour becomes significantly more competitive as a result of the creation of a single European market. As in our earlier partial equilibrium work, we find that the effects of '1992' differ quite markedly between these two interpretations of what '1992' may mean. We have also investigated the sensitivity of our results to change in the inter-industry distribution of the effects of policy, and find here only a moderate degree of sensitivity.

In short, our analysis confirms the central importance of the effects of

'1992' on market structure and competition, while suggesting that there remains much scope for improving our understanding of how to model the interaction between trade policy and industrial organisation.

Appendix: The model

Consumers in country j, $j = 1 \ldots J$, consume products which are produced in each country, so the number of product types available for consumption is $\sum_{i=1}^{J} n_i m_i$. Demands in each country are derived from a Dixit and Stiglitz (1977)-type welfare function, i.e. there is a CES aggregator of the form,

$$X_j^k = \left[\sum_{i=1}^{J} n_i^k m_i^k a_{ij}^{k(1/\epsilon^k)} x_{ij}^{k(\epsilon^k - 1)/\epsilon^k} \right]^{\epsilon^k/(\epsilon^k - 1)} \qquad j = 1 \ldots J \qquad (A1)$$

where a_{ij}^k are demand parameters describing the preferences of a consumer in country j for a product produced in country i. X_j^k can be regarded as a quantity index of aggregate consumption of the industry output. Dual to the quantity index is a price index, P_j^k, taking the form,

$$P_j^k = \left[\sum_{i=1}^{J} n_i^k m_i^k a_{ij}^k p_{ij}^{k(1 - \epsilon^k)} \right]^{1/(1 - \epsilon^k)} \qquad j = 1 \ldots J \qquad (A2)$$

and representing the price of the aggregate produce, where the p_{ij}^k are the prices of the individual varieties. The unit expenditure function is Cobb–Douglas, so

$$E_j = \prod_k (P_j^k)^{\beta_j^k} \quad j = 1 \ldots J, \quad \sum_j \beta_j^k = 1 \qquad (A3)$$

where the β_j^k give the share of industry k in country j expenditure.

Construction of the intermediate aggregators, Y_j^k, Q_j^k and F_j is exactly analogous.

Profits of firms are given by equation (5) of the text with cost function (2). The function G^k is nested CES. The function h^k takes the form,

$$h^k(z_i^k) = [c_0^k + c_1^k z_i^k + c_2^k (z_i^k)^{c_3^k}] \qquad (A4)$$

Returns to scale depend on the parameters $c_0^k \ldots c_3^k$. Thus, $c_0^k > 0$ is a fixed cost; $c_2^k > 0$, $c_3^k < 1$ implies decreasing marginal cost. Under the segmented market hypothesis firms choose the quantity they supply to each market, given sales of other firms in that market. The first order condition for profit maximisation takes the form,

$$p_{ij}^k(1 - t_{ij}^k)\left(1 - \frac{1}{e_{ij}^k}\right) = \frac{1}{m_i^k}\frac{\partial c_i^k}{\partial z_i^k} \quad i, j = 1 \ldots J \qquad (A5)$$

where e_{ij} is the perceived elasticity of demand and is given by

$$\frac{1}{e_{ij}^k} = \frac{1}{\epsilon^k} + \left(1 - \frac{1}{\epsilon^k}\right)s_{ij}^k, \quad i, j = 1 \ldots J \tag{A6}$$

s_{ij}^k is the share of a single firm from country i in the country j market for industry k.

Under the integrated market hypothesis firms choose total sales to the 7 EC markets, given total sales of their rivals. In this optimisation problem they anticipate that the allocation of all firms' sales between all markets will be such as to equate producer prices of a particular product in all markets, i.e. to satisfy the following equation,

$$p_{ij}^k(1 - t_{ij}^k) = p_{il}^k(1 - t_{il}^k), \quad i, j, l = 1 \ldots J \tag{A7}$$

NOTE

This research was supported by UK ESRC grant no. R000231763, by grants from the UK Department of Trade and Industry and the Southampton University Management School, and by the IT92 research programme at the CEPR, which is funded by the EC's SPES programme. We are grateful to Alan Winters and to participants in the Paris conference (16–18 January 1992) for comments on an earlier version.

REFERENCES

Commission of the European Communities (1989) *The Impact of the Internal Market by Industrial Sector: the Challenge for the Member States*, Brussels. Directorate General for Economic and Financial Affairs.

Department of Employment (1985) *New Earnings Survey, 1985*, London: DES.

Dixit, A. and J.E. Stiglitz (1977) Monopolistic competition and optimum product diversity, *American Economic Review*, 67, pp. 297–308.

Eurostat (1986) *National Accounts ESA, Input–Output Tables 1980*, Luxembourg: Office for Official Publications of the European Community.

  (1989a) *Structure and Activity of Industry, Annual Inquiry 1985, Main Results 1984/85*, Luxembourg: Office for Official Publications of the European Community.

  (1989b) *Structure and Activity of Industry, Annual Inquiry, Data by Size of Enterprise, 1984*, Luxembourg: Office for Official Publications of the European Community.

Gasiorek, M., A. Smith and A.J. Venables (1992) 'Completing the internal market in the EC: factor demands and comparative advantage, Chapter 2 in L.A. Winters and A.J. Venables (eds), *European Integration: Trade and Industry*, Cambridge, London: University Press, pp. 9–30.

Office of Population and Census Surveys (1984) *Census 1981, Economic Activity, Great Britain*, London: HMSO.

Piggott, J. and J. Whalley (1985) *U.K. Tax Policies and Applied General Equilibrium Analysis*, Cambridge: Cambridge University Press.

Pratten, C. (1988) 'A survey of the economies of scale', in *Research on the Cost of Non-Europe: Basic Findings*, vol. 2., Brussels: European Commission.

Smith, A. and A.J. Venables (1988) 'Completing the internal market in the European Community: some industry simulations', *European Economic Review*, **32**, pp. 1501–25.

Venables, A.J. (1992) 'Trade policy under imperfect competition: a numerical assessment', in A. Smith (ed.), *Empirical Studies of Strategic Trade Policy*, Chicago: University of Chicago Press for NBER.

Discussion

LARRY S. KARP

Policy-makers are keenly interested in estimating the economic effects of European integration. They want to know the likely magnitude of changes in employment, production, and trade that will result from '1992'. Aggregating estimates of such effects obtained from partial equilibrium models may be misleading: as factors adjust across sectors, input prices will change. In addition, many industries involve increasing returns to scale and imperfect competition, and these are important in determining the effects of integration. Assessing the magnitude of these effects thus requires a general equilibrium model of imperfect competition. Gasiorek, Smith and Venables' (hereafter GSV) Chapter 2 represents the most ambitious and successful attempt to date to provide such a model.

Most Computable General Equilibrium (CGE) models emphasise the distinction between tradeable and non-tradeable goods. The GSV model assumes that all goods are tradeable, and the important distinction is between those that are produced competitively and those that are produced in monopolistic sectors. The competitive sector is treated as a single aggregate, while there is considerable disaggregation within the monopolistic sectors. This division is consistent with the hypothesis that a large percentage of the effects of integration will be due to changes in the monopolistic sectors.

The extent of disaggregation of these sectors enables the authors to provide detailed estimates of the industry-specific effect of '1992'. This is precisely the sort of information that policy-makers want to see, and thus constitutes one of the strengths of the chapter. Unfortunately, it also creates the danger (which the authors acknowledge) that the reliability of the estimates will be exaggerated in policy discussions.

Considerable effort was made in using the data to obtain reasonable values for parameters of the model, but it is apparent that it was necessary to exercise a great deal of discretion along the way. Given that time, space, and readers' patience are all finite, the details of the decisions regarding the data were wisely not included in the chapter. As is the case for most CGE models, this means that readers are able to get a general picture of where the results come from, but only the authors know where the major weaknesses are.

In view of this, it would be interesting to see a more highly aggregated version of this model, one which contained perhaps only a couple of monopolistic sectors. It would have been easier to understand what was driving such a model, and sensitivity studies could have been presented economically. CGE models are quite useful in providing an overview of an economy, but are suspect when it comes to sectoral detail. A more highly aggregated model would focus policy-makers' attention on economy-wide results, rather than on the less reliable results for specific sectors. It would also be useful to see if the aggregate results of the current model were close to the results of the (suggested) aggregated model.

These sorts of concerns arise because of the nature of CGE models. The greater is the effort to provide detail, and thus to offer a policy-relevant model, the greater is the likelihood of getting the detail wrong. There are, however, two features of the model which deserve comment, and which are not inherent in this type of exercise. The first involves the description of imperfect competition, the second regards the manner in which integration is modelled.

The only source of imperfect competition is that producers of final outputs are able to influence prices by means of their choice of quantity. One reason for this assumption is to make the model tractable. A commodity can serve both as a final output or as an intermediate good. Demand for the final good can be easily obtained from the consumer's utility-maximisation problem, but the derived demand for inputs is harder to express. This makes it harder to model imperfect competition in the market for inputs than in the market for final goods.

Thus, assuming the same prices in the input as in the final demand markets makes the model easier to solve. However, the assumption does preclude the study of other types of imperfect competition which may be equally, or more, important. For example, the model cannot address questions of how European integration may affect vertical integration and control between upstream and downstream industries. Changes in the relations between these industries may be an important result of '1992'.

Economic integration is taken to mean that subsequent to '1992', firms will not be able to price discriminate across national boundaries. To the extent that markets become less segmented, it does seem plausible that the opportunities for price discrimination will diminish. However, it is not obvious why '1992' will have this effect over a broad range of industries. If there are cases where quotas limit the possibilities for arbitrage, and thus sustain price discrimination, then the removal of those quotas will indeed lead to the kind of integration described by the model.

A reduction in costs of moving goods from one country to another, brought about by reduction of tariffs or bureaucratic rules, will have a qualitatively different effect. If it were possible to price discriminate before '1992', then lowering transport costs (broadly defined) might either increase or decrease the incentive for price discrimination. For example, suppose that a firm is able to price discriminate in two markets, and selling in the second market involves an extra cost, per unit of sales, of t (the transport cost). The absolute value of the equilibrium price difference, $p_1 - p_2$, is a function of t, but the comparative statics are ambiguous: a reduction in t could lead either to an increase or a decrease in the price difference. If price discrimination was an important feature of pre-'1992' Europe, it would be helpful to explain why the '1992' reforms would reduce this discrimination. A reduction in transport costs does not provide an explanation.

The results of the model distinguish between the short run and the long run. In the long run free entry drives profits to 0, whereas in the short run profits may be positive or negative. It is interesting to note that in every case the welfare gains in the long run exceed those in the short run. For a variety of market structures (including Nash–Cournot oligopoly) free entry leads to a number of firms in excess of the socially optimal number. This result is even more pronounced if there are increasing returns to scale, so that a larger number of firms implies higher average costs. For many industries, it appears that '1992' will lead to a decline in the number of firms, and an increase in industry concentration. The resulting rationalisation of production more than compensates for the greater oligopoly power.

A considerable portion of the short-run welfare gain is explained by the cost decrease which is assumed to follow the '1992' reforms. Although this varies across industries, it appears that only about half of the welfare gain in the short run is due to adjustment of production. The percentage of welfare gain that is explained by the model (rather than assumed at the outset) is much higher in the long run. This underscores the conclusion that a substantial percentage of the potential welfare gain from '1992' will be due to industry restructuring. For many sectors this requires a decrease in the number of firms. It will be interesting to see if politicians and regulators will permit the bankruptcies and mergers that such a change implies.

The projected fall in net imports in the transport, food products, and textile sectors is noteworthy. Since automobiles, agriculture, and textiles present some of the most vexing problems in trade negotiations, this result may not be welcome news. At this point it is worth repeating that conclusions concerning individual sectors should be viewed with more scepticism than the conclusions for the aggregate economy.

This chapter addresses extremely important questions. The CGE modelling techniques it uses are, in principle at least, appropriate. Moreover, the chapter extends these techniques by including imperfect competition, and it makes a serious effort to use the data in a sensible manner. Studies of this sort provide a valuable addition to the research that is available to inform policy-making. However, I think that there is some danger of being swept away by the elegance and apparent power of CGE modelling. Too much is hidden in these models for the results of them to be regarded as more than suggestive of what might happen if a large number of assumptions are correct. One of the important uses of CGE models is to provide a discipline for thinking about large-scale reform, and to provide an incentive for the development of better partial equilibrium models.

3 Global production effects of European integration

JAN I. HAALAND and VICTOR D. NORMAN

1 Introduction

This chapter reports preliminary experiments with a general equilibrium world trade model developed to analyse the effects of EC integration on the global pattern of production and trade. The model is analogous to the Gasiorek–Smith–Venables (hereafter GSV) general equilibrium model of the EC (Gasiorek, Smith and Venables, 1991) and should be considered its twin. The GSV model is intended to shed light on the general equilibrium effects of integration on the EC countries themselves; our model tries to capture the external effects. The two models have the same theoretical basis and similar overall structure. The difference has to do with the model scope: in the GSV model each of the major EC countries is modelled explicitly, while the rest of the world is summarised in one region. Our model summarises the EC as one region consisting of a number of identical countries, but models the USA, Japan and EFTA explicitly.

The two essential features of European integration which are captured in the model are (1) reduction in real trade costs between European markets (simplified border formalities, lower costs following from harmonised product standards, etc.), and (2) integration of previously segmented markets (i.e. an end to intra-European price discrimination). This calls for a modelling framework with (initially) segmented markets and imperfectly competitive product markets.

The structure of the model (shown in Figure 3.1), which distinguishes 5 world regions – EC, EFTA, USA, Japan, and ROW[1] – is therefore one in which the EC and EFTA each initially consist of 6 separate (but, for simplicity, identical) countries and sub-markets. The USA, Japan, and ROW are modelled as fully integrated markets. Each country produces 12 traded goods and 1 non-tradeable from 3 primary factors, capital and 2 types of labour (skilled and unskilled). For simplicity, the non-traded

67

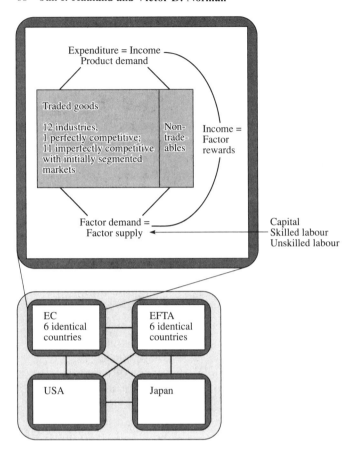

Figure 3.1   Structure of the model

good is assumed to be produced in a perfectly competitive industry. One of the traded goods is also perfectly competitive; the rest are produced in imperfectly competitive industries. Each imperfectly competitive industry is assumed to consist of a number of identical sub-industries. There is Cournot competition with differentiated products and free entry in each industry.

The model is calibrated to actual 1985 data for production and trade and to data from the mid-1980s for industry concentration.

We use the model to simulate the effects of the internal market in the EC and the effects of extending the internal market to a European Economic Area (EEA) comprising the EC and EFTA countries. In both cases, we compute the effects of a reduction in trade costs alone, and the combined effects of lower trade costs and market integration.

In the Chapter, we first give details of model structure (section 2) and calibration (section 3). Sections 4 and 5 present and discuss simulation results. In section 6 we discuss our results in relation to the question of whether the European internal market should be seen as a threat to Japan and the USA. We also discuss our industrial structure simulations in relation to the possible growth effects of the internal market.

2 Model structure

There are R regions, some of which (the EC and EFTA) consist of a number of identical countries and sub-markets. In each industry there are a number of producing firms in each region. Product differentiation is modelled along Spence–Dixit–Stiglitz lines, so that varieties are perfectly symmetric and there is a constant elasticity of substitution between all varieties. Products are used both in final consumption and as intermediate products.

2.1 Final demand

Demand is derived from a two level utility function. The top level, assumed to be Cobb–Douglas, determines demand for commodity aggregates; the bottom level, which is CES, determines demand for individual, differentiated products.

With a CES sub-utility function for the differentiated products from industry i, we can define a perfect price index for the industry,

$$P_i^m = \left(\sum_{r=1}^{R} N_{ir} a_{ir}^m p_{ir}^{m(1-\sigma_i)} \right)^{\frac{1}{1-\sigma_i}} \tag{1}$$

where P_i^m denotes the price index for industry i products sold in market (country) m, σ_i is the elasticity of substitution between product varieties in industry i, and p_{ir}^m is the price of an individual product variety from industry i, produced in region r and sold in market m. The a_{ir}^m are preference parameters which allow for national differences in preferences over product varieties of different origin. N_{ir} is the number of firms in region r, and thus the number of product varieties supplied by region r.

The aggregate demand, denoted C_i^m, for industry i in market m, given a Cobb–Douglas utility function, is simply

$$C_i^m = a_i^m \frac{Y^m}{P_i^m} \tag{2}$$

where Y^m is total income in market (country) m.

The demand for a product variety produced in region r, c_{ir}^m, is then

$$c_{ir}^m = a_{ir}^m \left(\frac{P_i^m}{p_{ir}^m}\right)^{\sigma_i} C_i^m \tag{3}$$

2.2   Production, factor demand and demand for intermediate goods

Goods are produced using the primary factors capital, skilled labour and unskilled labour, and an intermediate goods aggregate. The production technology has economies of scale for the goods produced in the imperfectly competitive industries, and constant returns for the others. Scale economies are modelled in terms of fixed costs and constant marginal costs.

The total cost function for a firm in industry i in region r is

$$B_{ir} = b_{ir}(W_i^r, Q^r)[x_{ir} + f_{ir}] \tag{4}$$

Where W_i^r is a price index of primary factors in region r, Q^r is a price index for intermediate goods used in region r, x_{ir} is output per firm of good i in country r, and f_{ir} captures fixed costs. The $b_{ir}(.)$ functions are CES functions

$$b_{ir}(W_i^r, Q^r) = [\lambda_{ir}^w(W_i^r)^{1-S} + \lambda_{ir}^q(Q^r)^{1-S}]^{\frac{1}{1-s}} \tag{5}$$

The factor price index is a CES index over the prices of capital and the 2 types of labour; so letting w_k^r denote the price of primary factor k in region r, we have

$$W_i^r = \left(\sum_{k=1}^{K} \beta_{ik} w_k^{r(1-s_i)}\right)^{\frac{1}{1-s_i}} \tag{6}$$

The intermediate input is modelled as a two-level CES aggregate: product varieties of different origin constitute an intermediate aggregate from each industry; these in turn combine to an aggregate intermediate good.

The intermediate aggregate from industry i to region r is described by a price index

$$Q_i^r = \left(\sum_{s=1}^{R} N_{is} \delta_{is}^r q_{is}^{r(1-\gamma_i)}\right)^{\frac{1}{1-\gamma_i}} \tag{7}$$

where q_{is}^r denotes the intermediate goods' price of a country s variety of good i supplied to market r. The price index for the intermediate aggregate used in region r is then an aggregate of these:

$$Q^r = \left(\sum_{i=1}^{I} D_i^r Q_i^{r(1-\Gamma)}\right)^{\frac{1}{1-\Gamma}} \tag{8}$$

The firm's demands for primary factors and intermediate goods are given by the partial derivatives of the total cost function with respect to factor prices and intermediate goods prices and need not be spelled out.

2.3 Pricing and competition

For the perfectly competitive industries, price equals marginal cost (which equals average cost). For the imperfectly competitive industries, the producer sales price is a markup over marginal cost. As there are trade costs – modelled in *ad valorem* terms – the consumer price p_{ir}^m in market m of a variety of good i from region r is given by

$$p_{ir}^m(1 - t_{ir}^m) = \text{markup}_{ir}^m b_{ir} \tag{9}$$

The markup differs between final and intermediate sales. For intermediate sales, we make (for simplicity) use of the Chamberlinian large-group assumption, so the markup reflects product differentiation only (i.e. firm market shares do not matter). Thus,

$$q_{ir}^m(1 - t_{ir}^m) = \frac{\gamma_i}{\gamma_i - 1} b_{ir} \tag{10}$$

Note that with this formulation, price differences between markets will exactly equal trade costs, so markets for intermediate goods will automatically be fully integrated internationally.

For final goods, the markup reflects both product differentiation and market shares. The model can be used to solve both for segmented and for integrated markets. In both cases, we assume Cournot competition.

With perfectly segmented markets, and a top-level elasticity of substitution of 1, the Cournot equilibrium markup becomes simply

$$\text{markup}_{ir}^m = \frac{\sigma_i}{\sigma_i - 1} \frac{1}{1 - \omega_{ir}^m} \tag{11}$$

where ω_{ir}^m is the share of a region r firm in the market for good i in market m.[2]

As an alternative to completely segmented markets, one can specify that a particular set of countries constitutes a fully integrated market. Full integration is here, as in GSV, defined as a case where the producer price for a given product must be the same in all parts of the integrated market.

As all market segments matter for the equilibrium prices in this case, the markup function becomes fairly complex. Following Haaland and Wooton (1992) it is, however, not too difficult to write down the equilibrium conditions, even though it may be difficult to find explicit solutions. The general conditions are given in the Appendix on pp. 86–7.

2.4 General equilibrium

The model is closed by factor market clearing conditions and an aggregate income identity. The factor market conditions are straightforward and need not be spelled out. The income identity requires some elaboration, because of the way in which trade costs are accounted for.

We assume that all trade costs are real costs. If so, one must specify a production technology for trade and transactions services. We do this by assuming that trade services subtract directly from utility, i.e. that the production function for trade services is identical to the utility function for final consumption. This can be seen as a general-equilibrium analogue of the 'iceberg' approach to trade cost modelling – it essentially means that consumers enjoy only a fraction of the quantities available, the rest 'evaporating' as trade costs.

3   Data and calibration

3.1   Data

The model has 12 traded goods, corresponding to the 2-digit NACE industrial classification, and 1 aggregate comprising all other goods and services. The latter are called non-tradeables, and are treated as such in the model. It should be noted, however, that this is unsatisfactory, both because there is some trade in non-manufactured goods initially and because the internal market is likely to lead to a significant increase in service trade. In a later version of the model we intend to disaggregate 'non-tradeables'.

Table 3.1 gives the input characteristics of the industries – the shares of value added in the value of production (these differ between regions; the numbers reported are the averages for all regions), the cost shares of the three factors, and the extent to which there are economies of scale.

Based on the factor cost shares, we have placed the tradeables in three groups according to relative factor intensities. The grouping is somewhat arbitrary (one could, for example, argue that transport equipment belongs in the labour-intensive group); so it should be stressed that this is done for reporting purposes only – the industries are not aggregated in the model.

Of the tradeables, 11 goods (NACE 17–49) are taken to be produced in imperfectly competitive industries, while 1 tradeable (NACE 13 + 15) and the non-traded aggregate are assumed to come from perfectly competitive industries. By assumption, then, there are constant returns to scale in the non-tradeables' sector and the perfectly competitive tradeables' sector. For the imperfectly competitive industries, concentration is measured by Herfindahl indexes. The market assumptions are summarised in Table 3.2, which also gives the Herfindahl indexes and the share of each good going to final demand.

Table 3.1. *Input characteristics*

NACE/Industry	Average value added share in production	Factor shares in value added			Returns to scale[a]
		Skilled	Unskilled	Capital	
Capital intensive					
13 + 15 Ores, metals, mineral prod.	0.38	0.28	0.41	0.32	0.00
17 Chemical products	0.31	0.39	0.28	0.33	0.15
36 Food products	0.31	0.31	0.40	0.30	0.04
47 Paper and printing prod.	0.35	0.33	0.42	0.24	0.13
Skill intensive					
21 Agric. & ind. mach.	0.38	0.38	0.46	0.17	0.07
23 Office mach. & prec. instr.	0.51	0.54	0.30	0.16	0.15
25 Electrical goods	0.36	0.41	0.43	0.16	0.10
28 Transport equipment	0.35	0.30	0.46	0.23	0.12
Labour intensive					
19 Metal prod.	0.33	0.31	0.49	0.20	0.07
42 Textiles, clothing and leather	0.35	0.30	0.51	0.19	0.03
48 Timber and other n.e.s.	0.41	0.32	0.51	0.17	0.05
49 Rubber and plastic prod.	0.36	0.31	0.45	0.24	0.05
Non-traded goods	0.65	0.22	0.62	0.16	0.00

[a] Percentage cost increase at one-half initial output.

Table 3.2. *Market characteristics*

NACE/Industry		Market structure	Average Herfindahl indexes				Share to final dem.
			EC	EFTA	USA	Japan	
Capital intensive							
13 + 15 Ores, metals, mineral prod.	T	PC					0.13
17 Chemical products	T	C	0.022	0.074	0.001	0.007	0.28
36 Food products	T	C	0.006	0.019	0.000	0.006	0.65
47 Paper and printing prod.	T	C	0.005	0.024	0.000	0.012	0.22
Skill intensive							
21 Agric. & ind. mach.	T	C	0.003	0.036	0.001	0.010	0.65
23 Office mach. & prec. instr.	T	C	0.103	0.090	0.014	0.082	0.65
25 Electrical goods	T	C	0.016	0.050	0.001	0.023	0.54
28 Transport equipment	T	C	0.120	0.033	0.014	0.060	0.67
Labour intensive							
19 Metal prod.	T	C	0.003	0.017	0.000	0.004	0.36
42 Textiles, clothing and leather	T	C	0.002	0.018	0.000	0.001	0.62
48 Timber and other n.e.s.	T	C	0.002	0.017	0.001	0.002	0.20
49 Rubber and plastic prod.	T	C	0.014	0.044	0.001	0.007	0.56
Non-traded goods	NT	PC					0.60

T = tradeable.
NT = non-tradeable.
C = Cournot.
PC = perfect competition.

Table 3.3. *Initial pattern of production, value added shares of GDP*

	EC	EFTA	USA	Japan
Capital intensive	**0.112**	**0.111**	**0.088**	**0.104**
13 + 15 Ores, metals, mineral prod.	0.034	0.046	0.026	0.040
17 Chemical products	0.024	0.021	0.019	0.025
36 Food products	0.036	0.019	0.021	0.031
47 Paper and printing prod.	0.018	0.025	0.022	0.008
Skill intensive	**0.079**	**0.055**	**0.079**	**0.108**
21 Agric. & ind. mach.	0.023	0.016	0.016	0.023
23 Office mach. & prec. instr.	0.008	0.012	0.016	0.012
25 Electrical goods	0.023	0.012	0.019	0.044
28 Transport equipment	0.025	0.015	0.028	0.029
Labour intensive	**0.060**	**0.068**	**0.043**	**0.089**
19 Metal prod.	0.020	0.026	0.016	0.039
42 Textiles, clothing and leather	0.020	0.016	0.010	0.023
48 Timber and other n.e.s.	0.011	0.019	0.010	0.015
49 Rubber and plastic prod.	0.009	0.007	0.007	0.012
Non-traded goods	**0.750**	**0.761**	**0.792**	**0.710**

The pattern of production in 1985 is shown in Table 3.3. Note that the perfectly competitive industries are very large relative to the imperfectly competitive ones. This should be kept in mind when looking at the magnitude of simulated general equilibrium effects – particularly the simulated effects on factor prices.

In addition to the four regions reported in Tables 3.2 and 3.3, the model has ROW as a fifth region. It plays no active role, however, and is included only to ensure overall trade flow consistency and to simplify a future extension of the model. In the simulations reported in this chapter, trade with the ROW region is kept constant.

3.2 Calibration

The model is calibrated along standard lines, in the sense that some parameters are specified exogenously, while the rest are determined in such a way as to make the model consistent with base-year data. The exogenously specified parameters are the top-level elasticities of substitution in cost and demand functions. On the demand side, all top-level elasticities are automatically unity by the choice of a Cobb–Douglas utility function. On the cost side, the elasticity of substitution between capital and both labour types is set at 0.8, while that between primary factors and the intermediate composite good is set at 0.3. The latter is an arbitrary choice; the former is consistent with a wide range of empirical studies. The substitution elasticity between different goods in the intermediate composite is also set arbitrarily, at 0.5.

Other parameters follow from calibration to data. At the industry level, the procedure is identical to the one used in partial equilibrium models of imperfect competition, see Smith and Venables (1988) or Norman (1989). As in these, calibration gives parameter values for the combined effects of trade costs and consumer preference for home-produced goods, but the breakdown into trade costs and preferences must be specified. Following Smith and Venables, we have arbitrarily set initial real trade costs within Europe at 10 per cent of the value of trade. For trade between Europe, Japan and the USA, real trade costs are set at 20 per cent of the value of trade.

The 2-digit industry classification is an aggregate classification, and concentration measures at this level will underestimate the true degree of market concentration. We have therefore assumed that each aggregate industry consists of a number of identical sub-industries, each with a correspondingly higher degree of concentration that indicated by the aggregate Herfindahl indexes. Specifically, since the effective number of firms in the industry is measured as the inverse of the Herfindahl index, the effective number of competing firms at the sub-industry level is simply the inverse Herfindahl index divided by the number of sub-industries.

The elasticities of substitution between product varieties in an industry are calibrated to make the initial industry equilibria consistent with zero profits.

To calibrate factor endowments, we need data on factor prices. We do not have detailed data on these, but have used rough indications (shown in Figure 3.2) based on different sources, the most important being wage data provided by the employers' federation in Sweden and Norway. Factor demands from each industry are then found as the derivatives of the total cost functions with respect to factor prices, evaluated at the stipulated factor prices; and total endowments are found as the sum of demands across industries.[3]

4   Effects of EC integration

Following Smith and Venables (1988), we have simulated the effects of trade cost reductions between EC countries and the combined effects of trade cost reductions and market integration. In both cases, the trade cost reduction is modelled as an equi-proportionate reduction in real trade costs for all goods from imperfectly competitive industries, the reduction

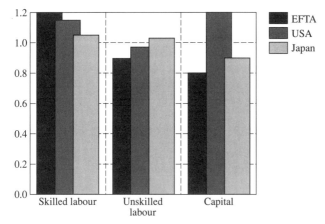

Figure 3.2 Factor price used in calibration (EC = 1)

being set arbitrarily at 2.5 per cent of the initial value of EC trade. In all simulations, we assume free exit and entry of firms, to maintain initial profitability levels.

The simulated effects on production are shown in Table 3.4. There are several noteworthy features. First, the effects for the EC as a whole are much smaller than the effects for individual EC countries reported in GSV (1991). NACE 23, Office machinery, may serve as an illustration. In the corresponding experiment with complete market integration, GSV obtain production changes ranging from + 46 per cent for the UK to − 7 per cent for Italy and − 16 per cent for the aggregate of the smaller EC countries. We get an estimate for the EC as whole of + 4.7 per cent. Since the GSV average effects (across EC countries) are of the same order of magnitude as our estimates, this suggests that GSV capture significant differences between EC countries in the competitive impact of the internal market; alternatively that there is significant (initially unexploited) comparative advantage *within* the EC.

Second, the effects of EC integration on Japan and the USA are very small, both in absolute terms and relative to the effects on the EC countries. It is particularly noteworthy that the EC real income gain is not offset by corresponding real income losses for Japan and the USA – with full integration, their loss is only around 0.05 per cent of their initial expenditures on the goods in question, as compared to a gain to the EC of 1.9 per cent. This confirms the European view that the internal market will not create a 'Fortress Europe'.

The effects on production and real income in the EFTA countries are

Table 3.4. *Effects on production, prices and welfare of EC integration, percentage change from base*

	EC		EFTA		USA		Japan	
	Lower transp. costs	Mkt. integration	Lower transp. costs	Mkt. integration	Lower transp. costs	Mkt. integration	Lower transp. costs	Mkt. integration
Production								
Capital intensive								
13 + 15 Metals	− 0.99	− 0.54	4.34	2.38	0.43	0.02	0.24	0.34
17 Chemical products	0.50	1.40	− 0.90	− 0.30	− 0.06	− 0.02	− 0.02	0.00
36 Food prod.	0.10	1.00	− 0.10	0.80	− 0.01	0.06	0.00	0.06
47 Paper	0.10	0.30	− 0.20	− 0.20	− 0.01	0.00	0.00	0.00
Skill intensive								
21 Prod. mach.	1.30	1.30	− 7.30	− 5.40	− 0.10	0.01	− 0.06	− 0.05
23 Office mach.	2.30	4.70	− 2.70	− 0.70	− 0.30	− 0.20	− 0.40	0.10
25 Electrical goods	0.70	2.10	− 2.10	1.00	− 0.04	0.03	− 0.07	− 0.05
28 Transport	1.10	4.50	− 0.70	− 4.20	0.00	− 0.03	− 0.10	− 0.60

Labour intensive								
19 Metal prod.	0.05	**0.30**	– 0.04	**0.02**	0.00	**0.00**	0.00	– **0.01**
42 Textiles, etc.	0.09	**0.05**	– 1.60	**0.00**	0.01	**0.10**	– 0.03	**0.00**
48 Timber	0.40	**0.40**	– 1.10	– **0.60**	– 0.03	**0.10**	– 0.03	– **0.01**
49 Plastics	0.08	**0.70**	– 0.20	**0.70**	– 0.01	**0.03**	– 0.01	– **0.01**
Non-tradeables	– 0.02	– **0.12**	– 0.01	– **0.01**	0.00	**0.00**	0.00	– **0.01**
Real factor prices								
Skilled labour	0.34	**0.62**	– 0.19	– **0.18**	– 0.02	– **0.01**	– 0.01	– **0.02**
Unskilled labour	0.26	**0.50**	– 0.09	– **0.14**	0.00	– **0.01**	– 0.01	– **0.02**
Capital	0.25	**0.57**	0.11	– **0.04**	0.01	– **0.01**	0.00	– **0.01**
Real income								
% of expenditures on tradeables	1.00	**1.90**	– 0.30	– **0.40**	– 0.02	– **0.04**	– 0.02	– **0.06**

quite significant, however. Given the dependence of EFTA countries on EC trade, that is not particularly surprising. Again, however, it confirms the view that freer trade within Europe is highly important to European countries but no serious threat to overseas production.

The third important conclusion to be drawn from Table 3.4 has to do with the overall pattern of EC production. Market integration will generally stimulate EC production of goods from imperfectly competitive industries, (a) because increased competition and lower prices will shift demand and resources from (initially) competitive to less competitive industries, and (b) because lower trade costs and fuller exploitation of scale economies releases real resources for increased production. That is reflected in the positive effect of integration on production in all the imperfectly competitive industries. Note that production of goods from perfectly competitive industries (metals and non-tradeables) declines.

That is not all. EC production increases by much more in engineering (skill-intensive) products than in other products from imperfectly competitive sectors, and the negative effects on production outside the EC are correspondingly larger for skill intensive goods. In percentage terms, the negative effect on engineering production is largest for EFTA; but in absolute terms, there could as well be significant, negative effects for the USA (particularly for office machinery) and Japan (particularly for transport equipment). It seems probable that this largely reflects the fact that the least competitive industries in the EC initially (office machinery and transport) are found in the engineering sectors. The factor price effects reflect these changes. Real factor prices will, not surprisingly, rise in the EC and fall elsewhere. More interestingly, the price of skilled labour will rise relative to other factor prices in the EC, while it will fall in EFTA, the USA and Japan.

5   Effects of EEA

Our second set of model simulations concerns the effects of the agreement between the EC and EFTA countries to establish a European Economic Area (EEA). If implemented, this agreement could extend the internal market to comprise all of Western Europe. As details of the agreement are not yet published, and as some aspects of the accord have to be renegotiated, it is unclear whether EEA will involve integration to the same extent as the internal market programme. For our purposes, however, we assume that EEA would involve the same for the EC–EFTA area as the internal market would involve for the EC. We have therefore carried out exactly the same set of simulations for an integrated EC–EFTA.

Table 3.5 reports the differential effects of EEA – i.e. the effects of extending the internal market to comprise the EFTA countries. All changes are reported as percentage point changes from Table 3.4. Thus, for example, when Table 3.5 reports an EEA effect on EC production of office machinery in the integration case of + 0.3 per cent, it means that EC production would increase by 5.0 per cent (the Table 3.4 effect of 4.7 per cent plus 0.3 per cent) relative to the base case as a result of Western European market integration.

Welfare effects are generally as should be expected. The EEA will primarily benefit the EFTA countries, and their welfare gain could be substantial. In the simulations, participation in the internal market gives an EFTA gain (compared to staying outside the internal market) equivalent to 3.3 per cent of their expenditures on traded goods; or, in relative terms, almost twice the gain that the EC will make from the internal market. The EC will also gain from the EEA, but the additional EC gain from inclusion of the EFTA countries is a modest 0.1 per cent of expenditures on tradeables. The USA and Japan will lose, but the numbers are very small.

As regards production, the most striking feature of Table 3.5 is the dramatic effect on the pattern of EFTA production. The EEA would mean a very substantial stimulus to EFTA production of skill-intensive (engineering) products, with a correspondingly large negative effect on production of capital-intensive metals and labour-intensive products, particularly textiles and clothing. The converse would be true for the EC, although the percentage (as opposed to the absolute) effects are naturally smaller, since EC production of each good is so much larger than that of EFTA.

There are two forces at work here. One is simply that the extension of the internal market to include EFTA will dampen some of the effects that an EC-only internal market would have on the division of labour between EFTA and the EC. The second, and more important, is that EEA will stimulate EFTA, as well as EC, production of skill-intensive goods.

The industrial structure effects are clearer from Table 3.6, which sets out the total effect on tradeables' production of Western European market integration, relative to base production. As is seen, production of skill-intensive (engineering) products will generally rise substantially both in the EC and EFTA, to some extent at the expense of US and Japanese production. At the same time, production of (capital-intensive) metals will shift from the EC and EFTA to Japan. Within Europe, production of labour-intensive products will shift from EFTA to the EC.

All of these changes reflect two distinct forces. One is the reallocation of resources from (initially) highly competitive industries to less competitive ones. Both the EC and EFTA have higher initial concentration ratios in

Table 3.5. *Differential effects of EEA, percentage point change from EC integration case*

	EC		EFTA		USA		Japan	
	Lower transp. costs	Mkt. integration	Lower transp. costs	Mkt. integration	Lower transp. costs	Mkt. integration	Lower transp. costs	Mkt. integration
Production								
Capital intensive								
13 + 15 Metals	0.54	**0.55**	− 4.87	**− 4.18**	0.28	**0.13**	0.18	**0.11**
17 Chemical products	0.10	**0.20**	1.30	**1.80**	− 0.02	**− 0.01**	− 0.01	**0.00**
36 Food prod.	0.10	**0.20**	− 1.40	**0.60**	0.00	**0.01**	0.01	**0.01**
47 Paper	− 0.40	**0.00**	2.60	**2.00**	− 0.01	**0.00**	− 0.01	**0.00**
Skill intensive								
21 Prod. mach.	− 2.20	**− 1.40**	25.20	**18.10**	− 0.20	**− 0.08**	− 0.14	**− 0.05**
23 Office mach.	0.40	**0.30**	1.10	**4.80**	− 0.10	**0.00**	0.00	**− 0.02**
25 Electrical goods	− 0.40	**− 0.40**	9.30	**10.60**	− 0.05	**− 0.03**	− 0.03	**− 0.05**
28 Transport	0.30	**− 1.10**	− 0.50	**23.00**	− 0.01	**− 0.02**	− 0.10	**0.00**
Labour intensive								
19 Metal prod.	0.15	**0.30**	− 0.16	**0.38**	0.00	**0.00**	0.00	**0.00**
42 Textiles, etc.	1.31	**1.05**	− 10.90	**− 6.60**	− 0.02	**0.00**	− 0.01	**0.00**

48 Timber	− 0.60	0.80	3.70	− 0.40	0.00	0.00	− 0.02
49 Plastics	0.42	0.40	− 2.30	− 1.10	− 0.01	0.00	0.00
Non-tradeables	0.01	0.00	− 0.01	− 0.30	0.00	0.00	0.00
Real factor prices							
Skilled labour	0.00	0.01	0.89	1.43	0.00	− 0.01	− 0.01
Unskilled labour	0.03	0.02	0.62	1.07	− 0.01	0.00	− 0.01
Capital	0.06	0.04	0.36	1.05	0.00	0.00	0.00
Real income							
% of expenditures on tradeables	0.10	0.10	2.10	3.30	− 0.01	− 0.01	− 0.02

Table 3.6. Total effect on production of EC integration and EEA, percentage change from base

	EC		EFTA		USA		Japan	
	Lower transp. costs	Mkt. integration	Lower transp. costs	Mkt. integration	Lower transp. costs	Mkt. integration	Lower transp. costs	Mkt. integration
Capital intensive								
13 + 15 Metals	− 0.46	**0.00**	− 0.53	**− 1.80**	0.71	**0.15**	0.42	**0.44**
17 Chemicals	0.60	**1.60**	0.40	**1.50**	− 0.08	**− 0.03**	− 0.03	**0.00**
36 Food prod.	0.20	**1.20**	− 1.50	**1.40**	− 0.01	**0.08**	0.00	**0.07**
47 Paper	− 0.30	**0.30**	2.40	**1.80**	− 0.01	**0.00**	− 0.01	**0.00**
Skill intensive								
21 Prod. mach.	− 0.90	**− 0.10**	17.90	**12.70**	− 0.30	**− 0.07**	− 0.20	**− 0.10**
23 Office mach.	2.70	**5.00**	− 1.60	**4.10**	− 0.40	**− 0.20**	− 0.40	**0.08**
25 Electrical goods	0.30	**1.70**	7.20	**11.60**	− 0.09	**0.00**	− 0.10	**− 0.10**
28 Transport	1.40	**3.40**	− 1.20	**18.80**	− 0.01	**− 0.04**	− 0.20	**− 0.60**
Labour intensive								
19 Metal prod.	0.20	**0.60**	− 0.20	**0.40**	− 0.01	**0.01**	0.00	**− 0.01**
42 Textiles, etc.	1.40	**1.10**	− 12.50	**− 6.60**	− 0.02	**0.10**	− 0.04	**0.01**
48 Timber	− 0.20	**1.20**	2.60	**− 1.00**	0.03	**0.10**	− 0.05	**− 0.03**
49 Plastics	0.50	**1.10**	− 2.50	**− 0.40**	− 0.02	**0.03**	0.01	**0.01**

the engineering industries than in other industries; we should thus expect market integration to have a greater, positive impact in those industries. The other relates to comparative advantage. With imperfectly competitive markets, comparative advantage will be less than fully exploited. As European markets become more competitive, therefore, we should expect reallocation of resources to industries in which Western Europe have latent, but less than fully exploited, comparative advantage. The simulation results suggest that engineering products could be examples of such goods.

6   Conclusions and extensions

The most important conclusion to be drawn from our simulations is that the internal market in Europe poses no threat to Japan or the USA. Market integration in Europe will benefit the EC significantly; it will be even more important to the EFTA countries if the EEA accord is implemented; but the (negative) effects on real incomes in Japan and the USA will be negligible.

The other striking conclusion concerns the effects of European integration on industrial structure in Europe. One of the original, major arguments for the establishment of a unified, internal market within the EC was that this would foster economic growth by shifting resources into rapid-growth industries – typically R&D or skill-intensive engineering sectors. The simulation experiments reported in this chapter lend some support to this argument. European integration will induce significant reallocation of resources into engineering industries, both in the EC and in EFTA (if the internal market is extended to include the EFTA countries). Since our model is a static one, however, we cannot say whether or not this reallocation will stimulate European economic growth. It could be an interesting extension to tie together general equilibrium simulations of our type and endogenous-growth simulations based on industrial cluster externalities of the Porter type.

In our model, non-manufactured goods are treated as one aggregate 'non-tradeable' good with perfectly competitive national markets. Since some of the major effects of European integration are likely to be found in service industries, this is highly unsatisfactory. An obvious extension, therefore, is to disaggregate 'non-tradeables' and model service industries as imperfectly competitive sectors producing goods which are traded internationally, or can become so.

Appendix: Cournot competition in integrated markets

In the model it is possible to specify which countries are part of the integrated markets, and which ones are outsiders. Hence, the model can treat 'pure' EC integration as well as integration between the EC and EFTA. Full integration is here, as in Smith and Venables (1988), defined as a case where the producer price for a given product must be the same in all parts of the integrated markets.

As all market segments matter for the equilibrium prices in this case, the markup function becomes fairly complex. Following Haaland and Wooton (1992) it is, however, not too difficult to write down the equilibrium conditions, even though it may be difficult to find explicit solutions.[4] The general conditions we have modelled are given from the following reasoning:

Let IR be the set of markets that are part of the integrated market, and let

$$\theta_{ir}^m = \frac{c_{ir}^m}{\displaystyle\sum_{s \in IR} c_{ir}^s}$$

be the share of a representative country r firm's total sales in the integrated markets sold in market segment m, where $m \in IR$. Let R_{ir}^h be the relative, expected market price reaction equivalent to the Cournot assumption from firm h. That is: when firm r increases its price marginally, it perceives the market price in the integrated market for a product from country h to increase by proportion R_{ir}^h (the same relative price change in all segments of the integrated market, by definition), in order to be consistent with the Cournot assumption for the overall integrated market.

Using this, and the properties of the demand functions and price indices, the perceived effect on the price level in market $m \in IR$ of a marginal price increase by a representative, individual firm from country r can be written:

$$\left(\frac{dP_i^m}{dp_{ir}^m}\right)^* \frac{p_{ir}^m}{P_i^m} = \omega_{ir}^m + (N_{ir} - 1)\omega_{ir}^m R_{ir}^r + \sum_{h \neq r} N_{ih}\omega_{ih}^m R_{ir}^h$$

where superscript * indicates that this is the perceived effect, given that we have Cournot competition and integrated markets. This can be written:

$$\left(\frac{dP_i^m}{dp_{ir}^m}\right)^* \frac{p_{ir}^m}{P_i^m} = \omega_{ir}^m(1 - R_{ir}^r) + \sum_{h=1}^{R} N_{ih}\omega_{ih}^m R_{ir}^h \qquad (A1)$$

The overall perceived price elasticity for a representative firm from country r (inside or outside IR) in the integrated market is:

$$\epsilon_{ir} = - \sum_{m \in IR} \theta_{ir}^m \left(\frac{dc_{ir}^m}{dp_{ir}^m} \right)^* \frac{p_{ir}^m}{c_{ir}^m}$$

Using (3) in the chapter plus the fact that we have a top-level elasticity of unity, implying that $P_i^m C_i^m$ is constant (if the firm disregards general equilibrium effects), the elasticity can be rewritten

$$\epsilon_{ir} = - \sum_{m \in IR} \theta_{ir}^m \left[- \sigma_i + (\sigma_i - 1) \left(\frac{dP_i^m}{dp_{ir}^m} \right)^* \frac{p_{ir}^m}{P_i^m} \right]$$

$$\epsilon_{ir} = \sigma_i - (\sigma_i - 1) \sum_{m \in IR} \theta_{ir}^m \left(\frac{dP_i^m}{dp_{ir}^m} \right)^* \frac{p_{ir}^m}{P_i^m} \tag{A2}$$

The R_{ir}^h for all h must be such that the accompanying perceived quantity reactions satisfy the Cournot assumption. Hence, from the individual country r firm's point of view, the market price reactions for each one of the other products must satisfy (remember that R_{ir}^h is the perceived price rise for products from firm h as seen from firm r):

$$\sigma_i R_{ir}^h - (\sigma_i - 1) \sum_{m \in IR} \theta_{ih}^m \left(\frac{dP_i^m}{dp_{ir}^m} \right)^* \frac{p_{ir}^m}{P_i^m} = 0 \qquad \text{all } r, h \tag{A3}$$

Note that it is the weights of firm h that matter for this expression. Since home-market dominance is central to the effects of market integration, the weights will typically differ between firms. (A1) and (A3) give us a complete set of equations to determine all the R_{ir}^hs.

Comparing (A2) and (A3) for $h = r$ (i.e. for competing products from your own country), it is easy to see that the elasticity must be $\epsilon_{ir} = \sigma_i(1 - R_{ir}^r)$, and the markup factors for the integrated case then become

$$\text{markup}_{ir} = \frac{\epsilon_{ir}}{\epsilon_{ir} - 1} = \frac{\sigma_i(1 - R_{ir}^r)}{\sigma_i(1 - R_{ir}^r) - 1} \qquad \text{all } r. \tag{A4}$$

This is by definition the same in all segments of the integrated market. Note that the markup depends only on R_{ir}^r; it is, however, necessary to solve the complete system of equations to find this.

NOTES

The model developed for this chapter is primarily the work of Jan I. Haaland. Victor D. Norman has participated in discussions of the modelling format, and the particular simulations presented in the chapter are the result of joint work, as is the chapter itself. We are extremely grateful to Michael Gasiorek, who has done almost all the data work. We are also very grateful to him, Alasdair Smith and

Anthony J. Venables for letting us construct a twin model to theirs, for letting us use their data, and for valuable discussions. We would also like to thank Richard Baldwin and Alan Winters for very useful comments on an earlier draft of the chapter.

The research for the chapter is financed by grants from the Norwegian Research Council for Science and Technology (NTNF) and the Norwegian Research Council for Applied Social Science Research (NORAS).

1 The rest of the world is included for accounting completeness only, and trade flows to and from the rest of the world are exogenous. In Figure 3.1, therefore, the ROW region is not included.
2 The derivation of (11) is tedious but straightforward, and can be found in the Appendix to Norman (1990). Note that since the top-level utility function is Cobb–Douglas, the industry price elasticity of demand is unity, which – as is seen from (11) – would give an infinite markup in the case of monopoly. As our industries are oligopolistic, this constitutes no problem in the model.
3 It should be noted that the factor prices used to calibrate factor endowments matter only for the units of measurement of endowments. We could have set all initial factor prices equal to unity in all regions, the only effect would have been that factor endowments could not have been compared across countries. So long as we do not allow for factor movements between regions, that would not matter for the simulation experiments.
4 Detailed proofs are not included below, they can be found in Haaland and Wooton (1992).

REFERENCES

Gasiorek, M., A. Smith and A.J. Venables (GSV) (1991) 'Completing the internal market in the EC: factor demands and comparative advantage', in L.A. Winters and A.J. Venables (eds), *European Integration: Trade and Industry*, London: Cambridge University Press.
Haaland, J.I. and I. Wooton (1992) 'Market integration, competition, and welfare', Chapter 5 in this volume.
Norman, V. (1989) 'EFTA and the internal European market', *Economic Policy*, **9**, pp. 432–66.
   (1990) 'Assessing trade and welfare effects of trade liberalization', *European Economic Review*, **34**, pp. 725–51.
Smith, A. and A.J. Venables (1988) 'Completing the internal market in the European Community: some industry simulations', *European Economic Review*, **32**, pp. 1501–25.

Discussion

RICHARD E. BALDWIN

The results projected by Haaland and Norman's Chapter 3 are interesting and potentially quite important, and I shall highlight three of them. First, the integration of Europe will benefit Europe but will have an almost imperceptible macroeconomic effect on the USA and Japan. Second, if EFTA does not join the EC via the European Economic Area (EEA), or some other arrangement, the '1992' integration of the EC will lead to a moderate decline in EFTA's industrial output. The source of this decline stems from the manner in which the '1992' programme will favour EFTA's major industrial competitors in the EC market. However, if EFTA does join with the EC either through EC membership or through the EEA agreement, then EFTA firms will also benefit from the market opening. As a result EFTA's GDP and industrial output will rise. Clearly this implies that it would be quite costly for EFTA not to join in the EC integration process.

The last result is that potential gains and losses are quite small compared to GDP. For instance, the projected real income gains for the EC from '1992' amount to less than one-quarter of 1 per cent of EC GDP. For comparison, this figure is less than one-eighth the size of the lower end of the Cecchini Report's range of 2.5–6.5 per cent. Nevertheless, the impact will fall primarily on the industrial sector, so it may be useful to state – as Haaland and Norman do – the gains and losses as a percentage of the tradeable (manufacturing) sector. Here the numbers are something like 2 per cent, which is much more in line with the results from other models. It is also important to note that the authors are not looking at the impact of '1992' on the non-industrial sectors of the economy, such as services.

There is one way in which I think the results could be usefully extended. To do this, I will first take a stab at isolating the key effect that is captured in the Haaland–Norman model. The Haaland–Norman model reflects the realities of modern business by assuming that manufacturing sectors are imperfectly competitive. In this sort of situation, a firm's profits and sales typically decline when some of its rivals gain a cost advantage. The size of the loss depends upon the size of its rivals' costs reduction and on the fraction of its rivals that get the reduction. We now see why EFTA loses from '1992'. The EC is the most important market for EFTA countries and in general the primary competitors to EFTA firms are EC firms. Assuming that '1992' makes intra-EC trade easier and cheaper, we see that it has the effect of giving a cost edge to a large fraction of EFTA's industrial rivals. The results, seen in Table 3.4, are a fall in EFTA's manufacturing output and real income.

Given that this is the key effect in the Haaland–Norman model, consider what would be the results of the EEA talks breaking down and EFTA splitting up, with some countries joining as full EC members and others not going through with the EEA agreement. In this case, the Haaland–Norman analysis suggests that the losses to the non-joining countries would be even larger than those stated in Table 3.5. The point is that when some of the EFTA countries with large manufacturing trade join the EC, the fraction of the industrial rivals to the non-joining EFTA nations that receive the costs advantage will be even larger. As argued above, this would cause even greater losses of market share and real income in the non-joiners than is predicted by Table 3.4. The gains to the joiners would be about the same.

I now wish to make two substantial critiques of the Haaland–Norman study.

The second of the two scenarios examined by the authors is not explicitly implied by '1992'. This experiment assumes that '1992' will lead all manufacturers to charge a uniform price across Europe. Currently, the prices of manufactured goods vary greatly across EC countries, even for virtually identical products such as automobiles. The reason for this sort of price discrimination is difficult to ascertain. In principle there already is free trade in manufactured goods, so significant price differences that do not reflect true costs should have been arbitraged away. In fact, a whole host of local laws, registration procedures, local restrictive business practices, etc. support the price discrimination. Since the authors (and everyone else who has worked in the Smith–Venables tradition of market integration) do not specify why price discrimination is possible, it is hard to evaluate the assertion that the Single Market Act will make it go away. Indeed, if the price differences do reflect local costs, or local regulations or restrictive practices that will not be affected by '1992', then clearly the gains predicted by the authors are overstated. It is a pity that the reader is not provided with a more substantial justification that the '1992' programme will actually lead to the changes assumed in the two scenarios. The same point applies to the impact of the EEA agreement.

My second critique applies mostly to the way the results are presented, although it also has something to say about the way the results should be interpreted. The construction of a model such as the Haaland–Norman one is a heroic task. Simply gathering consistent industry-specific trade and production data for the four regions must have been a formidable task and seems to have been done well. However when it comes to the scenarios, there was no careful collection of data on the industry-specific barriers that '1992' will eliminate. To take one example, the whole EC auto market will eventually be as open to Japanese imports as Belgium and Denmark currently are. The sales of Japanese cars, especially in France and Italy, should rise substantially. The authors do not allow for such industry-specific barriers in their scenarios. Intra-block trade costs are cut by the same percentage in all industries (2.5 per cent). I am not suggesting that I would have been able to get better industry-specific trade cost reductions. The 2.5 per cent is a reasonable average across industries. What I suggest is that industry-level results not be presented in such great detail, since much of the detail is probably spurious; the policy change is based on an average, so the average results on industry output should be the focus of the analysis. The authors' factor-intensity-based analysis of the effects is quite enlightening, so I would suggest basing the presentation on the averages of those three categories of industries.

4 The integration of financial services and economic welfare

CILLIAN RYAN

1 Introduction

Completion of the internal market in 1993 has focused attention on financial services, which are important both in their own right and for their role in fostering efficient trade and investment through the community. Not only are there large direct gains to be made through improvements in financial efficiency, but there are also likely to be indirect benefits in the goods and investment markets which are at the heart of the dynamics of '1992'.

Despite its importance, few estimates have been made of the impact of the integration of financial services. This chapter presents the results of a computer simulation of integration in the market for intertemporal financial services, using a computable general equilibrium model. This methodology is particularly suitable for studying discrete changes in regimes such as '1992', for which marginal econometric analysis may not be valid, and for studying industries where large data sets are not available.

The theoretical framework is based on Ryan (1991), which outlines a model in which intermediation services are necessary to facilitate trade. In applying this model, financial intermediaries are seen as facilitating three types of trade:

(a) long-term life-cycle-related intertemporal transfers
(b) short-term consumption-smoothing intertemporal transfers
(c) intra-temporal transaction-facilitating services.

While my long-term aim is to provide an integrated model for all three services, the present chapter outlines a model only for (a) and (b), the two intertemporal financial services, which together account for approximately 77 per cent of banking income and 60 per cent of costs in the major EC markets.[1]

92

The results support the broad conclusions of the simpler study conducted by Price Waterhouse (1988) in the context of the Cecchini (1988) report on '1992' – that the gains from market integration will be significant, that there are important differences between countries, and that these differences can be correlated with known features of economic structure and regulatory policies. These similarities suggest a robustness to the predicted gains despite the problems with the data and the many assumptions necessary in both exercises.

This chapter goes considerably further than the Price Waterhouse study, however; it examines the impact of financial integration on the demand for and allocation of resources in the economy and the impact of capital market integration; it provides estimates of the effects on output and employment both in financial services and in the rest of the economy, on international trade in financial services, and on economic welfare. In section 2 the theoretical model is outlined, while section 3 describes its calibration. Sections 4 and 5 respectively present the modelling of '1992' and the results of the integration. Section 6 discusses some sensitivity experiments and section 7 draws some conclusions.

2   The theoretical model

This section outlines a theoretical parable which can generate the two types of intertemporal trades identified above. Long-term, life-cycle consumption-smoothing trades capture the fact that people typically borrow while they are young, repay mortgages and build up pension-related savings in middle age and dis-save in old age. A significant portion of these savings are invested in industry via loans to enterprises or purchases of capital stock. In addition, agents also save (lend) and borrow for short-run, fungible consumption, such as holidays, Christmas and the purchase of consumer durables. Similarly, firms have uneven streams of payments and receipts resulting in short-run borrowing and saving.

At any given time we can observe stocks of assets and liabilities in the economy and flows of borrowing, lending, repaying and dis-saving, for both long- and short-run purposes. Furthermore, we can also observe that agents can be net borrowers in the long-run market while being net savers in the short-run market, and vice versa. This suggests a degree of independence between the two types of intermediation, which arises because long-term borrowing/lending often involves contractual commitments to repayments or savings which cannot be altered in the short run.

To model this pattern of behaviour and to reflect observable stocks and flows, we identify three types of time periods in the model:

(I)   Every agent is born into a generation, and there are three generations living at any point in time: the young generation, Y, who are net borrowers; the middle-aged, M, who are net savers; and the old or leisured generation, L, who are net dis-savers. Agents choose consumption in each generation G_g in order to maximise their life-time utility function defined as:

$$U = U(G_Y, G_M, G_L) \tag{1}$$

Life-time intergenerational consumption must satisfy the intergenerational budget constraint:

$$G_Y + \frac{G_M}{1 + r_g} + \frac{G_L}{(1 + r_g)^2} = I_Y + \frac{I_M}{1 + r_g} \tag{2}$$

where r_g is the intergeneration rate of interest and I_g is the income received in generation g.

(II) Within each generation there is a set of identical time periods, $t \epsilon$ $(1 \ldots n)$, within which the short-run (intertemporal) budget constraint must be satisfied. Within these time periods agents choose their recurring and fungible consumption, C_{Rg} and C_{Fg} to maximise $G_g(C_{gt}(C_{Rg}, C_{Fg}))$ subject to

$$(C_{Rg} + P_F C_{Fg}) = G_g^*/n \tag{3}$$

where G_g^* is the amount available for spending in generation g, P_F is the price of fungibles relative to that of recurring consumption, and agents are assumed to consume a constant fraction of their generational income in each t.

(III) Within every time period, t, there are two sub-time periods, the odd and the even $\{o, e\}$, in which agents may borrow or lend to fund fungible consumption and/or smooth out variable income opportunities; they must, however, settle their accounts in the following sub-time period. Agents thus choose odd- and even-period consumption of fungibles, O_g and E_g in order to maximize the intertemporal sub-utility function $C_{Fg}(O_g, E_g)$ subject to the short-run intertemporal budget constraint:

$$O_g + \frac{E_g}{1 + r_s} = I_o + \frac{I_e}{1 + r_s} = C_{Fg} \tag{4}$$

where r_s is the short-run rate of interest and where we assume for convenience that either I_o or $I_e = 0$: that is, agents are either odd- or even-period producers.

An agent's problem is thus to maximise

$$U = U[G_Y\{C_{Y1}(C_{RY}, O_Y, E_Y), \dots C_{Yn}(C_{RY}, O_Y, E_Y)\},$$
$$G_M\{C_{M1}(C_{RM}, O_M, E_M), \dots C_{Mn}(C_{RM}, O_M, E_M)\},$$
$$G_L\{C_{L1}(C_{RL}, O_L, E_L), \dots C_{Ln}(C_{RL}, O_L, E_L)\}],$$

subject to (2), (3), and (4) above.

Each generation is divided into two identical groups which are assumed to be born at the start of the odd and the even period respectively, in the first t period of the generation. This division is necessary to generate a continuous stream of short-run borrowing, lending, repayment and dis-saving at every instant in time.

Intertemporal trade follows the intermediation model set out in Ryan (1991) and is conducted exclusively by servicers. Thus, if goods' producers wish to consume a good in their non-productive period or more (or less) than their endowment in a generation, they must engage a servicer to trade on their behalf. Thus, for example, the short-run budget constraints for odd- and even-period producers are:

$$q_o = O_g + p_e E_g \quad \text{and} \tag{5}$$

$$q_e = p_o O_g + E_g \quad \text{respectively} \tag{6}$$

where q_i is the output of an agent producing in period i (measured in units such that its price in its 'own' period is unity) and p_j is the price of the other-period good, $i, j \in \{o, e\}$. The intertemporal interest rates which correspond to these intertemporal prices are $r_l = (1 - p_e)/p_e \times 100$ for lenders and $r_b = (p_o - 1) \times 100$ for borrowers. The corresponding budget constraint for servicers is:

$$p_{so} O_g + p_{se} E_g = (p_o s_o - s_e) + (p_e s_e - s_o) \tag{7}$$

where p_{sk} is the price of output in period $k \in (o, e)$ to a servicer for his or her own consumption, s_k is the quantity intermediated in period $k \in (o, e)$ and all prices are determined jointly by the demand for and supply of goods in both periods, the supply of services and the rate of transformation of servicers' joint output.

The competitive equilibrium for the fungible component of the short-run model is a labour allocation vector and a consumption vector for agents in each generation such that (in notation defined following equation (14)):

1 the (indirect) utility of an agent in a generation opting to produce in the odd or the even period is equal

$$V_g(1, p_e, q_{og}) = V_g(p_o, 1, q_{eg}); \tag{8}$$

2 the commodity markets clears,

$$\Sigma_g N_{og} q_{og} = \Sigma_g N_{og} O_g(1, p_e, q_{og}) + \Sigma_g N_{eg} O_g(p_o, 1, q_{eg})$$
$$+ \Sigma_g N_{sg} O_g(p_{so}, p_{se}, p_o s_o - s_e + p_e s_e - s_o) \tag{9}$$

$$\Sigma_g N_{eg} q_{eg} = \Sigma_g N_{og} E_g(1, p_e, q_{og}) + \Sigma_g N_{eg} E_g(p_o, 1, q_{eg})$$
$$+ \Sigma_g N_{sg} E_g(p_{so}, p_{se}, p_o s_o - s_e + p_e s_e - s_o) \tag{10}$$

3 the market for services clears,

$$\Sigma_g N_{sg} s_o = \Sigma_g N_{og} E_g(p_o, 1, q_{eg}) \tag{11}$$

$$\Sigma_g N_{sg} s_e = \Sigma_g N_{eg} O_g(1, p_e, q_{og}) \tag{12}$$

4 the factor market clears within each generation,

$$N_{og} + N_{eg} + N_{sg} = N_g \; \forall \; g, \tag{13}$$

and the utility of servicers is defined residually as

$$V_g(p_{so}, p_{se}, p_o s_o - s_e + p_e s_e - s_o) \tag{14}$$

where N_{ig} $i \epsilon (o, e, s)$ is the number of agents in sector i from generation g, N_g is the number of agents in generation g, $V_g(,)$ is the indirect utility of an agent from generation i, and $O_g(, ,)$ is the demand for O by an agent from generation g and the arguments of the latter functions are given by the budget constraints (5)–(7) above. The demand for E is similarly defined.

Agents can allocate themselves across sectors in the short run subject to income conditions imposed on servicers set out below, but are fixed within generations in the long-run model. All markets are assumed to clear at any instant and long-run intergeneration budget constraints must be balanced within an agent's lifetime. Thus the steady state of the complete model can be characterised by variants of Ryan (1990a) and (1991). As there are no dynamic interdependencies in the model, it is effectively an Arrow–Debreu instantaneous general equilibrium model with time-labelled goods, costly and endogenously determined trades, and 15 different types of consumers.[2] The problem thus reduces to a conventional one in which the resultant demands can be calibrated to long-run and short-run borrowing and saving.

3   Calibration

Assessment of the impact of completing the internal market on financial services is constrained by the perceived value of price and cost information to financial institutions, and the consequent paucity of suitable public information with which to conduct analysis.[3] In this section the model is calibrated to the available observable quantities and parameters for 6 European countries: Belgium, West Germany, France, Italy, the Netherlands and the UK. The choice of countries was constrained at the outset by the availability of intra-temporal transactions' service data. The programme employed is the Mathematical Programming System for General Equilibrium – MPSGE (Rutherford, 1989).

3.1   The data

The time period of the calibration, 1988, has been largely dictated by the availability of bank data. The two primary sources of this data are the International Clearing Bank Association (ICBA), covering individual banks' accounts in all the EC countries for the period 1987–9, and a less detailed OECD data set for the period 1978–86.

3.2   The utility function

The utility function employed is a nested CES utility function:

$$U = \sum_g \gamma_g [a_R C_{Rg}^\sigma + a_F (a_o O_g^\tau + a_e E_g^\tau)^{\sigma/\tau}]^{\phi/\sigma} \tag{15}$$

In order to perform simulations we need to fit numbers to the parameters, ϕ, σ, τ, (which depend on the elasticity of substitution), a_R, a_F, a_o, a_e, γ_g (which depend upon rates of time preference and the expenditure shares of recurring and fungible goods), and the quantities consumed; we also need to obtain relative prices for a budget constraint. This process is discussed below and the final configuration is outlined in the Appendix on p. 116.

3.3   Consumption

While data on some quantity variables (or categories of consumption) suggested by the theoretical model are extremely good, others are not directly observable. Although it is usual in this sort of model to calibrate parameters rather than quantities, in this case better results were obtained by using conventional parameter values and calibrating certain consumption variables.

The even-period producer's consumption of the odd-period good corresponds to short-term loans. This data comes from the European Commission's Cronos data base and is defined as short-term bank advances to commercial enterprises and private persons for under 1 year and, in exceptional circumstances, up to 2 years. We cannot use short-term deposits in a corresponding fashion because they are usually substantially larger than short-run borrowings due to individual liquidity and precautionary motives. The other consumption variables – for example, the odd-period producer's consumption of the odd-period good – are not directly observable, as they depend upon the income which the consumer has allocated to discretionary or fungible spending purposes. Thus short-term lending and unobserved fungible consumption are calibrated using the elasticities and parameters detailed below.

Recurring expenditure is the residual between the calibrated expenditures on fungible consumption and GNP minus investment (which is properly a component of permanent consumption). Differences between countries in the desire to borrow and lend, due to differences in either tastes or income, are partly captured by differences in the shares of recurring expenditure and fungibles.

Problems also arise in identifying the components of permanent expenditure. For example, inter-generational borrowing depends on accommodation purchase and renting patterns, education and training policies, tax progression and life-cycle income patterns in each country. On the savings side we need to add subscriptions to pension funds and ownership of capital stock to long-run bank assets. There are also problems in dividing these amounts between the accumulating balances of the middle-aged and the declining balances of the old.

To circumvent these problems I employ a measure of the old's consumption as a measure of their income on the assumption that all their income comes from returns on lending and investment or from dis-saving or capital sales. It is defined as the gross return on savings made in the corresponding period in the previous generation – that is, the current date lagged 25 years – and it is calculated as the old's share of final consumption and government expenditure net of transfers using Eurostat Demographic Tables (3C, Table 11). Using the rate of time preference and the elasticity of substitution, I can then calculate consumption in the other two generations.

I use a common income profile over the EC. Adopting Psacharopoulos and Layard's (1979) income profiles from the British Household Survey, I assume that income when middle-aged is 2.2429 times greater than when young. Generations are defined as 15–40, 40–65, and 65 + . Consumption by under 15s is allocated to the young and the middle-aged according to the age of the mother in Eurostat Tables (3C, Table 9).

3.4   *Elasticities of substitution and time preference parameters*

Estimates of the elasticities of intertemporal substitution can be obtained from several papers which investigate life-cycle models of consumption. Tobin and Dolde (1971) find that an elasticity near 0.66 is needed to match the life-cycle pattern of individuals. Friend and Blume (1975) derive estimates nearer to 0.5, while Hansen and Singleton (1983), using aggregate stock market and consumption data, and Kehoe (1984), in an analysis of the current account using international data, find values close to 1.

An alternative source for the elasticity of substitution lies in the empirical microeconomic literature which estimates consumer demand systems including variables such as consumer durables and housing. This literature suggests that the long-run, intertemporal elasticity of substitution is relatively low (housing real interest elasticities are typically less than 0.2) while consumer durables and recreation services tend to have somewhat higher elasticities.[4] As a consequence, I have opted for an elasticity of 1 for the short-run intertemporal function and an elasticity of 0.5 for the long-run inter-generation consumption function. The intra-temporal elasticity of substitution, σ, is fixed at 1.2, based on Theil (1981) and Deaton (1975).

The other significant variables in the calibration of the intertemporal utility function are the rates of time preference. These, along with the elasticity of substitution above, determine the parameters of the utility function and hence the demand functions. I use the long-run (10-year) average real rate of interest as the time preference parameter.

3.5 Interest rates

Interest rates for this model are real tax-adjusted interest rates.[5] Short-run rates are taken from the OECD *Bulletin of Financial Statistics*.

As was noted above, the relevant long-run rate is the cost of a 25-year loan or the return on a 25-year investment. Since long-run life-cycle decisions tend to involve contractual obligations which can be varied in the short run only by incurring severe transactions costs, the appropriate rate would appear to be a weighted average of the relevant rate over several years. For borrowing, I use the mortgage interest rate from the OECD *Bulletin of Financial Statistics* for the period 1983–90 (on the basis that consumers' expectations of future rates were relevant to decisions in 1988). The relevant rate for lending (or sale of capital) is based upon the return on long-term government bonds and stock market returns over the period 1980–90, weighted by their share of the sum of financial assets in the OECD banking statistics (OECD, 1985; 1987) and capital stocks estimated from the BDS data base or EC Input–Output tables.

3.6 Growth rates

The growth rate for the inter-generational model is the 25-year equivalent of the average growth rate between 1970 and 1990. The growth rate for the short-run model is that for 1987–8.

3.7 Allocation of agents to generations and sectors

Agents are allocated across generations in 1988 using Eurostat Demographic Tables (3C). Actual interest rates charged by intermediaries to members of a generation reflect the probability of survival across generations. Hence, past and projected survival rates from Eurostat 3C are also employed in order to take account of the declining membership of each generation as they increase in age.

Within a working generation, employment in the banking sector is estimated by its share of the economy's inputs. The detailed discussion of how this is done is postponed to section 3.9 on bank output below. The remaining agents are allocated across the sectors producing goods so that welfare is equalised across the odd and even time periods.

3.8 Goods' output

Ideally, we would like a detailed multi-input model of production in order to study the impact of integration on different factors of production. Unfortunately, reliable measures of relative factor usage in financial services compared with the rest of the economy do not exist, but Ryan (1991) demonstrates that the comparative static properties of the intermediation model are independent of the structure of goods production. Thus, I use a simple single-input production function in all sectors. The productivity of the goods' sector is determined by the aggregate value added figure *less* financial services from the EC Input-Output Tables.

3.9 Measuring bank outputs and inputs

The value added figure for financial services in each country is more difficult to determine. A variety of measures in the banking literature suggests that there are substantial differences in efficiency across countries.[6] However, the validity of these international comparisons is suspect for two reasons. First, there are substantial differences in the range and types of business conducted by major banks in each country; the usual method of comparing efficiencies across countries using the largest 5 or 10 institutions in each country can thus be quite misleading. Second, even where banks provide the same set of services, costs will differ if they provide different levels of services due to differences in tastes. For example, while automated services may be less costly to provide than manual ones, if there is domestic resistance to the usage of these services then domestic banks may appear to have relatively higher costs.

Brenton and Ryan (1992) have attempted to take account of these two problems by estimating the differences in costs attributable to differences in the levels of various types of service using the widest possible range of institutions operating in the banking sector in each country. The results did not support the thesis that differences in efficiencies across countries could be explained by either of the problems cited above. Thus, efficiency is determined by simply observing the inputs required in each country to service existing demand in the long- and short-run model.

For the long-run model, where life-insurance and pension funds must be included, I use input figures for the domestic financial services sector from the EC Input-Output Tables adjusted for the share of long-run intermediation and the degree of non-life insurance using Price Waterhouse's (1988) estimates. In the case of the short-run model I use OECD input data adjusted for the share of short-term loans as a fraction of total assets. Average costs of short-run and long-run financial intermediation are based on data from the Federal Reserve Banks' Functional Cost Analysis Program.

4   Modelling '1992'

There are many reasons why pre-trade price differences may obtain across countries. In the context of European financial services, the most frequently cited are differences in national regulations and differences in productivities, rather than factor endowments or returns to scale.[7] In so far as differences in costs are due to management efficiency and worker productivity then competition and market integration, including establishment by other EC banks and takeovers and mergers, ought to force relative efficiencies to converge.

If efficiency skills and expertise are fully 'transferable' then European efficiency will converge to that of the most efficient pre-1992 producer. This may be somewhat idealistic, both because the transfer of the skills may be limited and because '1992' does not involve a commitment to harmonise *all* banking regulations. In Price Waterhouse (1988), convergence was represented by assuming that prices in the more costly countries partially converge to the average of the four lowest prices for any given service. In the simulations below I report results for the case where all countries adopt best-practice techniques and, by way of comparison, an exercise where I assume that bank efficiency in each country rises towards the average of the four most efficient countries by the same percentage as Price Waterhouse (1988) assumed that prices would fall in each country towards the average of the four lowest European prices.

Even with identical productivities and margins, interest rates could still differ across countries due to differences in growth rates, tastes, etc.

Pan-European banks and improved capital flows ought to generate a common EC price for savings and lending. These new rates will result in some borrowers and savers gaining and some losing, but will result in an overall welfare gain. This convergence is perhaps more plausible than that of efficiencies.

In order to see the adjustment path followed in each economy, integration is simulated in three experiments, each of which consists of 3 steps. In the first step the productivity of the banking sector is harmonised across the EC and the model is re-run. Second, factors are reallocated between the financial and the goods' producing sectors within each economy. The factors are redistributed such that the return to resources employed in the banking sector within each country is maintained at the original level and the return to the two types of goods' producers is equalised. In the third step the markets for the 6 countries are integrated, generating common real borrowing and lending rates.

The first experiment is performed on the short-run component of the model, the second on the long-run component, and the third on the combined model where the long-run model and short-run effects are integrated.

In the integrated market we would also expect that measures of earnings or profitability would converge between members. The problem is to discern the point to which they would converge. In the initial simulations, where banking productivity is improved in the less efficient countries, factors are reallocated such that the initial value of earnings per unit of input is maintained in each country. The common level of earnings in the integrated model falls in the middle of the range in Table 4.1.

5   The results

5.1   Intertemporal service provision after '1992'

The first task of the analysis of '1992' is to identify who is likely to provide financial services after integration. This is difficult when differences in pre-integration efficiencies are due to such intangible sources of comparative advantage as management efficiency or worker productivity. Thus, if a country is less efficient due to the insulating effect of existing regulation, domestic producers may respond rapidly in the face of increased EC competition. However, evidence suggests that management efficiency and worker productivity reflect past investment in human capital and learning by doing, and therefore that domestic banks may take some time to accumulate the appropriate skills.[8] Domestic firms may thus take some time to respond to increased competition and, initially at

Table 4.1. *Relative efficiency of financial intermediaries in short-run markets*

	Efficiency	Returns
Belgium	32.3	2.80
France	16.3	1.63
Germany	31.7	3.22
Italy	15.1	1.13
Netherlands	28.4	2.53
United Kingdom	26.0	3.06

Notes:
Efficiency = Value intermediated per unit of input.
Returns = Gross earnings per unit of input.

least, the more efficient EC servicers are likely to provide intermediation services either directly or indirectly via a takeover or the supply of management services to domestic banks.

The efficiency measures reported in Table 4.1 are calibrated by the model by comparing the resources employed in short-run intermediation in each country with trades demanded in the base case. The relative ranking is consistent with many of the rankings found in the banking literature. From Table 4.1, Belgian and German banks appear to be the most likely to be able to provide these services in the post-'1992' environment.

Table 4.1 also reports the measure of gross earnings per unit of input; these are derived from the implied margins on borrowing and lending in the short-run model divided by total inputs and they reflect earning power in each market rather than efficiency. The model does not seek to explain or justify the level of these margins. In particular, it does not seek to explain whether they are generated by regulation or by imperfect competition.

5.2 Effects on sectoral allocations

Ryan (1991) shows that a necessary, though not sufficient, condition for service employment to contract as service technology improves is that the intertemporal elasticities of substitution are 1 or less. The evidence cited in the calibration of the model suggests that this is the case for all the intertemporal elasticities. Thus, contrary to common perceptions, as banks become more efficient service employment contracts, and market integration will not, at least in the intertemporal market, generate sufficient new business to maintain current employment, let alone justify an expansion in the service sector.

5.3   The short-run model

In the first step of the integration procedure, the service efficiency observed in Belgium is imposed in each country while the number of service producers remains unchanged. In all countries the service component of the intertemporal price is driven to zero – that is, competitive pressure between institutions within a country reduces borrowing and saving costs to their 'pure' intertemporal price. This is most surprising for the German case where there is little difference between its efficiency and that of Belgium. Thus, a rise in efficiency of as little as 1.8 per cent has severe adverse effects on the level of profitability in a competitive market. Price Waterhouse (1988) assumed that there would not be any loss of producer surplus in their welfare calculations and concentrated instead on consumer surplus; my result suggests that producer losses in these services would be significant. If so, we would expect integration and factor redeployment to take place almost simultaneously, and thus I immediately redistributed factors to generate meaningful returns to servicers. The results are reported in Table 4.2.

Table 4.2 reports the simulations for 3 possible levels of efficiencies. The first row for each country is the effect of imposing the Belgian level of efficiency. The second and third rows present the results obtained by simulating the partial efficiency gains suggested by Price Waterhouse. They reported a band of possible price effects for each country on the assumption that the higher priced countries would move partially towards the average of the four lowest. The lines PWU and PWL thus correspond respectively to the efficiency equivalent of their upper and lower price bounds.

The welfare gains from 1992 reported here are significantly in excess of the increase in the output of goods, because utility depends not only upon the quantity of goods consumed but also on their intertemporal mix. Since the improvement in service efficiency reduces the cost of borrowing and lending, generating an increase in inter-period trade, the compensating variation is a function of the changes both in inter-period trade and in output. France and Italy ultimately gain the most from this exercise, because of their relative inefficiency in the initial calibration; however, they are also likely to experience the most severe adjustment problems in the financial services sector.

The results of the Price Waterhouse-type exercise are of interest in putting the gains reported here in perspective. The consumer surplus

Table 4.2. Gains from equalising efficiencies in the short-run market with factor redistribution

% change:	Output	Inter-period trade	Labour employed in services[b]	Change in interest rates	Compensating variation[c]	Price Waterhouse consumer surplus[c]
Belgium	–	–	–	–	–	685
Germany	0.018	0.30	– 5.34	– 0.28	1555	4619
France	0.129	2.49	– 50.3	– 2.51	8785	3683
PWU[a]	0.084	1.54	– 32.1	– 1.50	5049	
PWL[a]	0.038	0.69	– 14.4	– 0.67	1822	
Italy	0.135	1.75	– 53.9	– 2.10	10811	3996
PWU	0.111	1.28	– 36.3	– 1.63	8022	
PWL	0.030	0.62	– 20.3	– 0.84	3810	
Netherlands	0.041	0.75	– 13.2	– 0.59	552	347
PWU	0.011	0.43	– 3.5	– 0.34	284	
PWL	0.000	0.00	0.00	0.00	0	
United Kingdom	0.060	0.91	– 22.1	– 0.76	3228	5051
PWU	0.038	0.55	– 11.2	– 0.25	1276	
PWL	0.004	0.12	– 2.4	– 0.08	193	

Notes:
[a] PWU and PWL are the upper and lower levels of efficiency corresponding to the range of partial price movements towards the projected Price Waterhouse 1992 price level.
[b] Labour employed ir. short-run intertemporal financial services.
[c] Measured in million ECU.

measures reported by Price Waterhouse are the estimated gains from all the services they considered, whereas my compensating variation is a measure of the gains from the partial '1992' experiment for short-run intermediation services, which accounts for only between 10 per cent and 30 per cent of bank business. The magnitude of the gains reported here suggest that the Price Waterhouse figures are an under-estimate, probably because they exclude the effects of integration on total output and the gains made by depositors.

Although efficiencies have been equalised in Table 4.2, differences in interest rates could still obtain due to differences in tastes, income or growth rates across countries. In Table 4.3, therefore, the results of the full integration of the short-run market are reported. This entails new (common) equilibrium interest rates for borrowing and lending. Whether borrowers or lenders in a country gain or lose depends both upon how this new interest rate compares with the base case rate *and* the welfare effects of the more efficient service technology. Thus, in the case of France and Italy there is a decrease in lending due to a fall in the equilibrium return to lenders, but the reallocation of resources away from the service sector (increasing both recurring and fungible consumption) is sufficiently large to lead to an overall welfare gain.

In Germany both borrowers and lenders gain from full integration relative to the previous case in Table 4.2 because interest rates fall for the former and rise for the latter. Italian borrowers and lenders, by contrast, both lose for the opposite reason. The large gains reported for lenders in the UK is caused by the fact that the real interest rate for lending in the base case was negative and becomes positive in the post-'1992' integrated market. A similar phenomenon also helps to boost the German gains.

Changes in relative returns will cause agents to switch their borrowing/lending patterns. Thus, initially, lenders in Belgium, France, Italy and the Netherlands will switch to borrowing while borrowers in the UK and Germany will switch to lending. The extent to which this occurs and the resultant effect on interest rates depends on the ability of agents to switch. The model employed the assumption that agents can switch costlessly, which for some range of borrowers and lenders is probably appropriate. However, in the fully integrated model this can lead to some countries specialising as borrowers or lenders in the short run, which is unrealistic. Unfortunately there is no way of quantifying the extent to which borrowers and lenders can switch. Some provisional experiments suggest that the redistribution of German and UK borrowers to lending would dominate the market outcome given the relative importance of Germany and the size of the gains for UK lenders. This causes additional shifts in saving and borrowing patterns within countries, and the gains

Table 4.3. *Gains/losses from the integration of the EC market, relative to base*

		Change in interest rate	% Change in inter-period trade	Change in consumer surplus	Change in servicers' income[b]	Service consumption[c]	Minimum change in trade[d]
Belgium[a]	l	-2.76	-2.84	-3805.8	-10.21	781.1	7.7
	b	-4.13	3.81	5445.1			
Germany	l	1.66	1.69	2514.0	-21.0	6578.6	75.2
	b	-0.91	0.11	1314.9			
France	l	-0.21	-0.8	550.5	51.87	4355.1	-29.5
	b	-0.27	2.62	5859.3			
Italy	l	-0.18	-1.74	791.3	117.54	5533.9	-68.4
	b	-0.07	0.37	1159.5			
Netherlands	l	-0.59	-0.54	-147.4	-0.98	1462.7	9.0
	b	-1.97	1.86	693.5			
United Kingdom	l	5.21	5.65	5875.63	-19.73	3018.9	9.4
	b	-0.94	-0.49	-142.83			

Notes:
[a] The effect on lenders and borrowers is denoted by l, lenders; b, borrowers.
[b] Consumption ascribed to domestically resident servicers.
[c] Earning per input of resident servicers, in million ECU.
[d] Change in net national lending, assuming domestically resident servicers and stable output growth in each country, in million ECU.

and losses reported in Table 4.3 are indicative of their potential importance.

Full integration also generates a common level of returns to inputs which lies in the middle of the spectrum reported in Table 4.1; the changes in servicers' income reported in Table 4.3 reflect this. Thus, returns in the two high margin markets, Germany and the UK, fall substantially while those in France and Italy rise.

The simulation in Table 4.3 shows countries being net borrowers or lenders at any instant. The extent of this intra-EC borrowing and lending will depend upon tastes, the rate of economic growth, the variance of output across countries and which country is supplying the intermediation services. In the initial calibration such intra-EC trade was not distinguished, as suitable data was not available, but the interest rates and calibrated parameters implicitly supported the existing level of trade. The trade figures reported in Table 4.3 thus reflect the incremental effect of integration on the volume of intra-EC borrowing and lending when output is stable over time and services are provided by domestic banks.

Of course, intertemporal intra-EC trade will be greater if services are supplied from abroad (either directly or via the provision of management services). Thus, much of the service consumption reported in Table 4.3 may be located in one or a few countries. If so, the intra-EC trade figures need to be adjusted to reflect the extent of service imports from other EC suppliers. In the extreme case where all services are provided by Belgium and Germany, intra-EC intertemporal and service trade would rise by ECU 15 291 million.

The trades reported in this exercise would result in temporary current account and permanent merchandise account deficits or surpluses. It must be emphasised, however, that these are market-clearing, welfare-maximising trades and ought not to be a concern to monetary and fiscal authorities nor be the object of corrective macroeconomic policies.

5.4   *The long-run model*

In the second experiment the efficiency of Belgian banks is imposed in the long-run model. However, while the returns to the service sector in each economy are reduced, prices are not driven to zero in this case. The effects of equalising efficiencies when service resources are redistributed to maintain the returns to service inputs are reported in Table 4.4

The striking result is the difference in the ranking of beneficiaries in this model compared with the short-run model. There are a number of reasons for this. The base efficiency measure for each country depends on the demand for intertemporal services and inputs to the service sector, which

Table 4.4. *Gains from equalising efficiencies in the long-run model*

	Goods' Output (% change)	Inter-period trade (% change)	Financial services' employment[a] (% change)	Interest rate (% change)	Compensation variation[b] (% change)
Belgium	–	–	–	–	
Germany	0.05	0.97	– 0.98	1.0	2038
France	0.62	4.55	– 4.81	5.0	7516
Italy	0.08	0.47	– 1.75	0.5	256
Netherlands	0.41	6.50	– 6.96	7.7	2696
United Kingdom	0.97	7.83	– 8.55	12.1	11 877

Notes:
[a] Labour employed in long-run intertemporal financial services.

E

in turn are sensitive to the demographic structure and the rate of growth. Thus, in contrast to the short-run model, the large growth rates in the Italian economy, and to a lesser extent in the French economy, result in greater demand for intertemporal services, justifying the larger proportion of resources employed in the financial sector. Conversely, the low UK growth rate has the effect of reducing the apparent efficiency of UK financial services. However, a caveat must be entered for the UK as the correction for the London international insurance market (based on figures cited in Price Waterhouse, 1988) may be under-estimated, resulting in an upward bias to the estimated employment in banking in the UK.

Tables 4.5 and 4.6 report the results of integrating EC markets for the long-run model. Table 4.5 reports the effect on intertemporal borrowing, lending and capital purchases in 1988 relative to the base case. They suggest that the effects of integration will vary considerably across economies. One interesting result is that a rise in savings in a country will not necessarily affect borrowers and sellers of capital symmetrically. Thus, in Belgium a rise in savings is associated with a rise in borrowing by the young, but a reduction in both the returns to and the realisation of assets by the old. A significant portion of the increase in savings (and the loss of income by servicers) is thus flowing to other EC countries, as can be seen from Belgium's current account surplus in Table 4.6.

As in the short-run case the interpretation of the degree of intra-EC trade in the integrated market depends on the location of the servicers in the equilibrium. However, even assuming that all domestic residents are serviced by domestic servicers, Table 4.6 shows a surprisingly large degree of inter-generational trade between EC countries in the integrated market. This in turn has important implications for both the capital and the current account.

The simulation in Table 4.6 results in a current account deficit of 7.7 per cent of GNP in the UK in 1988 while the remaining countries have deficits or surpluses in the range of 1–4 per cent of GNP. Given the time scale in the long-run model these deficits and surpluses could take up to 25 years to balance themselves. However, once again it must be emphasised that these are market-clearing, welfare-maximising trades which are entirely consistent with the long-run intertemporal budget constraints and ought not to be a concern to monetary and fiscal authorities.

As before, there is no reason to suppose that all intermediation is performed by domestic servicers and that it is entirely consistent with the model that services are supplied from abroad. In the most extreme case we could suppose that all financial servicers were Belgian, resulting in an increase in service-related intra-EC trade of as much as 6.3 per cent of EC

Table 4.5. *Changes in borrowing and lending in the integrated long-run market in 1988, %*

	Belgium	Germany	France	Italy	Netherlands	United Kingdom
Young	1.0	−4.9	−1.4	9.7	−4.9	22.1
Middle	1.3	1.9	0.7	−0.4	1.4	−0.4
Old	−13.0	1.1	0.9	−7.3	1.1	4.3
Service income	−0.8	0.3	2.3	2.3	0.1	−2.9

Table 4.6. *Net inter-country borrowing and lending as a result of long-run market integration in 1988*

	Domestic surplus[a]	Servicers' consumption	Minimum surplus as % of GNP[b]
Belgium	8607	5027	2.97
Germany	76 483	40 080	3.81
France	55 813	36 323	2.50
Italy	25 308	31 918	− 1.02
Netherlands	15 690	8165	3.94
United Kingdom	− 38 385	21 898	− 7.73

Notes:
[a] Difference between domestic production and consumption by non-servicers.
[b] Difference between domestic surplus and domestic servicers' income, assuming all financial services are supplied by domestic residents.

output and correspondingly greater deficits and surpluses on merchandise and capital accounts.

5.5   *The full model*

The results from equalising efficiencies in the full model are reported in Table 4.7. By and large the quantity changes in the two separate exercises are small enough that the gains in the combined long-run and short-run models are almost additive. The one item worthy of note is the effect on labour employed in financial services. This figure takes into account the changes in each component of the model and their relative importance as a fraction of financial services output. They thus represent the projected percentage loss of *total* financial service employment in each country.

6   Sensitivity analysis

The operation of the computer model necessitated time-consuming manual redistributions of factors between sectors. A complete set of sensitivity experiments has thus not been feasible; instead, I studied the initial perturbation of the base-case model to assess the impact of a selected number of imposed parameters and values.

6.1   *Varying the elasticity of substitution*

While the elasticities of substitution were employed in the initial calibration of quantities in the model, the sensitivity exercise takes these

Table 4.7. *Total gains from equalising efficiencies in domestic markets*

% change in:	Goods' output	Total inter-period trade	Financial services' employment	Compensating variation
Belgium	–	–	–	
Germany	0.068	1.466	– 2.69	3592
France	0.750	7.044	– 11.89	16 301
Italy	0.231	2.215	– 17.08	11 068
Netherlands	0.457	7.251	– 5.89	3248
United Kingdom	1.031	8.737	– 17.96	15 105

quantities as given and examines the effect of changing the elasticities of substitution in the various experiments. Varying the intertemporal elasticities of substitution between 0.4 and 1.5 and the elasticity of substitution between recurring and fungibles between 0.8 and 1.4 has only a minor effect on the quantities demanded and the redistribution of factors required to restore service margins to their base values.

Two factors which were important were the initial input figures for the banking sector and the elasticity of transformation of service outputs. As was noted in section 3 above, there are a variety of bank efficiency measures employed in the bank literature, but none of them commands universal acceptability. The differences in the relative rankings are often explained by recourse to differences in banking practices and the effect of regulation across markets. However, initial attempts by Brenton and Ryan (1992) to take account of differences between countries were not successful in resolving the contentious variations in efficiency measures. Even if one does not accept the relative rankings outlined here, the experiments still provide an example of what market integration might imply.

6.2   Varying the elasticity of transformation

The second figure of importance was the rate of transformation of the joint service output of borrowing and lending. This figure is important as a low elasticity of transformation forces a large portion of the costs of intermediation on to the shorter side of the market, reducing intertemporal trade within countries and significantly altering the servicers' consumption bundle.

There is very little evidence with which to make a judgement about the rate of transformation of servicers' output in European markets. There is a common perception in banking that deposit collection is considerably more costly than lending, and informal discussions with bankers also suggest that bundling and unbundling deposits and loans are costly. Linear programming and econometric estimates in Nelson's (1985) and Ferrier and Lovell's (1990) studies of the US market suggest that deposits are as much as twice as costly as loans to administer.

I employed a range of elasticities from 0 to 10 and found that as the elasticity fell from 1 to 0 intertemporal trade within countries was progressively and significantly reduced for any given input allocation to the service sector. For example, the inter-period trade volumes for the Belgian efficiency exercise reported in Table 4.2 fall by 7 per cent in the case of Italy and 2 per cent in the case of France. However, the trade volumes in the integrated market reported in Table 4.3 are virtually unaffected (falling by less than 0.5 per cent).

This result obtains because asymmetries in demand in domestic markets result in servicers employing greater resources in order to match borrowers and lenders and to ensure a smooth consumption path for themselves. In the fully integrated market, demand is more symmetric, which releases these resources to be directly employed for the benefit of producer-consumers. Thus, in a fully integrated market the elasticity of service output transformation is less important. Hence, as the transformation of service output becomes more costly, free capital mobility and access to other EC financial markets becomes relatively more important for welfare gains than rights of establishment by EC banks in otherwise restricted domestic markets.

7   Conclusions

In the report on financial services Price Waterhouse (1988) are at pains to point out the dangers of taking their figures too literally and emphasise that 'the exercise can only be regarded as illustrative and hypothetical'.[9] This qualification applies no less in the present exercise. The limited nature of the data which are freely available on financial services means that assumptions have to be made which are inevitably subjective and contentious. Nonetheless the results here, which derive from a very different methodology from that of Price Waterhouse, tend to support the latter's conclusions that the consequences of market integration are important for the EC as a whole, and that there are considerable variations across countries.

Yet the model goes considerably further and suggests that the potential gains are significantly larger than those estimated by Price Waterhouse. This is because the model encompasses a much broader range of potential effects. First, it includes the potential benefits for depositors as well as for borrowers. Second, it considers the effects on financial service providers, and suggests that integration will, initially, have deleterious effects on bank returns. In particular, I find that while the demand for intertemporal financial services will grow, this growth will not be sufficient to offset the efficiency gains and hence that it will not be possible to employ all the resources currently engaged in this type of financial services. There will thus be a significant redistribution of factors away from the financial services' sector and, ultimately, additional welfare gains due to increased output of other goods.

Third, in addition to measuring the gains from improved bank efficiencies the model measures the concomitant benefits of an integrated European market for capital, and estimates the benefits and losses to borrowers and depositors in each country. In particular, it demonstrates that certain sectors may be significantly worse off as a result of integration and that certain countries face significant increases in their investment and trade finance costs.

Fourth, it examines who is likely to provide financial services in the integrated market and provides estimates of the likely intra-EC trade effects on the current and capital accounts of the balance of payments. The deficits and surpluses on the merchandise and capital accounts are an integral part of this model, reflecting market-clearing, welfare-maximising choices and thus ought *not* to be the subject of corrective macroeconomic policy.

It is obvious that the model presented here is far from complete, both in the depth of its analysis and in the scope of the services considered. Realism would be enhanced by the separation and modelling of final consumer and government demands and the intermediate demands of producers. This is probably more important in the long-run than in the short-run model, as one would expect that the lower intermediation costs and the changes in the capital stock would influence the long-run rate of growth. Incorporating existing international capital flows would also add greatly to the model; however, this is currently constrained by the lack of detailed data on inter-EC trade flows in financial services.

Perhaps the more urgent development, however, is the inclusion of a model of intra-temporal services and the possibility of economies of scope. Intra-temporal services, although smaller than the services considered here, are important for facilitating trade in goods and services and it is possible that the growth in the scale and range of these services as a result of integration might accommodate the redundant factors from the intertemporal financial services.

Appendix: Calibration

$$U = \sum_g \gamma_g [a_R C_{Rg}^\sigma + a_F (a_o O_g^\tau + a_e E_g^\tau)^{\sigma/\tau}]^{\phi/\sigma} \tag{15}$$

Top level

Parameters: γ_g depends on rate of time preference derived from the long-run interest rate
$\phi = 1$ (elasticity of inter-generational substitution, 0.5)

Quantities: estimate of leisured (old) consumption derived from National Income and demographic data; young and middle-aged consumption follow from assumptions above

Middle level

Parameters: a_R, a_F Calibrated by model
$\sigma = 6$ (elasticity of substitution between recurring and fungibles, 1.2)

Quantities: C_{rg} and C_{fg} sum to national income minus gross investment; C_{rg} is the residual given C_{fg} from lower level

Lower level

Parameters: a_o, a_e Depends on rate of time preference
$\tau = 0$ (Short-run elasticity of substitution, chosen equal to 1, therefore function becomes Cobb–Douglas)

Quantities: Observe short-term borrowing by individuals and enterprises; given the parameters above, the remaining quantities are then determined

NOTES

I wish to thank Professor Edward Gardener, Phil Molyneux, Andy Mullineux, John Teppitt and Mike Lloyd Williams for their valuable insights on banking and the members of the IT92 programme, especially Jacob Kol and Alan Winters. Finally, my thanks to Ian Wooton with whom the original Intra-temporal Financial Services model was devised and from which this chapter developed. I am, of course, responsible for all the assumptions and errors in the chapter.

1 Figures based upon OECD (1987) and Federal Reserve Banks Functional Cost Analysis statistics.

2 Three generations, each containing borrowers, lenders, repayers, dis-savers, and servicers. The repayers and dis-savers are necessary to balance the income stream of the financial servicer.

3 For example, the Price Waterhouse/Cecchini study of financial services was constrained to compute the welfare gains on the basis of a series of prices collected confidentially from a limited sample of banks in the community and an estimate of demand for financial services based on a US insurance study.

4 See Deaton (1975), Theil (1981) and Phlips (1983).
5 The tax adjustment is based on marginal tax rates from Price Waterhouse tax reports making allowances for exceptions where noted.
6 For some examples of this see the exchange between Fanning (1981), (1982) and Frazer (1982). For more recent measures see Conti (1989) and Conti and Maccarinelli (1991).
7 See Ryan (1990b).
8 See Ryan (1990b).
9 CEC (1988), Part C, Section 5, p. 89.

REFERENCES

Brenton, P. and C. Ryan (1992) 'Bank services and relative efficiencies in European financial markets', University of Birmingham, mimeo.

Cecchini, P. *et al.* (1988) *The European Challenge 1992*, Aldershot: Gower.

Commission of the European Communities (CEC) (1988) 'The economics of 1992', *European Economy*, **35** (March), Brussels: European Commission.

Conti, V. (1989) 'Margins, costs and strategic prospects in banking: an international comparison', paper presented at the International Conference of Commercial Bank Economists, Zurich (June).

Conti, V. and M. Maccarinelli (1991) 'Optimal size in banking: theoretical issues and empirical results', paper presented at the International Conference of Commercial Bank Economists, San Francisco (June).

Eurostat (1988) *Demographic Statistics, Population and Social Conditions*, 3C, Luxembourg: EC.

(1991a) *Money and Finance*, 4E, Luxembourg: EC.

(1991b) *Eurostat Review*, Luxembourg: EC.

Deaton, A. (1975) *Models and Projections of Demand in Post-War Britain*, London: Chapman & Hall

Fanning, D. (1981) 'The human asset approach to bank rankings', *The Banker* (November) pp. 31–4.

(1982) 'The human asset approach to bank rankings – further evidence', *The Banker* (July) pp. 61–6.

Federal Reserve Bank System (1989) 'Functional Cost Analysis Program: National Average Report – Commercial Banks', Washington, D.C.: Federal Reserve Bank.

Ferrier, G.D. and C.A.K. Lovell (1990) 'Measuring cost efficiency in banking: econometric and linear programming evidence', *Journal of Econometrics*, **46**, pp. 229–45.

Frazer, P. (1982) 'How not to measure bank productivity', *The Banker* (August) pp. 103–5.

Friend, I. and M.E. Blume (1975) 'The demand for risky assets', *American Economic Review*, **65**, pp. 900–22.

Hansen, L.P. and K.J. Singleton (1983) 'Stochastic consumption, risk aversion and the temporal behaviour of asset returns', *Journal of Political Economy*, **91**, pp. 249–65.

Kehoe, P.J. (1984) 'Dynamics of the Current Account: Theoretical and Empirical Analysis', *Working Paper*, Harvard University.

Nelson, R.W. (1985) 'Branching, scale economies and banking costs', *Journal of Banking and Finance*, **9**, pp. 177–91.

OECD (1985) *Costs and Margins in Banking, Statistical Supplement 1978–1982*, Paris: OECD.

(1987) *Bank Profitability, Statistical Supplement, Financial Statements of Banks, 1981–1985*, Paris: OECD.

(various issues) *Financial Statistics Monthly, Part 1*, Paris: OECD.

Phlips, L. (1983) *Applied Consumption Analysis*, Amsterdam: North-Holland.

Price Waterhouse (1988) *The Cost of Non-Europe in Financial Services*, Research into the Costs of Non-Europe, Basic Findings, vol. 2, Luxembourg: EC.

Psacharopoulos, G. and R. Layard (1979) 'Human capital and earnings, British evidence and a critique', *Review of Economic Studies*, **46**, pp. 485–503.

Rutherford, T.F. (1989) *MPSGE-Mathematical Programming System for General Equilibrium*, University of Western Ontario, mimeo.

Ryan, C. (1990a) 'Short-Run Gains and Losses and International Trade in Intermediation Services', *Working Paper*, University of Wales, Bangor.

(1990b) 'International trade in financial services', *World Economy*, **13**(3), pp. 349–66.

(1991) 'International and Interregional Trade and Intermediation Services', *Working Paper*, University of Wales, Bangor.

Tobin, J. and W. Dolde (1971) 'Wealth, Liquidity and Consumption in Consumer Spending and Monetary Policy: The Linkages', *Monetary Conference Series*, **5**, pp. 99–146, Boston: Federal Reserve Bank of Boston.

Theil, H. (1981) *International Consumption Comparisons*, Amsterdam: North-Holland.

Discussion

JACOB KOL

1   Introduction

Financial integration includes free capital movements and the freedom to provide financial services: the two elements can hardly be conceived independently (Padoa Schioppa, 1990). The free movement of capital within the EC is one of the explicit objectives of the '1992' programmes, and in 'The economics of 1992' the CEC (1988) underlines the 'unique importance' of integrating the financial markets. As a result, an increase in efficiency is expected of the financial sector itself and of the other sectors using financial services.

2   Model and analysis

Ryan uses a calibrated general equilibrium model, in which financial services provide:

1 short-term consumption-smoothing intertemporal transfers, and
2 long-term life-cycle related intertemporal transfers.

This setting of the model reflects a focus on financial services for final consumption rather than for intermediate deliveries to other industries. According to the CEC (1988) the former services account for only 20 per cent and the latter for well over 50 per cent of total output of the financial services sector. Price Waterhouse (1988) reveals, however, that most intermediate deliveries are made within the financial sector – i.e. are inter-bank lending. If these are excluded, final sales account for 56 per cent of extra-sector sales, or 65 per cent if Italy, where retailers rather than banks offer finance for durables, is excluded. Nonetheless, as Ryan concedes, the separate modelling of intermediates would be useful.

Apart from methodology, Ryan's study differs in many other respects from the report by Price Waterhouse underlying the chapter on financial services in 'The economics of 1992'. The analysis in Price Waterhouse (1988) is based on estimates in 8 EC countries of 16 representative financial products including banking, insurance and brokerage services. Ryan uses an index of efficiency – measured as value intermediated per unit of input – for the banking sector as a whole for 6 EC countries. These and other differences render the findings of the two studies difficult to compare.

Both, the Price Waterhouse and the Ryan study assume that upon financial integration among EC countries convergence will occur, at least to some degree, in terms of prices and efficiency in the financial sector. Both studies agree further that such convergence will be due predominantly to increased competition rather than to the exploitation of economies of scale. This is well in line with findings in the literature that in banking operations economies of scale are very limited beyond a small minimum efficient size and that economic gains from financial integration in the EC will come largely from increased competition (Benston *et al.*, 1982; Shigehara, 1991).

3   Additional elements

Additional with respect to the expected degree of convergence some variants are offered, central to Ryan's analysis is the case that efficiency of the banking sector in the EC will converge to the highest level of efficiency, presently found in Belgium and Germany. The Price Water-house study is deliberately more cautious; it argues that upon financial integration the potential fall in prices will be realised only partly, because even with the fullest implementation of the 1992 programme and of competition policies, the resulting financial markets will always fall substantially short of being fully integrated and perfectly competitive (CEC, 1988). Since both the Price Waterhouse and the Ryan study agree that increased competition is the main force behind convergence, the Price Waterhouse study has an advantage in that it distinguishes within banking various sub-sectors, which have a different exposure to competition.

In this perspective, foreign competition needs to be mentioned. The presence of foreign banks in the EC and the possibility of their broader entry into the EC financial markets will increase competiton further and contribute to the efficiency gains of the 1992 programme (Shigehara, 1991).

Finally, increased competition in the banking sector has often led to a tendency to concentration, by acquisitions, mergers and takeovers, in order to preserve profit margins and to secure continuity. This tendency in the EC financial market may very well deflect convergence to the highest efficiency level or the lowest price (De Jong, 1991; Shepherd, 1986).

4   Conclusions

Ryan's study on the financial sector is a welcome contribution to the analysis of the effects of the EC 1992. The focus of the study could be more explicit on intermediate financial services to other industries, rather than on final consumer demand.

Increased competition is rightly taken as the main force behind convergence to a higher level of efficiency of the financial sector in the EC. In this perspective the study could benefit from considering more explicitly:
1 different types of banking services with a different exposure to competition,
2 the presence of foreign banks and their role in stronger competition, and
3 the process of concentration by acquisitions, mergers and takeovers probably easing competitive pressure.

Evaluation of these elements could provide a foundation for the assumptions on the degree of convergence and the ultimate level of efficiency which are central to Ryan's study.

REFERENCES

Benston, G.J., G.A. Hanweck and D.B. Humphrey (1982) 'Scale economies in banking: a restructuring and reassessment', *Journal of Money, Credit and Banking*, **14**, pp. 435–56.

Commission of the European Communities (CEC) (1988) 'The economics of 1992', *The European Economy*, **35** (March) Brussels: European Commission.

De Jong, H.W. (1991) 'Competition and combination in the European market economy', in P. de Wolf (ed.), *Competition in Europe*, Dordrecht: Kluwer Academic.

Padoa Schioppa, Tommaso (1990) 'Financial and monetary integration in Europe: 1990, 1992 and beyond', *Group of Thirty, Occasional Papers*, **28**, New York.

  (ed.) (1991) 'Europe after 1992: three essays', *Essays in International Finance*, **182** (May), Princeton University.

Price Waterhouse (1988) 'The Cost of Non-Europe in Financial Services', Research into the Costs of Non-Europe, Basic Findings, vol. 2, Luxembourg, EC.

Shepherd, W.G. (1986) 'The banking industry', in W. Adams (ed.), *The Structure of American Industry*, New York: Macmillan.

Shigehara, K. (1991) 'The external dimension of Europe 1992: its effects on relations between Europe, the United States and Japan', in Padoa Schioppa (ed.) (1991).

Part Three
Modelling market integration –
partial equilibrium

5 Market integration, competition, and welfare

JAN I. HAALAND and IAN WOOTON

1 Introduction

A number of the applied studies of the potential effects of the '1992' programme for single industries focus on the effects of changing from segmented, national markets to a fully integrated European market (see, for example, Smith and Venables, 1988 and Norman, 1989). The present chapter is motivated by these applied studies, and the purpose is to shed light on the various channels of price and welfare effects of such market integration.

For several results in the theory of international trade under imperfect competition it is crucial to make the distinction between segmented and integrated markets. In segmented markets firms consider each (national) market separately, and can charge different prices in each. With integrated markets such price discrimination is not possible, say, as a result of the potential for private arbitrage between markets. Market segmentation is the essential assumption of models of trade based on reciprocal dumping (see, for example, Brander, 1981 and Brander and Krugman, 1983) since, in the simplest versions of such models, the possibility of price discrimination between markets is the only reason for international trade. More recent studies of the effects of trade policies in imperfectly competitive markets reveal that the distinction between segmented and integrated markets is crucial for many of the results (see Markusen and Venables, 1988 for a summary).

International trade in the applied models that incorporate imperfect competition is partly motivated by reciprocal dumping, so that whether markets are segmented or integrated must be central to their results. The applied analyses examine the market equilibria in both situations, and go further, reporting the price and welfare effects of changing from segmented to integrated markets. Smith and Venables (1988) initiated this line of research and their results show that for the internal market in the

EC to yield substantial gains it is necessary to achieve more than simply reduced trade costs. The largest gains in their study appear when the market structure is altered from one with segmented, national markets to a situation with full market integration and no price discrimination between markets. Norman (1989) shows the same tendency in a similar model, in which Norway and Sweden are included in addition to the EC. However, Norman's study also shows that full market integration is not equally important in all industries and countries.

The story behind these results, which we shall call the 'conventional wisdom', is as follows. For most industries in most of the European countries it is typically the case that the producers have high market shares in their home markets and lower shares in the other European countries. With imperfectly competitive markets, this gives the firms much more market power in their domestic markets compared to foreign ones and, as a consequence, they can charge higher prices at home than abroad – that is, they can indulge in reciprocal dumping. Market integration implies that such dumping is no longer possible; firms compete not in segmented, national markets, but rather in one, integrated, European market. Market power then depends not on shares in individual markets, but on the share of the integrated market, and firms will typically lose power at home compared to what they held in the segmented case. Hence, home-market prices will go down, and the consumers will gain. International trade still occurs due to product differentiation, but it is reduced because there is no longer a basis for pure reciprocal-dumping trade. Hence, there is also a source of further potential gains through the reduction of real trade costs.

In this chapter we look in more detail into the mechanisms behind market integration. It is often taken for granted that market integration is similar to enlarging the market and thereby reducing the difference in market power between various sub-markets. One important result of our analysis is that this is not true; as long as there remains some kind of trade costs or biased preferences, an integrated equilibrium is not identical to equilibrium in a single market.

It is, for instance, often assumed that since price discrimination is no longer possible, producer surpluses must go down and consumer welfare up as a consequence of integration. We show, however, that this is not necessarily the case; the outcome depends on trade costs, preference biases, and the degree of competition (the number of firms) in each sub-market. As the inability to price discriminate applies to a firm's competitors as well as to itself, the whole situation is altered, and the outcome may well be that the integrated equilibrium is less competitive than the equilibrium in segmented markets with dumping. It may even be that all prices rise as a consequence of integration.

The plan of this chapter is as follows. In section 2 we present the structure of a simple model of international trade in a market with trade between symmetric countries. We stick to the dichotomy of segmented versus integrated markets, and we limit the analysis to one form of imperfect competition, Cournot competition.[1] It is a standard model with no new features; nevertheless, we find it useful to spell out the equilibrium conditions in some detail, in particular those with integrated markets which have not been discussed previously in the literature. In section 3 we analyse the price effects of market integration. These are quite complex and hence, for welfare assessments, we switch in section 4 to a stylised numerical model that focuses on the dimensions discussed in the theoretical analysis. These are the degree of competition in the markets, the level of the trade costs between markets, and the degree of substitutability between products, all of which turn out to be central to the effects of integration on prices, consumer welfare, and producer profits.

2 The model

We work with a very simple, partial equilibrium model of an industry characterised by Cournot competition. Each firm produces a different variety of a differentiated product. There are n firms in each of $m + 1$ countries (thus there are m foreign countries).

2.1 Demand

There is a single representative consumer in each country who maximises her utility through consumption of the goods produced by the industry. The quantity index, or utility function, is:

$$X = \left\{ n(a_h x_h)^{\frac{\sigma - 1}{\sigma}} + mn(a_f x_f)^{\frac{\sigma - 1}{\sigma}} \right\}^{\frac{\sigma}{\sigma - 1}} \tag{1}$$

where subscript h indicates home-produced goods and f foreign-produced (imported) goods, x_i is the consumed quantity of each variety of good of type i, a_i is the preference parameters and $\sigma > 1$ is the elasticity of substitution. All varieties of goods from any country have the same preference weights. The model has a strong element of *symmetry*: each country is identical in structure, and the preference weights on all goods from foreign countries are the same. Hence, we need only distinguish between home goods and foreign goods. The price index (or the unit expenditure function) dual to (1) is:

$$P = \left\{ n \left(\frac{p_h}{a_h} \right)^{1-\sigma} + mn \left(\frac{p_f}{a_f} \right)^{1-\sigma} \right\}^{\frac{1}{1-\sigma}} \qquad (2)$$

where p_i is the consumer price for (each) good of type i. With Y as the total expenditure on differentiated products, the consumer maximises X subject to the budget constraint:

$$PX = Y \qquad (3)$$

Demands for individual varieties of the good are given by:

$$x_i = a_i^{\sigma-1} p_i^{-\sigma} P^{\sigma-1} Y, \qquad i = h, f \qquad (4)$$

Given the symmetry of the model, x_f refers both to the demand for imported goods in the home market and to the demand in each of the foreign markets for varieties produced in the home country. It is often convenient to work in terms of market shares. The market shares of each variety of home-produced and foreign (imported) goods, respectively, are defined to be:

$$s_h \equiv \frac{p_h x_h}{Y} = \frac{1}{n} \left\{ 1 + m \left(\frac{a_f}{a_h} \frac{p_h}{p_f} \right)^{\sigma-1} \right\}^{-1},$$

$$s_f \equiv \frac{1 - n s_h}{mn} \qquad (5)$$

The total share of the market given to domestic goods is $n s_h$, while the remainder, $(1 - n s_h)$, is the share of the market for foreign goods. The price index has the properties that:

$$\frac{\partial P}{\partial p_h} \frac{p_h}{P} = s_h,$$

$$\frac{\partial P}{\partial p_f} \frac{p_f}{P} = s_f \qquad (6)$$

2.2   Producer behaviour

We focus on the optimal choices for a representative firm, say firm 1, which we call the active firm.[2] Producers maximise profits, with demand given from (4). Firms make the familiar Cournot assumption that all other producers hold their quantities constant. Thus the active firm assumes that:

$$\frac{dx_{ki}}{dx_{1i}} = 0, \qquad \text{for all } k \neq 1 \text{ and } i = h, f$$

where x_{ki} is the output of firm k in market i. Technology is very simple: there is a constant marginal cost, b, and a fixed cost. In the active firm's home market, the price that the producer receives, q_h, equals that paid by the consumers, p_h. For sales abroad, there is an *ad valorem* trade cost, t (the same in all countries), and this drives a wedge between the consumer price of imported goods, p_f, and the price received by their producer, q_f, such that $q_f = (1 - t)p_f$.

Profit-maximising firms set their prices as a markup over marginal costs:

$$q_i = \frac{\epsilon_i^*}{\epsilon_i^* - 1} b, \qquad \text{for } i = h, f \tag{7}$$

where the perceived price elasticity in market i is defined as:

$$\epsilon_i^* \equiv - \left(\frac{dx_{1i}}{dp_{1i}}\right)^* \frac{p_{1i}}{x_{1i}}, \qquad \text{for } i = h, f \tag{8}$$

where p_{1i} is the consumer price for firm 1's variety in market i. The asterisk indicates that this is the perceived effect, given the Cournot assumption. With segmented markets, there is a separate perceived elasticity for each market: with integrated markets the firm sets only one price, so the perceived elasticity is defined by (8), with x_1 being the active firm's total sales. Using (4), the perceived elasticity for segmented markets may be rewritten as:

$$\epsilon_i^* = \sigma - (\sigma - 1)\left(\frac{dP}{dp_{1i}}\right)^* \frac{p_{1i}}{P} \tag{9}$$

The perceived elasticity in a market is thus a function of the perceived responsiveness of the price index to a change in the price of the active firm's variety.

With integrated markets, the active firm must consider the consequences of its actions on both its home and foreign markets simultaneously. Let P_h and P_f be the price indices, as defined in equation (2), for the active firm's home market and each of its export markets, respectively. That is, P_h is the price index for consumers in the active firm's home country, while P_f is the price index in foreign countries into which the active firm's variety is imported. Then the perceived elasticity with integrated markets may be written as:

$$\epsilon^* = \sigma - (\sigma - 1) \sum_{i=1}^{m+1} \theta_{1i} \left(\frac{dP_i}{dp_{1i}}\right)^* \frac{p_{1i}}{P_i} \tag{10}$$

where θ_{ki} is defined as the volume share of market i in firm k's total sales; that is:

$$\theta_{ki} \equiv \frac{x_{ki}}{\sum_{j=1}^{m+1} x_{kj}}$$

The perceived elasticity of demand in the integrated-markets equilibrium is thus a function of a weighted sum of the perceived price index responsiveness in each market in which the variety is sold.

Now consider the expected market prices' effects for goods from the other firms that are consistent with the Cournot assumption that these competitors will not adjust their outputs. We must distinguish between home and foreign firms. Let R_h be the expected response in the consumer price of a competing home firm to a change in the active firm's consumer price, while R_f is defined to be the relative price response of a foreign firm. Thus:

$$R_h \equiv \left(\frac{dP_h}{dp_{1i}}\right)^* \frac{p_{1i}}{P_h};$$

$$R_f \equiv \left(\frac{dP_f}{dp_{1i}}\right)^* \frac{p_{1i}}{P_f}$$

(11)

Using an expression similar to (9), the Cournot assumption in the segmented markets case for a competitor of each type in the active firm's home and foreign markets can be written as:

$$\sigma R_k - (\sigma - 1)\left(\frac{dP}{dp_{1i}}\right)^* \frac{p_{1i}}{P} = 0, \qquad \text{for } i, k = h, f$$

(12)

Similarly, for integrated markets, the Cournot assumption may be written in a similar way to (10) as:

$$\sigma R_k - (\sigma - 1) \sum_{i=1}^{m+1} \theta_{ki} \left(\frac{dP_i}{dp_{1i}}\right)^* \frac{p_{1i}}{P_i} = 0, \qquad \text{for } k = h, f$$

(13)

Comparing (10) and (13), and remembering that $\theta_{1i} = \theta_{hi}$ because the active firm is a typical home firm, we see that the perceived elasticity in integrated markets can be rewritten as[3]

$$\epsilon^* = \sigma(1 - R_h)$$

(14)

It is easy to see that this also holds for the segmented equilibria, where the R_h may differ between markets. We have yet to find R_h. The perceived change in the price index in a market as a result of the change in the active firm's price will be a combination of the direct effect of the price change and the effect of perceived price changes made by the firm's competitors. Differentiating (2), and substituting (6) and (11), yields:

$$\left(\frac{dP}{dp_{1i}}\right)^{*}\frac{p_{1i}}{P} = s_i + (n-1)s_i R_h + (1-ns_i)R_f \tag{15}$$

We use (12) or (13) together with (15) to find the equilibria.

2.3 Equilibrium in segmented markets

From (12), we see that $R_h = R_f = R$. (15) then becomes

$$\left(\frac{dP}{dp_{1i}}\right)^{*}\frac{p_{1i}}{P} = s_i + (1-s_i)R$$

where R may differ between the markets. Together with (12) and (14), this yields

$$\epsilon_i^{*} = \frac{\sigma}{1+(\sigma-1)s_i}, \qquad \text{for } i = h, f \tag{16}$$

and, from (7), we find the familiar expression (see, for example, Norman, 1989) for prices in segmented markets:

$$q_i = \frac{\sigma}{\sigma-1}\frac{1}{1-s_i}b, \qquad \text{for } i = h, f \tag{17}$$

Since market shares do depend on the relative prices, these are not parameters, of course. It is, nevertheless, convenient to think in terms of market shares, in particular when we are going to compare the segmented equilibria with the integrated one. The market share formulation also shows clearly how there is a basis for reciprocal dumping when market shares for home firms and foreign firms differ; for example, due to trade costs or a home-good bias in the preferences.

If the number of firms grows and competition increases, market shares approach zero and the perceived elasticity goes towards σ for all firms in all markets. Hence increased competition reduces the basis for dumping in the segmented equilibrium; this is important when we compare segmented and integrated equilibria with different numbers of firms.

2.4 Integrated equilibrium

With integrated markets price discrimination is not possible; hence, the producer price must be the same for sales in all markets, and consumer prices can differ only with the trade costs. In a completely symmetric world, such as the one we study here, this also fixes relative prices between home and foreign goods and hence, in turn, the market shares. However, integration implies that all markets must be considered simultaneously –

both in firms' profit-maximisation decisions and in the formulation of the Cournot assumption.

The overall elasticity is given by (14), but (13) shows that R_h and R_f may now differ from each other, since they depend on weighted averages of the markets and the firms evaluate the relative importance of the markets differently. To find the perceived elasticity, we must thus solve for R_h and R_f, using (13) and (15).

Due to the symmetry between the markets, it is sufficient to keep track of the effects in the active firm's home market and in a representative foreign market. Hence we use

$$\theta_i \equiv \frac{x_i}{x_h + mx_f}, \qquad \text{for } i = h, f$$

Define the active firm's weighted-average market shares as follows:

$$\bar{s}_i \equiv \theta_i s_h + (1 - \theta_i) s_f, \qquad \text{for } i = h, f \tag{18}$$

where the s_i are the shares in the integrated equilibrium, as defined by (5). Using these and (15), the two equations in (13) can be written

$$\sigma R_h - (\sigma - 1)[\bar{s}_h + (n-1)\bar{s}_h R_h + (1 - n\bar{s}_h) R_f] = 0,$$
$$\sigma R_f - (\sigma - 1)[\bar{s}_f + (n-1)\bar{s}_f R_h + (1 - n\bar{s}_f) R_f] = 0 \tag{19}$$

From these we find R_h and, using (14), we then get

$$\epsilon^* = \sigma \frac{\left(\dfrac{\sigma}{\sigma - 1}\right) - n(\bar{s}_h - \bar{s}_f)}{\left(\dfrac{\sigma}{\sigma - 1}\right) - (n - 1)(\bar{s}_h - \bar{s}_f) + \sigma \bar{s}_f} \tag{20}$$

This cannot be transformed into an easily interpretable price equation: it is, however, possible to write the integrated-equilibrium producer price in an expression analogous to that for segmented markets, equation (17). Thus:

$$q = \frac{\sigma}{\sigma - 1} \frac{1}{1 - s_{eq}} b \tag{21}$$

where

$$s_{eq} \equiv \frac{1 + \delta}{n(m + 1 + \delta)}, \tag{22}$$

and

$$\delta \equiv \frac{\bar{s}_h - \bar{s}_f}{\sigma \bar{s}_f}$$

Despite their inability to price discriminate between markets, firms do not treat each national market segment equally, as they would in a single market, because preference biases and trade costs still exist.[4] In a single market, in the absence of these differences between national market segments, firms would have equal shares of each market segment $s \equiv 1/\{n(m + 1)\}$, the inverse of the total number of varieties. In the integrated markets equilibrium, each firm does get s on average, but behaves as if its share equals s_{eq}.

One way to interpret (22) is as follows: from (19) it is not too difficult to see that $R_h = (1 + \delta)R_f$. But the competitors count only through their influence on market conditions; hence, the integrated equilibrium must be identical to equilibrium in an 'equivalent single market' where each foreign firm counts as $1/(1 + \delta)$ home firms. Hence in the 'equivalent single market' there are n home firms and $nm/(1 + \delta)$ foreign firms. All firms are identical, and their market shares are s_{eq}, the inverse of the total number of firms in this 'equivalent single market'. If $\delta \neq 0$, then s_{eq} differs from s, s_{eq} being an increasing function of δ. We can determine that $\delta > 0$ whenever there is a bias (due to preferences or impediments to trade) for home market goods. Thus $s_{eq} > s$, that is, trade impediments make the integrated market less competitive than the equivalent single market and, from (21), the larger is δ, the higher will producer prices be in the integrated markets equilibrium relative to that of a single market. It should, however, be remembered that δ is endogenously determined. Hence, it is not straightforward to see how the price in the integrated equilibrium depends on the parameters of the model.

3   Effects of integration

We will use this model to study the effects of market integration for profits and consumer surplus. Overall welfare assessments are not explicitly included; they follow from the effects on profits and consumer surplus, plus any transfer payments if trade costs are tariffs rather than real costs (see, for example, Venables, 1990c). The relative sizes of these effects, and hence aggregate welfare may, however, depend on the exact parameter value in the utility and profit functions, and we do not want the results to depend on an arbitrarily chosen parameter. We thus stick to disaggregated welfare assessments, for which the qualitative results are robust to specific parameter values. In this section we briefly discuss the relevant dimensions, based on the model description above. The discussion shows that it is difficult to get firm results from theoretical considerations alone, and in section 4 we use a numerical model to illustrate the arguments. Even though we are going to focus primarily on welfare effects, it is fairly obvious that the key issue in understanding the effects of integration is related to what happens to prices and competition. Indeed, the main motivation behind integration in the sense discussed here is that it will force firms to behave more competitively, and thus lead to consumer gains through lower prices and increased consumption: the study of prices is thus the key.

3.1   Prices

From (17), we see that with segmented markets there is an element of dumping, with $p_f(1 - t) < p_h$, as long as firms have larger market shares in their home markets than abroad. This will typically be the case if there are trade costs (real or artificial) or a bias towards home-produced goods in preferences. In our model dumping occurs as long as

$$T \equiv 1 - (1 - t)\frac{a_f}{a_h} > 0 \tag{23}$$

Following Smith and Venables (1988) we will call T the total tariff equivalent.[5] As dumping in this sense stems from the fact that firms exploit their market power in the home market, one would expect market integration to result in a reduction of home-market prices. However, it is not quite so straightforward. From (17) and (21), we see that the integrated producer price lies between the segmented producer prices if $s_f < s_{eq} < s_h$. Now, as $s_f \leq s \leq s_h$ and $s < s_{eq}$ whenever $\delta > 0$, then $s_f < s_{eq}$. It is less obvious that the second inequality, $s_{eq} < s_h$, holds and our discussion will focus on that. In order to do so, it will be useful to introduce a new term, $\gamma \equiv s_h - s_{eq}$. This is the 'share difference' between segmented markets equilibrium and that of the solution for integrated markets. If $\gamma > 0$, the home-market price will fall with integration.

Let $\rho \equiv q_h/q_f$, the endogenously determined relative producer price in the segmented equilibrium. For $\rho = 1$, the producer prices in the two types of market are the same, as they must be (by definition) for integrated markets. In the segmented case, dumping implies that $\rho > 1$; and the higher is ρ, the more dumping there is. We can write $s_h = s(\rho, T, n, m)$, with $s_T > 0$ and the remaining partial effects negative. But ρ is endogenous and it is not too difficult to find that $\rho = \rho(T, n, m)$, with $\rho_T > 0$, $\rho_n < 0$, $\rho_m < 0$. That is, the indirect effects of the parameters T, n, and m work through ρ in such a way as to *dampen* their direct effects on s_h.

In the integrated equilibrium, firms have an equal share of the market, s. But, as we have seen, this is not the appropriate measure to use in determining producer prices: from (21), q is a function of s_{eq}, which is not the same as the simple measure of market share due to the influence of the δ term. The complexities stem from the fact that the integrated equilibrium is *not the same* as the equilibrium in a single market. With differentiated products there are still different market segments, and the producers may care more about some segments than others, due both to differences in preferences and to trade policies. If there are high trade costs, firms perceive it to be very costly to retain market shares in the foreign markets when dumping is not possible. Hence the integrated equilibrium may be one in which all firms stick to their own home markets and care less about exports.

We can show that $\delta = \delta(T, t, m)$, where $\delta_T > 0$, $\delta_t > 0$, $\delta_m \leq 0$ (with inequality when $\delta > 0$). Note that it is not only the total tariff equivalent that influences δ, but also its composition (unlike the case for the determination of ρ). Thus an increase in t raises δ both directly and through an increase in T. Even when the tariff equivalent is held constant, a shift in its composition towards increased trade costs (away from a preference bias for home-market goods) will still expand δ.

In summary, dumping ($\rho > 1$) acts pro-competitively in the segmented markets equilibrium and home-market biases ($\delta > 0$) reduce the competitiveness of the integrated markets solution. We have yet to demonstrate that these influences can be sufficiently large to reverse the market-share inequality, such that $\gamma < 0$ and the home-market price rises as a result of market integration. What is immediately clear however is that, for the polar cases of $T = 0$ and $T = 1$, $\gamma = 0$. Thus when either there are no impediments to trade or trade barriers are prohibitive, the integrated markets equilibrium is indistinguishable from that of the segmented markets case.

In order to begin to understand what occurs between these extremes, consider the special case of a bilateral monopoly (that is, $n = 1$ and $m = 1$) in which $t = 0$. Hence, all home-market bias arises from preferences, not trade barriers. In this case γ is a function only of T and the elasticity of substitution, σ. Table 5.1 shows how γ varies with different values of the parameters. From Table 5.1, it is clear that we may well have $\gamma < 0$, implying that the home-market price rises as a consequence of integration. Thus, in this special case, all consumer prices may rise from market integration.

Our next task is to loosen these restrictions and consider the sign of γ under more general assumptions. Instead of a bilateral monopoly, let n and m take any arbitrary fixed values (that is, there is still no entry or exit). Now, let t be non-zero and consider the effects of the composition of the tariff equivalent term, T.

Table 5.1. *Share difference,* $\gamma \equiv s_h - s_{eq}$, $m = 1$, $n = 1$, $t = 0$

Tariff equivalent T	Elasticity of substitution, σ				
	2	4	6	10	20
0.0	0.00	0.00	0.00	0.00	0.00
0.2	0.02	0.03	0.02	-0.01	-0.18
0.4	0.05	0.02	-0.05	-0.24	-0.38
0.6	0.06	-0.07	-0.22	-0.30	-0.30
0.8	0.05	-0.17	-0.20	-0.19	-0.18

Proposition 1
For a given tariff equivalent, T, γ is a decreasing function of the trade cost, t.

Proof
For a given T, all individual market shares are given, both in the segmented and the integrated case. But s_{eq} is an increasing function of δ, itself an increasing function of t, for given T. $\square$

Hence, the higher are the trade barriers, the less likely it is that the home-market price falls with integration.

Next, let us consider the importance of the number of firms in each domestic market.

Proposition 2

$$\frac{ds_{eq}}{dn} \frac{n}{s_{eq}} < \frac{ds_h}{dn} \frac{n}{s_h} < 0$$

Proof
From (22),

$$\frac{ds_{eq}}{dn} \frac{n}{s_{eq}} = -1$$

since δ is independent of n. From (5) and the properties of ρ, we have

$$\frac{ds_h}{dn} \frac{n}{s_h} = -1 + \frac{ds_h}{d\rho} \frac{d\rho}{dn} \frac{n}{s_h} > -1 \quad \square$$

Hence, an exogenous increase in n reduces s_{eq} relatively more than it lowers s_h. So if $\gamma \leq 0$, the greater is n the more limited is the home-price rise from integration. If $\gamma > 0$, we cannot rule out the possibility that γ

falls with an increase in n. Of course, for large n, domestic markets are always highly competitive and, hence, the effects of integration are very limited.

3.2 Welfare

For welfare assessments both the home price and the foreign price matter; and this discussion shows that it is not unlikely that we end up with a moderate price fall for home goods and a sharp price rise for imports, such that the overall effects for consumers and producers are not obvious.

The removal of dumping possibilities reallocates sales between markets and reduces trade and thus lowers trade costs; hence there is an aggregate gain through reduced real trade costs; whether this appears as profits or consumer surpluses or as a combination of the two again depends on the exact conditions regarding competition and protection. If there are many domestic firms, competition ensures that the cost reduction benefits the consumers through lower prices; if there are few firms the gain may appear entirely as profits.

3.2.1 Consumer surplus
Consumers' welfare will be measured by the utility function in (1). With Y exogenously given (as consumption of the numéraire good is predetermined), the consumer surplus is determined by prices alone; if integration lowers the average consumer price, as measured by the price index $P(\cdot)$ the consumers are better off, and vice versa. If P^S is the price level in segmented equilibrium and P^I the one in the integrated equilibrium, we have

$$\frac{X^I}{X^S} = \frac{P^S}{P^I}$$

This may be rewritten as:

$$\frac{P^S}{P^I} = \left(\frac{1 + m(1 - T)^{\sigma - 1}}{1 + m[\rho(1 - T)]^{\rho - 1}}\right)^{\frac{1}{\sigma - 1}} \left(\frac{1 - s_{eq}}{1 - s_h}\right) \tag{24}$$

We discussed above, whether the market share equivalent in the integrated solution was smaller than the home market share in the segmented case. Here we see that this is not sufficient to ensure consumer surplus gains of integration. With $\rho > 1$, the expression in the first parentheses is less than unity; hence, we need more than a marginal reduction in home-market prices to make sure that the overall expression is positive.

The reason is, of course, that import prices typically go up, and the fall in home-market price must make up for that.

3.2.2 Profits
It is commonly claimed that as the segmented case allows the firms to price discriminate, whereas that is not possible in the integrated case, profits must necessarily be higher in the segmented solution. This is, however, not correct. Since integration means that no firms are allowed to price discriminate, the whole competitive situation is altered, and profits may go up or down as a consequence of integration. In isolation, the fact that a firm cannot price discriminate reduces profits and leads to a reallocation of sales from the former low-price markets (abroad) to the high-price market (at home). But since this is true for all firms, the foreigners will reallocate their sales from our market to their own home markets, and this tends to increase our profits. The total effect depends on the exact competitive situation, as the discussion of price determination above clearly indicates. Indeed we have seen that all producer prices may go up, and then profits clearly increase. But even in the more normal case in which the home-market price falls and the export price rises, profits may go up since both markets matter, and since the reallocation of sales between markets saves trade costs for the firm. The numerical results below show that only when there are several firms in each country can we be sure that competition is strong enough to reduce profits and increase consumer surpluses when we go from segmented to integrated markets.

4   Numerical examples

In this section we will illustrate the effects of integration along the dimensions discussed above by presenting results from a stylised numerical model. The model is constructed in accordance with the model specification above: there are a number of identical economies trading with each other in segmented markets that are then integrated. As the economies are identical we focus on prices and welfare effects in one country. Throughout the discussion we look at prices and welfare measured relative to the levels in the segmented equilibrium. Hence, the absolute levels of the variables are not important. Fixed costs of production are disregarded, so that effectively there are constant returns to scale; the profits we report are based on price *less* marginal costs, and represent the contribution to fixed costs. As long as we ignore entry and exit, this is legitimate.

Table 5.2a shows the effects of integration between 2 countries with 1 firm in each country and an elasticity of substitution of 2 between the

Table 5.2. *The effects of integration, % change from segmented equilibrium*

(a) Elasticity of substitution, $\sigma = 2$

	Integrated relative to segmented			
Trade costs	Home price	Foreign price	Consumer surplus	Profits
0.0	0.0	0.0	0.0	0.0
0.1	− 2.4	2.9	− 0.1	0.2
0.2	− 4.4	6.9	− 0.6	0.7
0.3	− 6.0	12.4	− 1.6	1.8
0.4	− 6.9	20.2	− 3.2	3.5
0.5	− 6.8	31.8	− 5.7	6.1

(b) Elasticity of substitution, $\sigma = 5$

	Integrated relative to segmented			
Trade costs	Home price	Foreign price	Consumer surplus	Profits
0.0	0.0	0.0	0.0	0.0
0.1	− 3.1	5.4	− 0.5	1.4
0.2	− 4.0	14.8	− 2.5	5.9
0.3	− 0.9	31.9	− 7.5	14.4
0.4	10.8	66.7	− 18.1	27.3
0.5	43.7	150.1	− 36.9	43.4

varieties. This is the simplest textbook version of reciprocal dumping between national 'monopolies' at the outset, and we require that dumping is no longer permitted in the integrated solution. There are no biases in demand and all trade costs are summarised in the tariff rate, t. As we do not discuss tariff revenues it is not important whether this is a tariff or a trade cost; it is, however, assumed that the rate stays the same in the segmented and the integrated equilibria.

Table 5.2a shows results for various trade costs. The second and third columns show percentage changes in the consumer prices of home-produced goods and imports in the integrated equilibrium relative to the segmented one. As expected, the home price goes down and the foreign price rises; the rise in the foreign price is, however, very strong, due to the fact that, with these parameter values, there is a substantial amount of dumping in the segmented equilibrium.

The next two columns show the welfare effects, the percentage changes in consumer surplus and profits, respectively. This example clearly shows that the welfare effects are not necessarily as the 'conventional wisdom' suggests. In this case, producers gain and consumers lose from integration; and the reason is simply that the segmented case *with dumping* is, in a sense, more competitive than the integrated case; when price discrimination is no longer possible, it becomes too costly for firms to retain their high shares in the foreign market.

We now examine further how these results depend on the elasticity of substitution, σ. There are two opposing effects from increasing this. First, the competitive pressure increases, since varieties are closer substitutes, and hence there is less room for price differences. On the other hand, the effects of trade costs and protection are stronger. Integration, with the same producer price in all markets, implies that the consumer prices are forced to differ by the trade costs, and the higher is the elasticity of substitution, the more will demand for foreign goods go down with integration. Hence, if there are only a few domestic firms their market power may increase as a consequence of integration.

Table 5.2b shows the most extreme example of this. This table is identical to Table 5.2a except that we now have $\sigma = 5$, rather than 2. There is no bias in preferences in this case, and the results clearly illustrate how integration combined with remaining trade costs may give the domestic firm a market power that it did not have in the segmented equilibrium with dumping.

For low trade costs, the development is similar to the one in Table 5.2a, differing only in the magnitude of the changes. For higher trade costs, however, the situation is completely different. At some stage the tariff becomes almost prohibitive for the foreign producer, and the market equilibrium appears to shift from a duopoly to (almost) a domestic monopoly. In this example the change occurs from a trade cost around 0.3; from there on prices rise dramatically and the changes in consumer and producer surpluses shift accordingly.

From section 3.1, we know that these price results are affected by the composition of T, as well as by the degree of competition in the markets. The welfare consequences of this are illustrated in sub-sections 4.1–4.3.

4.1   Tariff versus biased preferences

Figure 5.1 plots consumer surpluses and profits for the model above, as the composition of the total tariff equivalent (see (23)) switches between tariffs and home-market preferences. The tariff equivalent is set at 0.5 so that the left-hand side of the diagram coincides with the last row in Table

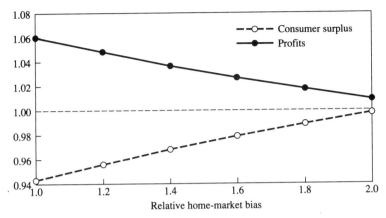

Figure 5.1 Relative effects of market integration, tariff equivalent = 0.5, 2 countries, 1 firm per country

5.2a with trade cost at 0.5 and no biases in preferences. The elasticity of substitution is equal to 2. As we go from left to right the proportion of the tariff equivalent coming from preferences increases, with the extreme right-hand side corresponding to free trade.

Figure 5.1 demonstrates the effects stated in Proposition 1: as the tariff rate is reduced, s_{eq} is reduced while s_h is unaltered, and the price changes are attenuated.

4.2   The number of firms

In Figure 5.1 it is still the case that consumers lose and producers gain from integration. We know from Proposition 2 that increasing the number of firms will affect the integrated solution relatively more than the segmented one, so Figure 5.2 shows the welfare effects with a larger number of firms ($n = 2$) in each country.

Two effects should be noted. First, the effects in the no-bias case (left-hand side) are smaller than before, as predicted by Proposition 2, because the difference between segmented and integrated equilibria is smaller. Second, we can now generate the 'conventional wisdom', in which consumers gain and producers lose. In fact, we also see that it is possible for both producers and consumers to gain; this is because trade costs are saved when firms switch their sales towards more home-market sales. Whether this is a gain for the country as a whole depends on whether we talk about real trade costs or only income transfers through reduced tariff revenue.

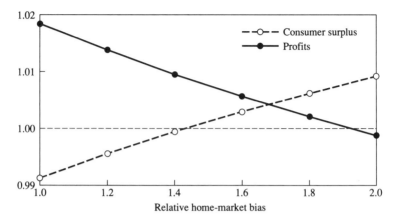

Figure 5.2   Relative effects of market integration, tariff equivalent = 0.5, 2 countries, 2 firms per country

4.3   Home versus foreign competition

As well as the total number of firms, it also matters whether competition comes from home firms or foreign firms. Since all foreign competitors face the trade costs, and hence will tend to lose market shares in an overseas market when they are not allowed to dump, an increase in the number of foreign firms (or in the number of identical countries in the model) does not increase the competitive pressure to the same extent as an equivalent rise in the number of firms in each country would do. This is illustrated in Figure 5.3, in which two different situations are shown. In both cases the

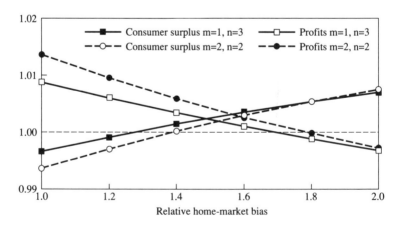

Figure 5.3   Relative effects of market integration, tariff equivalent = 0.5, elasticity = 2, total number of firms = 6

Table 5.3. *The effects of integration, % change from segmented equilibrium*
$T = 0.5$, $t = 0.1$, $m = 1$

| | Integrated relative to segmented | | | | | |
| | $\sigma = 2$ | | $\sigma = 5$ | | $\sigma = 10$ | |
Number of firms	Consumer surplus	Profits	Consumer surplus	Profits	Consumer surplus	Profits
1	− 1.1	1.8	− 28.8	25.3	− 90.5	68.0
2	0.6	0.2	0.6	5.8	− 10.7	21.5
3	0.5	− 0.1	3.0	− 1.0	− 1.3	4.9
5	0.4	− 0.2	2.8	− 4.2	0.4	− 0.5
10	0.2	− 0.2	1.6	− 4.0	0.3	− 1.2

total number of firms in the world is equal to 6, one set of lines shows the welfare effects if there are 3 countries and 2 firms in each, the other if there are 2 countries and 3 firms in each. The results demonstrate how domestic competition is necessary to ensure consumer gains from integration.[6] With few domestic firms the integrated equilibrium may be less competitive than the segmented one, in the sense that profits rise and consumer surplus declines with integration. This effect is less when the level of the tariff equivalent is the result of home-market biases, rather than of trade impediments.

4.4 Number versus substitutability between varieties

Finally, Table 5.3 indicates how sensitive are the welfare effects with respect to the elasticity of substitution and the number of firms in each country. Table 5.3 is constructed for the case of 2 countries (that is, $m = 1$) and with the tariff equivalent fixed at $T = 0.5$ with trade costs set at $t = 0.1$, and it reveals two significant results. First, the chances for producers to gain and consumers to lose from integration are higher the fewer firms there are in each country and the closer substitutes are the goods. But it is worth noting that such effects occur not only for the case of international duopoly, as in Table 5.2. With $\sigma = 10$, we get the same pattern (of producer gain and consumer loss) in a world with 6 firms. As calibrated elasticities often greatly exceed this level (see, for example, Smith and Venables, 1988), such an outcome may then be more than merely a theoretical possibility. It should be observed that, in Table 5.3, the bulk of the total tariff equivalent arises from biased preferences. From

Proposition 1, we know that this tends to increase consumer gains and reduce profits, relative to a situation with a higher trade cost, t. Hence, if anything, the parameter choice that we have made biases the results in support of the conventional wisdom.[7]

Secondly, Table 5.3 shows that, although we get a sign pattern in accordance with the conventional wisdom for a large number of firms, the effects of integration in such cases are small when σ is high. This reflects the fact that, with a large number of firms and not too much product differentiation, there is little basis for dumping in the segmented case and only a limited scope for exploitation of market power. Hence, the difference between the segmented markets equilibrium and the integrated market one is small, as long as we remain in a completely symmetric world.

5   Conclusions

The effects of market integration, defined as a move from segmented, national markets to an integrated international one, have been central to a number of recent studies of potential gains from the '1992' programme. The expected gains from market integration come from the fact that, at the outset, firms enjoy large market shares and thereby substantial market power in their home markets, while their export-market shares are much smaller. With integrated markets, a firm's market power depends on its position in the overall market; hence the possibility of exploiting its dominant position in its home market is expected to be reduced.

In this chapter we show that, while this indeed may be the case, the opposite may also happen. The integrated equilibrium may be one in which the consumer prices of *all* products are higher than in the segmented case. If goods are differentiated and there are trade costs or national preference biases, then the equilibrium in integrated markets differs from that in a single market. Hence, even if the average market share in the overall market is smaller than that in the home market in the segmented case, this is not sufficient to ensure that the price of domestic goods will go down. The point is that, with integrated markets and no dumping possibilities, it becomes more expensive to serve the foreign market, and the competitive pressure from foreign firms (facing a cost or preference disadvantage) will go down. Hence, even though an integrated equilibrium yields lower prices for home goods than in a segmented case without dumping (if such a case were possible), it does not necessarily yield lower prices than in a segmented equilibrium with dumping; and this should be the relevant basis of comparison. Our results show that the probability of all prices rising from market integration is greater the higher are each of trade costs, the bias in preferences towards home goods, and the degree of concentration in the market (that is, the fewer firms there are).

In applied models of this type, data limitations have meant that preference biases and trade barriers cannot be separately observed. Instead, all that can be calibrated is the combined effect, as measured by the tariff equivalent (see, for example, Smith and Venables, 1988 and the discussion in Norman, 1989). This measure has then been allocated arbitrarily between its two components. We have shown that these two components have qualitatively different effects on the integrated markets equilibrium. Hence, for applied work, it is important to attempt to distinguish between the two.

For welfare assessments, the 'conventional wisdom' says that consumers will gain and producers will lose from integration. This is obviously not always true; if all prices go up, the reverse is true. However, even in the more 'normal' case of a fall in the home-market price, we know that the foreign price will increase, since there are no dumping possibilities. Hence, for consumers to gain we need more than a marginal reduction in the home price, since it must outweigh the rise in the import price.

A similar story applies for the effects on profits. Again, the degree of protection (or preference biases) and the degree of concentration in the markets are the central parameters. Another way to see this is as follows: we know that there is a certain quantity of 'wasteful' trade in the segmented equilibrium, and that this disappears in the integrated case. Hence, if trade is costly, there are gains from integration, in the sense that the overall costs go down. The distribution of these gains – and, indeed, whether the cost reduction represents a welfare gain at all in a second-best world – depends on how competitive the markets are. With few firms in each country, the firms manage to capture the benefits of the fall in costs, and may even increase the prices, since the competitive pressure from foreign firms declines. With many firms in each country, on the other hand, any cost reductions are passed through to the consumers.

In this chapter we have focused on how integration affects competition; in doing so we have worked with a model with a given number of firms, and in which the firms are symmetric in terms of production costs. There are at least two related topics that may be important. First, with increasing returns to scale, free entry and exit imply that the overall number of firms, and hence overall production costs, may be affected by market integration. This tends to yield welfare gains through more efficient production. On the other hand, fewer firms implies that the exploitation of market power may go up, and the total welfare effects are not clear. Second, there may be asymmetric costs between firms, and thus elements of trade based on comparative advantage in addition to the intra-industry trade we have studied here. It is not obvious how the exploitation of comparative advantage is affected by market integration; this will have to be a topic for future research.

Of course, in applied models all of these effects are present. Hence, when such models yield large gains from market integration, this may be due to one or both of these alternative effects; even though the story usually told to explain the effects is the one related to market power and increased competition.

NOTES

The research for this paper was supported by grants from the Alfred P. Sloan Foundation, the Norwegian Research Council for Science and the Humanities (NAVF), and from the British Council. We are grateful to our discussant, Konstantine Gatsios, and to the editor for comments and suggestions to improve the chapter. Any remaining deficiencies are our own responsibility.

1 A strand of theoretical work that looks more carefully into the game between firms competing simultaneously in multiple markets (see Ben-Zvi and Helpman, 1988 and Venables, 1990a) suggests that the appropriate game is one in which firms realise that there are links between the markets, but not as close links as the integrated market hypothesis suggests. Hence Venables (1990a), for example, studies a two-stage game in which the segmented and the integrated solutions come out as special cases, but the 'preferred' game is one that lies somewhere between these cases.
2 We try to economise on notation but we shall on occasion distinguish between the actions of the active firm and those of its home and foreign competitors.
3 This is valid only for $n > 1$: that is, when there are domestic competitors. All of the results that follow are, however, correct for $n = 1$ as well.
4 It is the existence of these market differences that permits firms to price discriminate in the segmented markets equilibrium.
5 In calibrated models, such as that of Smith and Venables (1988), data on market shares in the segmented equilibrium are used to define T. The extent of trade barriers and relative preference biases are not independently observed. See also Norman (1989) for discussion of this.
6 Essentially, with the same total number of firms, domestic competition yields a higher γ than competition from foreign firms.
7 For the cases of $\sigma = 2$ and $\sigma = 5$, this is confirmed by comparing the first row of Table 5.3 with the final rows of Table 5.2a and 5.2b, respectively.

REFERENCES

Ben-Zvi, S. and E. Helpman (1988) 'Oligopoly in segmented markets', *NBER Working Paper*, **2665**, Cambridge, Mass.: NBER.
Brander, J.A. (1981) 'Intra-industry trade in identical commodities', *Journal of International Economics*, **11**, pp. 1–14.

Brander, J.A. and P.R. Krugman (1983) 'A reciprocal dumping model of international trade', *Journal of International Economics*, **15**, pp. 313–21.

Markusen, J.R. and A.J. Venables (1988) 'Trade policy with increasing returns to scale and imperfect competition: contradictory results from competing assumptions', *Journal of International Economics*, **24**, pp. 299–316.

Norman, V. (1989) 'EFTA and the internal European market', *Economic Policy*, **9**, pp. 423–66.

Smith, A. and A.J. Venables (1988) 'Completing the internal market in the European Community: some industry simulations', *European Economic Review*, **32(7)**, pp. 1501–25.

Venables, A.J. (1990a) 'International capacity choice and international market games', *Journal of International Economics*, **29**, pp. 23–42.

(1990b) 'The economic integration of oligopolistic markets', *European Economic Review*, **34**, pp. 753–73.

(1990c) 'Trade policy under imperfect competition: a numerical assessment', CEPR, *Discussion Paper*, **412** (April).

Discussion

KONSTANTINE GATSIOS

The completion of the European internal market will result in segmented national markets becoming integrated into one market. Quite naturally, over the last few years the study of the welfare effects of such a dramatic change has been a popular line of research among economists at both a theoretical and an applied level.

Chapter 5 by Haaland and Wooton contributes to this literature and, in particular, to its theoretical strand. The model employed is very close to that of Smith and Venables (1988). There are Dixit–Stiglitz type of preferences, product differentiation and monopolistic competition between symmetric firms operating under a constant marginal cost and a fixed cost. Unlike Smith and Venables' study, however, the aim here is to shed doubt on the popular premise that a move from segmented to integrated markets is necessarily pro-competitive, resulting in consumer gains and producer losses.

This premise, sometimes referred to as 'conventional wisdom', stems from the standard textbook case in which price discrimination exercised by a monopolist in a given market generates higher profits and lower consumer surplus, as compared to the case of no discrimination.[1] The reason why this result may not carry through in more general models, like the one here, is easy to see.

In a segmented markets equilibrium firms can price discriminate between home and foreign markets. In an integrated markets equilibrium they can no longer do so, despite the fact that the factors that segment markets and allow price discrimination to occur in the first place (here, trade costs and preference biases) are still present. Put differently, although in an integrated markets equilibrium firms still face, in essence, different market segments, they cannot translate this into different pricing policies. It is therefore clear, almost by definition, that an integrated markets equilibrium is different to a single market equilibrium, since in the latter case any sort of trade impediment, like those mentioned above, is absent. Although this observation is fairly obvious, it nonetheless provides the background explanation for obtaining results which stand in contrast to the 'conventional wisdom', namely that producers may gain and consumers may lose due to market integration.

The identification of the theoretical possibility of such adverse welfare effects, although not surprising (after all, we are dealing with a second-best world), is worth making. However, the most useful and interesting contribution of the chapter is that it investigates the role of different factors that give rise to such effects. This is conducted in sections 3 and, especially, 4 with the aid of specific numerical examples. The discussion of different possibilities revolves around three central parameters: the degree of protection (in terms of trade costs and preference biases), the degree of competition and the elasticity of substitution in consumption. In Table 5.3, for instance, it is shown that for a given level of trade costs and preference biases, the fall in consumer surplus in the integrated equilibrium relative to the segmented one is greater the smaller the number of firms and the larger the degree of substitutability in consumption. The reverse happens with profits.

A final comment. The literature on 'new trade theory' has by now provided us with a fairly good understanding of the interrelations between imperfect competition, trade patterns and welfare (for a review see Helpman and Krugman, 1989). In particular, the analysis of market integration in the context of imperfectly competitive product markets – to which this chapter has contributed – has been more or less exhaustive (see, for instance, Markusen and Venables, 1988; Venables, 1990; and Winters, 1988). What we seem to understand less satisfactorily, however, are the mechanisms through which firms can successfully discriminate between different sub-markets. This is a central question in the analysis of economic integration, yet our theories on this issue seem to lack sufficient depth. At the same time there is a need to look more closely into aspects of market integration such as regulation (product standards, financial and professional services), competition policy, public procurement and state aids. Cooperation between member states in such areas may actually prove to be more important for welfare and economic efficiency considerations than the mere removal of trade barriers (see, for instance, Gatsios and Karp, 1992). It may also prove to be more difficult.

NOTES

1 What happens to social surplus, however, is another matter. This, for instance, will be the highest possible if the monopolist can perfectly price discriminate between consumers and capture all consumer surplus.

REFERENCES

Gatsios, K. and L. Karp (1992) 'The welfare effects of incomplete harmonisation of trade and industrial policy', *Economic Journal*, **102**, pp. 107–19.

Helpman, E. and P. Krugman (1989) *Trade Policy and Market Structure*, Cambridge, Mass.: MIT Press.

Markusen, J.R. and A.J. Venables (1988) 'Trade policy with increasing returns to scale and imperfect competition: contradictory results from competing assumptions', *Journal of International Economics*, **24**, pp. 299–316.

Smith, A. and A.J. Venables (1988) 'Completing the internal market in the European Community: some industry simulations', *European Economic Review*, **32(7)**, pp. 1501–25.

Venables, A.J. (1990) 'The economic integration of oligopolistic markets', *European Economic Review*, **34**, pp. 753–73.

Winters, L.A. (1988) 'Completing the European Internal Market', *European Economic Review*, **32**, pp. 1477–99.

6 Pharmaceuticals: who's afraid of '1992'?

GERNOT KLEPPER

1 Introduction

The market for pharmaceuticals is probably the most strongly segmented and highly regulated market in the EC – witness the large price differences between countries. At the same time, the pharmaceutical industry in some countries such as Germany and the UK belongs to the most successful sector of the economy.

In studies of the internal market in 1992 the prospects for a unification of the markets for pharmaceuticals have been seen as not too bright (CEC, 1988a). The expectations about the success of the planned directives of the Commission of the EC were muted, although some convergence of price levels was predicted, but the potential path for prices in the process of unification and the resultant welfare effects remained unexplored (CEC, 1988b). In 'The Economics of 1992' a convergence of prices to a community average was assumed, resulting in a fall of spending on pharmaceuticals of ECU 720 million or to some 3 per cent in total expenditure.

This chapter develops a framework within which the likely outcomes of measures taken towards an internal market can be analysed. It first introduces some features of pharmaceutical markets in terms of industry characteristics and demand regulations, and summarises the proposed measures by the Commission of the EC. In section 3 it presents a simple model of a price discriminating monopoly which is exposed to price controls in one market and which faces limited arbitrage between the markets. Changes in regulations concerning arbitrage and price controls are then investigated (section 4) and the impact of moves towards unified markets on welfare are discussed (section 5). The chapter concludes with some speculations about the likely process of creating an internal market for pharmaceuticals as laid out by the directives of the EC and further planned directives.

150

2   Industry and market structure

2.1   Main industry characteristics

The European pharmaceutical industry can best be characterised by its dual structure. On the one hand, there are small companies which do not develop new drugs, have small R&D budgets and sell mostly to local markets. They make up the bulk of the 2200 pharmaceutical companies in Europe. The European market is dominated, however, by around 60 internationally operating, large, research-oriented companies of which about 30 are of European origin. They control some 70–80 per cent of the market in France, Germany, Italy and the UK and account for most of the ECU 4–5 billion spent on R&D.

These large international firms rely to a considerable extent on intra-firm trade and production in local affiliates such that trade statistics reveal only a small proportion of the internationalisation of the market for pharmaceuticals. It has been estimated that while in 1984 imports into the EC amounted to about ECU 1.2 billion, sales by local affiliates of non-EC companies amounted to ECU 7.7 billion (CEC, 1988b). This emphasis on local production has two causes. It is often claimed that the national authorities which regulate pharmaceutical markets and control demand discriminate against imports, thus forcing foreign companies to establish local facilities. The other cause relates to the technology of producing pharmaceuticals.

Developing new drugs requires large investment in R&D adding up to, for example, DM 2915 million (1980) in Germany, i.e. 14.6 per cent of German industry turnover (BPI, 1990). This is about one-third of total R&D spending in the EC (CEC, 1988b). It is estimated that the development of one new pharmaceutical entity costs about DM 250 million. Since R&D projects have a low probability of success large companies choose to work simultaneously on 8–10 projects in order to spread the risk. In addition, research facilities require a minimum efficient scale for libraries, animal testing, laboratories, etc. so that the R&D facilities tend to be in one centralised place, usually the headquarters of the company. Once the chemical entity has been developed, it is necessary to prepare the active ingredients and convert them into dosage form. The latter step involves few economies of scale and can be decentralised. The marketing of drugs is then a purely local activity. The production technology can therefore roughly be characterised as one which involves sizeable fixed costs but otherwise constant marginal costs.

The demand for pharmaceuticals is determined by complex interactions between patients, physicians, and different health insurance systems. The

Table 6.1. *Estimation of relative drug prices from different studies,*
UK = 100

	1974*	1981*	1982*	1983*	1984*	1985*
Belgium	143	73	66	103	69	70
Denmark	n.a.	n.a.	143	154	99	n.a.
France	80	69	57	76	52	77
FRG	288	128	159	164	124	120
Greece	n.a.	n.a.	n.a.	73	n.a.	n.a.
Italy	85	65	62	57	58	72
Netherlands	n.a.	n.a.	140	145	114	113

* Data from years shown.
Source: Taken from CEC (1988b), Table 4.2

choice of an ethical, i.e. by prescription only, drug – the dominating market segment – is largely made by the physician who is privileged to prescribe drugs, but he does not pay for it. Patients, the consumers of pharmaceuticals, have little incentive to respond to price differences of drugs, so the national and local health institutions who bear the costs have had to seek alternative ways to control the cost of pharmaceutical therapies. Except for Germany, Ireland, the Netherlands, and the UK, all EC countries use direct price controls. Other measures include controls on total expenditure, positive or negative lists, and direct negotiations between health systems and the pharmaceutical industry.

Table 6.1 shows that the different approaches to cost control have resulted in drastic price differences between high-price countries like Denmark, Germany and the Netherlands (which incidentally do not control prices) and low-price countries like Italy and France which limit prices. Spain and Portugal, which are not included here, also have low prices.

2.2   Barriers to trade

The major regulations for pharmaceuticals concern health aspects. Every pharmaceutical has to pass a registration procedure before it can be sold in a national market. Proof of safety, efficacy and quality have to be supplied by the producer. In addition, packages, labels, patient information leaflets and dosages must be approved. These characteristics together define a pharmaceutical product in a national market. Strictly speaking, this means that two products sold in two different countries with different patient information leaflets or different labels but identical chemical ingredients are treated as different products. The admission process of pharmaceuticals thus unintentionally produces perfect market segmentation if viewed from a legal standpoint.

In reality, this view has been contested. Since the late 1970s companies have appeared which have tried to arbitrage pharmaceuticals from low-priced to high-priced countries, mostly to Germany, the Netherlands and the UK. These companies bought, for example, German pharmaceuticals in France or Italy and exported them to Germany, or they bought Italian pharmaceuticals in Italy and exported them parallel to the exports of the producers to Germany. These re-imports and parallel imports are estimated to be rather small, amounting to ECU 150 million in the EC in 1985 (CEC, 1988b). For Germany a market share of 1 per cent has been quoted (SVR, 1987) which – according to industry representatives – has remained fairly constant. Companies specialising in re-importing pharmaceuticals report that producers respond quickly to increased arbitrage by lowering prices in high-priced markets. The model in section 3 also indicates that a low volume of re-imports and parallel imports does not necessarily indicate low pressure on market segmentation.

In Germany, arbitrage is undertaken by approximately 5 to 6 large firms and a larger number of small firms. Since these firms are required to be registered as pharmaceutical producers and since their re-imported or parallel imported products have to go through the national registration, arbitrage activities cannot be performed on a hit-and-run basis. It is impossible to assess exactly the cost structure of arbitrage firms, but there seem to be some setup costs, with marginal costs being relatively flat until the producers of the arbitrage products actively try to prevent arbitrage. Marginal costs may then become very steep.

The European Court ruled in 1976 that re-imports and parallel imports did not need a separate admission procedure – which is time consuming and expensive – if the products were identical. If there are therapeutically relevant differences between the products, however, then a new admission is necessary. This statement is at the heart of many court rulings concerning re-imports and parallel imports. National regulations differ substantially. In the Netherlands, a simplified registration procedure can be used by arbitrageurs if the pharmaceutical has the same chemical compounds and the same dosage. This procedure is frequently used (Hart and Reich, 1990, p. 250). Germany does not have a special admission procedure for re-imported pharmaceuticals; it requires, however, that the re-importing firm be registered as a pharmaceutical producer with all the responsibilities for safety of the drugs which it sells. A court ruling in 1989 reinforced the barriers for arbitrage since it required that in order to be identical products, re-imported pharmaceuticals needed to have identical names to those sold in Germany. The federal court (Bundesverwaltungsgericht) decided that the products 'Methorexat' sold in Germany and 'Methorexate' sold in Italy, which except for the last letter are otherwise identical, cannot be treated as identical products. Arbitrage is therefore made very costly since the re-imported product must go through the complete admission process.

Taken together, these regulations in countries with high prices for pharmaceuticals mean that it is fair to conclude that arbitrage inside the EC is still considerably restricted. It is costly since the imported products often have to be repackaged, or since wholesalers in the exporting countries do not deliver products to exporters, or since companies have reacted to court rulings by exploiting the possibilities of product differentiation in order to keep markets segmented as much as possible. National admission processes which undoubtedly are necessary for health and safety reasons therefore provide the basis for market segmentation. The question is then whether the measures taken by the EC will attack this situation and will move pharmaceutical markets toward a unified internal market without segmentation.

Market segmentation is also a necessary condition for the sustainability of price control measures which are taken by the majority of countries. The measured price differences (see Table 6.1) therefore represent a mixture of price discrimination imposed by profit-maximising firms and price controls imposed by national health institutions. Elimination of national price controls will therefore not necessarily lead to uniform prices within the EC. It is even an open question whether price differences will be larger with than without price controls. Whether European directives towards easier arbitrage opportunities under unchanged price control regimes will be sustainable is also unknown. The analysis below may shed some light on these issues.

2.3   Initiatives towards an internal market

The Commission of the EC has in the past introduced a number of measures to harmonise pharmaceutical markets. Their intended aim is to secure a safe supply of pharmaceuticals without limiting the development of the European pharmaceutical industry and the free movement of goods within Europe. Whereas in the past a producer could register a drug only with the national authority of the country in which the product was sold, a multi-country registration procedure has now been introduced.

The multi-country procedure gave pharmaceutical companies the option of obtaining registration of a pharmaceutical product for the entire EC by supplying first 5 and, since 1983, only 2 national registrations to the European Commission for Proprietary Medicinal Products (CPMP), which then evaluates the documents supplied by the company and gives a positive or negative recommendation to the member countries for accepting the national registrations in their countries without further delay. This procedure has not been used very much; the pharmaceutical industry accused it of being too time-consuming. In 1987 the CPMP was given more power through the rule requiring that national registration processes for high-technology drugs such as drugs produced with biotechnology be also processed by the CPMP, i.e. a European-wide registration is automatically prepared.

Despite these efforts to harmonise registration procedures, the final decision still remains with the national authorities. This also means that pharmaceutical firms still have the option of obtaining only national admissions for their products. They can thus choose the degree of product differentiation and market segmentation through 'spurious' product differentiation such as slight changes in the name of a drug, different packaging, different dosage or different patient information.

New initiatives towards a harmonised registration within the EC work in three directions (Hart and Reich, 1990): first, the establishment of the principle of mutual recognition of registration; second an expansion of the competence of the CPMP, yet without giving it registration authority, and finally the creation of a pan-European admission agency, the 'European Medicines Agency'. The last proposal of the Commission of 1990 on a 'Future System for the Free Movement of Medicinal Products within the European Community' envisages an obligatory pan-European registration for biotechnically produced drugs and an optional one for high-technology and new drugs. A decentralised procedure with mutual recognition of admissions is planned for drugs not in the two groups just mentioned but with a European dimension; national authorities are therefore responsible only for drugs with a local market.

The so-called 'Transparency Directive' addresses the question of price controls. The Commission does not challenge price controls in general but aims at making price control measures more transparent for those involved in the process by setting time limits on procedures or giving companies more rights to challenge price controls. Under these rules price controls can still be imposed; they may, however, be accompanied by higher political costs if the decision processes become transparent and the alleged discrimination of foreign firms can be documented. If the initiatives and plans by the Commission of the EC towards an internal market for pharmaceuticals are accepted and implemented a first step towards a unified market will be made. Through the pan-European registration of biotechnology products market segmentation will be ruled out. For other products companies may still have the option of segmenting markets through national registration. Whether the European court will challenge some of the national rules concerning arbitrage through re-imports and parallel imports is hard to predict, but some harmonisation between, for example, German and Dutch rules will probably come about, resulting in lower costs of arbitrage. Price controls, on the other hand, seem likely to prevail.

The question is then what the impact of such regulatory measures will be on pharmaceutical markets in Europe. What will happen to price discrimination by firms? Will prices rise or fall? Will price controls persist as arbitrage becomes easier? Another issue arising from a unified market with possibly uniform prices is the welfare issue. Consumer surplus will fall in countries whose prices increase, but even on a Community level it is not clear whether a move from the current system which is inefficient to a unified market which is also inefficient will raise or lower welfare. In order to clarify these questions and to answer some of them, I now develop a simple model of a price discriminating firm faced with price controls in one market but not in the other.

3   A Model of price discrimination, price controls, and arbitrage

3.1   Market segmentation

Suppose a firm produces an ethical drug which is protected by patents and serves a specific therapeutic group. There may be some substitutes in that market segment, but essentially the firm will have a monopoly – especially if it supplies the most advanced pharmaceutical for curing this specific illness. The firm is assumed to produce just 1 pharmaceutical and to sell in 2 markets, 1 and 2. It has a cost function of the form

$$c(x) = F + c \cdot x \tag{1}$$

where F is fixed cost (R&D, etc.)
$\quad c$ is marginal cost, and
$\quad x$ is the volume of production;

hence there are constant marginal costs and increasing returns to scale.

The firm's profit if it can price discriminate between markets will then be given by

$$\pi(p_1, p_2) = x_1(p_1)p_1 + x_2(p_2)p_2 - c(x_1(p_1) + x_2(p_2)) \tag{2}$$

where $x_1(p_1)$ and $x_2(p_2)$ are the demand functions in market 1 and 2. Profit maximisation yields the following first order conditions

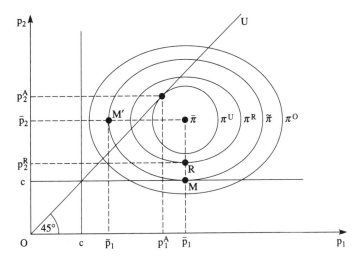

Figure 6.1   Third degree price discrimination with price controls

$$\frac{p_2}{p_1} = \frac{1 + \dfrac{1}{\epsilon_1}}{1 + \dfrac{1}{\epsilon_2}} \tag{3}$$

where ϵ_1 and ϵ_2 (≤ -1) are the respective demand elasticities in the 2 markets. Equation (3) shows that prices in the market with lower demand elasticities (in absolute terms) will be higher. For the following it is assumed without a loss of generality that $\epsilon_2 > \epsilon_1$, hence $p_1 > p_2$.

Under a regime without market segmentation, the firm will set a uniform price p_0 such that its marginal revenue in both markets together will equal its marginal cost, i.e.

$$p_U\left(1 + \frac{1}{\epsilon_U}\right) = c \tag{4}$$

where ϵ_U is the price elasticity in the combined market.

Suppose now that prices are controlled by a regulatory agency in country 2 which fixes p_2 at p_2^R. Since the pharmaceutical producer faces constant marginal costs and the demand functions are independent, the price in market 1 will remain at p_1 whereas $p_2 = p_2^R$. This result is illustrated in Figure 6.1. $\bar{\pi}$ represents the profit-maximising price combination $(\bar{p}_1, \bar{p}_2)$ under third degree price discrimination. The isoprofit line labelled π^R goes through the price pair $(\bar{p}_1, p_2^R)$ when prices are controlled in market 2. The tangency point of the isoprofit line π^U with the 45° line, represents the equilibrium without market segmentation. π^0 denotes price combinations where profits of the firm are zero if both markets are served. Under the demand constellation of the model, however, prices in market 2 can be lowered only to c through controls. Beyond that, the firm will cease to supply that market but will still make profits in market 1. Thus equilibrium could not lie on π^0 but below c.

3.2   Arbitrage

Suppose now that markets are only imperfectly segmented. Goods can be arbitraged between markets at some costs. There are arbitrageurs who supply parallel imports or re-imports by buying in the low-price market and selling in the high-price market. In order to perform this activity they have additional costs of repackaging, of distribution, of sourcing, etc. which may parametrically depend on the institutional structure of the markets. The profit function of an arbitrageur would be

$$\pi^A(x_A, a) = (p_1 - p_2) x_A - c(x_A, a) \tag{5}$$

where x_A denotes the quantity which is bought, resp. sold, in the two markets and $c_A(\cdot)$ is the cost function of arbitrage parameterised with a. It is assumed that the cost function is convex, i.e. $c' = \partial c/\partial x_A > 0$, $c'' > 0$ and $\partial c/\partial a > 0$.

Under the assumption that the arbitrageurs do not believe that they can influence prices the profit-maximising arbitrage x_A will be given by

$$p_1 - p_2 = c'(x_A, a) \tag{6}$$

The supply function of the arbitrageur in market 1 will then be given as the inverse of (6),

$$x_A = x_A(p_1 - p_2, a) \tag{7}$$

with $x'_{A1} > 0$, $x'_{A2} < 0$, $x'_A > 0$, where x'_{Ai} denotes the partial differential of the supply function with respect to p_i, and $x'_A = \partial x_A/\partial(p_1 - p_2)$. The signs follow from the strict convexity of the cost function.

The pharmaceutical firm will now recognise the behaviour of arbitrageurs which itself depends on the extent of the firm's own price discrimination among the two markets. Profits of the pharmaceutical firm then become

$$\begin{aligned}
\pi(p_1, p_2, a) = {} & p_1[x_1(p_1) - x_A(p_1 - p_2, a)] \\
& + p_2[x_2(p_2) + x_A(p_1 - p_2, a)] \\
& - c[x_1(p_1) + x_2(p_2)] - F
\end{aligned} \tag{8}$$

Maximisation with respect to p_1 and p_2 then yields first order conditions

$$0 = p_1 \left[1 - \frac{1}{\epsilon_1} \left[1 - \frac{x_A}{x_1} (1 + \epsilon_A) \right] \right] - c \tag{9}$$

$$0 = p_2 \left[1 - \frac{1}{\epsilon_2} \left[1 + \frac{x_A}{x_2} (1 + \epsilon_A) \right] \right] - c \tag{10}$$

ϵ_1 and ϵ_2 are defined as the market demand elasticities net of arbitrage. ϵ_A denotes the reaction elasticity of arbitrage with respect to the price dispersion, i.e.

$$\epsilon_A(a) = \frac{\partial x_A(p_1 - p_2, a) \cdot (p_1 - p_2)}{\partial(p_1 - p_2) \cdot x_A(p_1 - p_2, a)} > 0 \tag{11}$$

The familiar condition on third degree price discrimination given in (3) is then transformed into

$$\frac{p_1}{p_2} = \frac{1 + \dfrac{1}{\epsilon_2} \left[1 + \dfrac{x_A}{x_2} (1 + \epsilon_A(a)) \right]}{1 + \dfrac{1}{\epsilon_1} \left[1 - \dfrac{x_A}{x_1} (1 + \epsilon_A(a)) \right]} \tag{12}$$

A comparison of the first order conditions under price discrimination without arbitrage (equation (3)) and with arbitrage (equation (11)) shows that arbitrage reduces the wedge between the two prices. The degree of reduction then is determined by the two brackets on the right-hand side of equation (12).

The degree of price discrimination by the pharmaceutical firm depends on the extent to which arbitrage is made costly by the regulations for the marketing of drugs in a country and by the barriers to re-imports or parallel imports. It is thus implicitly assumed that the producer has exhausted his ability to impose costs on the arbitrageurs. This effect is captured by the parameter a. Suppose a high a represents strict regulations such that the costs of arbitrage are high. Then the extent of arbitrage will fall as a increases, $\partial x_A / \partial a < 0$ and consequently $\partial \epsilon_A / \partial a < 0$. Hence, as a falls, i.e. the costs of arbitrage fall, the bracket in the numerator of equation (12) increases and it falls in the denominator. In other words, the perceived price elasticity of the pharmaceutical firm in market 2 falls and it rises in market 1. Since $\epsilon_2 > \epsilon_1$, the perceived elasticities will eventually equalise as a falls and price discrimination will cease to exist. Conversely, as a increases the perceived elasticities will deviate and price discrimination will increase.

In Figure 6.2 the line $\pi^U \bar{\pi}$ indicates the optimal price discrimination under alternative costs of arbitrage. The comparative static results for alternative costs of arbitrage are

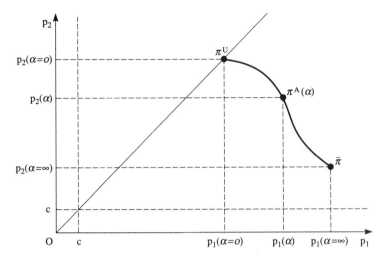

Figure 6.2   Third degree price discrimination with arbitrage

$$\frac{dp_1}{da} \quad \begin{cases} \geq 0 & \text{if } 2x_2' + (p_2 - c)x_2'' \leq 0 \\[2mm] < 0 & \text{if } 2x_2' + (p_2 - c)x_2'' > 0 \end{cases} \tag{13}$$

and

$$\frac{dp_2}{da} \quad \begin{cases} \leq 0 & \text{if } 2x_1' + (p_1 - c)x_1'' \leq 0 \\[2mm] > 0 & \text{if } 2x_1' + (p_1 - c)x_1'' > 0 \end{cases} \tag{14}$$

The path of profit-maximising allocations under different arbitrage opportunities has a negative slope as in Figure 6.2 if both demand functions are not too convex. The curve $\pi^U \bar{\pi}$ could have a positive slope, i.e. with relaxed arbitrage opportunities prices in both markets fall, if the demand in market 1 is very inelastic. It is also apparent that the sign of the slope of the path $\pi^U \bar{\pi}$ is independent of the cost structure of arbitrage.

3.3   Price controls with arbitrage

The introduction of price controls in a model with perfectly segmented markets leads to lower prices in the market in which the controls are imposed but prices in the unconstrained market are not affected. This follows immediately from the first order conditions of profit-maximi-

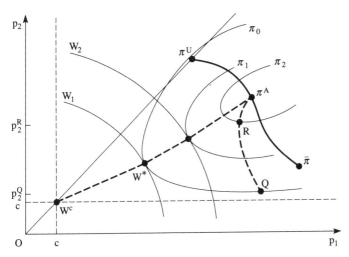

Figure 6.3   Price discrimination with arbitrage and price controls

sation and is illustrated in Figure 6.1. Under arbitrage this independence disappears since price controls increase the price dispersion between the two markets such that arbitrage will increase in order to exploit the new profit opportunities. Producers will consequently adjust prices in the market without price controls such that their profits are maximised given the behaviour of the arbitrageurs.

If prices in market 2 are changed by the authorities of that country, the pharmaceutical producer will adjust p_1 such that

$$\frac{dp_1}{dp_2^R} = - \frac{(p_1 - p_2)x_A'' + 2x_A'}{2x_1' + (p_1 - c)x_1'' - 2x_A' - (p_1 - p_2)x_A''} \qquad (15)$$

The denominator is identical to the first diagonal term of the second order condition and is negative. The sign of the numerator potentially depends on the sign of x_A'' which is ambivalent and which represents the shape of the marginal cost curve of arbitrage.

If the arbitrage supply function, i.e. the marginal cost curve, is concave, then the sign of equation (15) is uniquely positive, hence a reduction of the price in market 2 through administered price ceilings will be accompanied by a reduction in the price in the uncontrolled market. If however $x_A' < 0$ and $(p_1 - p_2)x_A'' < -2x_A'$ then prices may be raised in market 1 as a response to lower prices in market 2. This could happen if the marginal cost curves of the arbitrageurs was sufficiently convex.

In Figure 6.3 an example is given where price controls at p_2^R initially induce a reduction of the price p_1 in market 1 such that R is the optimal allocation. If the price in market 2 is further reduced to p_2^Q, then the optimal decision by the producer will be to raise the price of good 1 in order to compensate for the losses in market 2. The reason for such a result comes from the fact that as p_2 falls arbitrage will increase *ceteris paribus* resulting in a lower p_1. If, however, the marginal cost curves of the arbitrageurs are sufficiently steep then it becomes profitable for the producer to reduce the supply in market 1 since this reduction is not matched by increased arbitrage.

The introduction of arbitrage and price controls could therefore lead to either a rise or a fall in prices in the uncontrolled market. Which occurs is essentially an empirical issue which is determined by the shape of the marginal cost curve of arbitrage. Since arbitrage involves buying large amounts of the commodity in the low-price market, it will not go unnoticed by the producer if the market share of re-imported goods or parallel imports increases. Companies specialising in the re-import of pharmaceuticals report increasing difficulties in buying large quantities from one wholesaler and often have to rely on a large number of smaller suppliers. Such evidence suggests that a convex marginal cost curve for arbitrage is more likely than a concave one. This, in turn, would indicate that increasing arbitrage going hand in hand with stricter price controls could be accompanied by rising prices in market 1.

3.4   Oligopolistic markets

Pharmaceutical companies usually supply many different products in several market segments, i.e. different therapeutic groups. Sometimes there is only one producer supplying a dominating drug, in other cases there are very few; very rarely, however, is there a larger number of suppliers. The question is therefore whether the result which has been derived for a monopoly in a market segment also holds for an oligopolistic market structure. One can show that the same results can also be derived in a Cournot–Nash framework.

Suppose there are two producers, K and L, which both sell in the two markets, 1 and 2, having the same characteristics as before. The supply of the two oligopolists is (x_{K1}, x_{K2}) and (x_{L1}, x_{L2}). Under Cournot behaviour each producer will choose those quantities which maximise his profits given the output of the other producer and given the arbitrage which takes place between the two markets. The profit of producer K is

$$p_1(x_{K1} + x_{L1} + x_A)x_{K1} + p_2(x_{K2} + x_{L2} - x_A)x_{K2} - c(x_{K1} + x_{K2}) \quad (16)$$

and correspondingly for producer L. Arbitrage is determined corresponding to (6) by

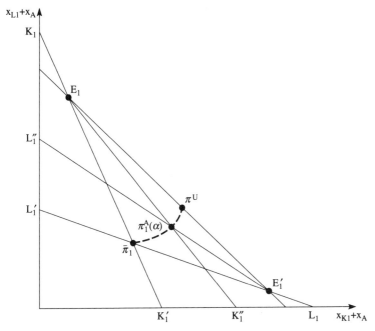

Figure 6.4 Reaction functions under different arbitrage opportunities in market 1

$$p_1(x_{K1} + x_{L1} + x_A) - p_2(x_{K2} + x_{L2} - x_A) = c'(x_A, a) \qquad (17)$$

Under Cournot behaviour each producer maximises profits subject to the constraint of the arbitrage between the two markets. The resulting reaction functions are illustrated in Figures 6.4 and 6.5. Figure 6.4 represents the market with the high prices. Without arbitrage the Nash equilibrium is $\bar{\pi}_1$ where the reaction functions $K_1 K'_1$ and $L'_1 L_1$ intersect. In the presence of arbitrage, the reaction functions cannot uniquely relate, say, x_{L1} to x_{K1}, but instead one must work in terms of the total market supply, i.e. $x_{K1} + x_A$ in market 1 and $x_{K2} - x_A$ in market 2. For a specific arbitrage opportunity parameterised by a, the resulting equilibrium market supplies are represented by $\pi_1^A(a)$ in Figure 6.4 and the corresponding supply in market 2 is $\pi_2^A(a)$ in Figure 6.5.

The comparative static results are the same as in the monopoly. If arbitrage becomes more costly, i.e. $da > 0$, then

$$\frac{dx_A}{da} = \frac{-\pi_{11}\lambda p_2'^2}{\Delta} - \cdot - \frac{\partial c''(x_A, a)}{\partial a} < 0 \qquad (18)$$

where π_{11} is the second derivative of the constraint maximisation (16) and

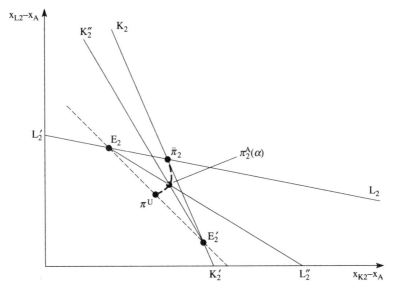

Figure 6.5   Reaction functions under different arbitrage opportunities in market 2

(17), Δ is the determinant, and λ is the Lagrangian multiplier. For each producer the response of the sum of arbitrage supply and his own supply is also negative, i.e.

$$\frac{dx_A}{da} + \frac{dx_{K1}}{da} = \frac{p_1'}{\Delta}\left[\frac{\partial c''(x_A, a)}{\partial a}\lambda p_2'^2 + \pi_{2A}^2 p_1'\frac{\partial c'(x_A, a)}{\partial a}\right] < 0 \qquad (19)$$

where p_1' is the first derivative of the demand function in market 1.

From equation (19) one can immediately see that with increased costs of arbitrage the price in market 1 rises. Whether the price in market 2 rises or falls depends on how the demand of the arbitrageurs changes relative to the change in the supply of the producers. As in the monopoly case, this is not uniquely determined. Hence, the price discrimination equilibria as illustrated in Figure 6.2 carry over to the oligopoly.

In the case of price controls the profit maximisation of each firm as given by equation (16) and the constraint (17) has the additional constraint that the price in market 2 must remain below p_2^R:

$$p_2(x_{K2} + x_{L2} - x_A) \le p_2^R \qquad (20)$$

The comparative static results of this maximisation also reveal that as the price controls are loosened, i.e. $dp_2^R > 0$, the price difference will be reduced. Whether the price in market 1 falls or rises again depends on the slopes of the demand functions in the two markets.

4   Welfare effects

The welfare effect of third degree price discrimination has been investigated by Schmalensee (1981) and Varian (1985). Varian derives bounds on the welfare change of different degrees of price discrimination and on the difference in welfare between uniform pricing and profit-maximising price discrimination. The basic necessary condition for an increase in welfare when a firm is moving from uniform pricing to price discrimination is that the sum of outputs in both markets must increase. This result depends on profits of the firm as well as on consumer surplus. In analysing the welfare effects of price controls at some given regulation of arbitrage the results of Schmalensee and Varian can be used. One has only to employ the additional assumption that arbitrage takes place in a perfectly competitive environment with zero profits. Then the welfare of the overall region – assuming quasi-linear utility – is given by

$$W(p_1, p_2, a) = \int_{p_1}^{\infty} x_1(v)\, dv + \int_{p_2}^{\infty} x_2(v)\, dv + \pi(p_1, p_2, a) \tag{21}$$

where $\pi(p_1, p_2, a)$ is defined by (8).

Figure 6.3 illustrates the results. W^C represents the welfare maximum although at negative profits. W_* is the welfare optimum under a zero profit restriction illustrated by the isoprofit contour π_0. The dotted line $W_* \pi^A$ contains the welfare optima under alternative profit constraints and given arbitrage opportunities a. These optima all involve some degree of price discrimination. They could, however, be achieved only through price controls in both markets. The line $\pi^A RQ$ corresponds to equilibria under alternative price control measures in market 2. One can show that the isowelfare contours W_1 and W_2 have negative slope for prices above marginal costs and therefore the tangency points with the isoprofit contours have a negative slope as well. The points along $\pi^A RQ$, however, are defined by zero slopes of the isoprofit contours; consequently the price control equilibria $\pi^A RQ$ always involve a loss of profits relative to the profit constrained welfare maxima $W_* \pi^A$. It is also apparent that – as is likely for the pharmaceutical market – with increasing price controls overall welfare will first increase as long as prices in both markets fall, i.e. consumer surplus rises faster than profits fall. But after equation (15) has turned negative, i.e. after the producer reacts to price controls with higher prices in market 1 because of high costs of arbitrage, then welfare can fall as price controls become tighter. From the arguments about the likely slope of the line $\pi^A RQ$ above, one can conclude that 'small' price controls increase welfare but 'large' price controls probably lower welfare.

The welfare analysis of changes in the regulatory framework which determine the costs of arbitrage as represented by the parameter a are

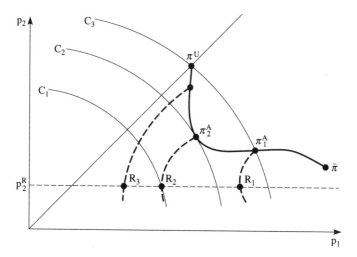

Figure 6.6   Changes in arbitrage under price controls

more difficult to analyse. Changes in a without price controls move profits along the line $\pi^U\bar{\pi}$. Such movements are accompanied by new isoprofit contours and by new isowelfare contours which contain the profits of the producing firm. It is therefore impossible to compare the welfare of two equilibria determined by alternative a, i.e. alternative regulatory regimes. One can, however, illustrate the impact of a on consumer surplus alone.

In a situation without price controls anything can happen to consumer surplus for both countries together when a is varied. The shape of the line $\pi^U\bar{\pi}$ determines the welfare effect. In Figure 6.6 easier arbitrage first goes hand in hand with an increase in consumer surplus, but beyond π_2^A consumer surplus begins to fall. Uniform prices then may or may not yield higher consumer surplus than perfect price discrimination for which the bounds on welfare are given by Varian (1985).

The sign of consumer surplus changes can be predicted when price controls are imposed. If the price in market 2 is restricted to p_2^R (see Figure 6.6) and this control is not lifted as arbitrage becomes liberalised, then price and welfare in market 2 is fixed while consumers in market 2 benefit from increased arbitrage. Total differentiation of the first order condition for profit maximisation with respect to p_1 yields

$$\frac{dp_1}{da} = \left[\frac{\partial F_1(p_1, p_2^R, a)}{\partial p_1}\right]^{-1} \left[\frac{\partial x_A}{\partial a} + (p_1 - p_2)\frac{\partial^2 x_A}{\partial(p_1 - p_2)\partial a}\right] > 0 \quad (22)$$

with

$$F_1(p_1, p_2^R, a) = x_1(p_1) + (p_1 - c)\frac{\partial x_1}{\partial p_1} - x_A - (p_1 - p_2^R)\frac{\partial x_A}{\partial (p_1 - p_2^R)} = 0$$

being the first order condition $\partial \pi / \partial p_1$.

Figure 6.6 illustrates this case. Without price controls easier arbitrage would move the price discriminating prices from π_1^A to π_2^A and finally to π^U. Whereas these movements are accompanied first by a rise in consumer surplus and later by a fall, the equilibria under prices controlled at p_2^R which are represented by the intersection of the p_2^R line with the dotted lines yield increasing consumer surplus throughout. It should be mentioned, however, that the profits of the pharmaceutical firm fall and eventually it will make negative profits. Before such a situation arises the firm may also stop supplying market 2 and set the price in market 1 as in the unconstrained case. This situation occurred recently when a German pharmaceutical company stopped supplying the Greek market because the price controls and the induced arbitrage opportunities were unacceptable for that firm.

5   The likely impact of harmonisation

The Commission of the EC has addressed the two pre-eminent issues, namely market segmentation and price controls in directives on market transparency and on the authorisation of medicinal products. The directives in both issues will certainly not create an internal market for pharmaceuticals; they will rather induce some slight moves towards a unified European market. Two immediate questions then arise: what will happen to prices in the national markets, and what will be the likely welfare effects of moves towards unification?

The transparency directive requires national authorities to lay open their procedures and guidelines in controlling and authorising prices of pharmaceuticals. Although not a ban on price controls, it is hoped that the new regulations will pressure national authorities to end discriminatory practices and will therefore lead to less restrictive price-setting for products from foreign countries. According to market insiders, companies already get more freedom to price their newly introduced products according to their own interests. Arbitrageurs also report that new products now exhibit lower price differences than in the past.

The model presented here does not uniquely predict the outcome of an easing of price controls. One can, however, expect that in cases where price differences are large and the arbitrage cost function is strongly convex, allowing prices to rise in the controlled market will be accompanied by falling prices in the unrestricted market as is commonly expected. If, on the other hand, arbitrage can be expanded relatively easily then it is more likely that the optimal response of pharmaceutical companies to rising controlled prices will be to raise prices in the unrestricted market. The outcome of the transparency directive will then be falling consumption accompanied by rising prices in both markets.

The welfare impact of the transparency directive depends on price responses as well. The welfare of the EC overall may slightly increase through movements from, for example, Q to R in Figure 6.3 if the path $\pi^A RQ$ has a sufficiently negative slope between R and Q. It is more likely, however, that welfare will decline because the losses of consumer surplus in the price controlled market and possibly the unrestricted market will not be outweighed by increasing profits of the pharmaceutical companies.

The existing procedures for the authorisation of pharmaceuticals and the proposed procedures leave open alternative ways for pharmaceutical companies to introduce new products. With the exception of biotechnology products they can still choose national authorisation thus allowing them to segment markets by obtaining different national admissions for the same chemical entity, e.g. under different names. One can therefore predict that as long as price discrimination is sufficiently profitable – e.g. because of price controls or because of different demand elasticities – community procedures such as multi-state registration will not be used extensively. Still, arbitrage will be alleviated somewhat in the future.

It has been shown that institutional changes which facilitate arbitrage represent movements along the path between perfect price discrimination and uniform pricing such as $\pi^U \bar{\pi}$ in Figure 6.6. Since the present situation also entails price controls the starting point will be an allocation like R_1 (Figure 6.6). If price controls remain in place the new admission procedures will move prices from R_1 to R_2, i.e. only prices in unrestricted markets fall. In that case profits will fall and consumer surplus will increase. If, on the other hand, price controls are partially lifted as well this will be represented by a move from R_1 towards some point along the line $R_2 \pi_2^A$. The impact on consumer surplus will be ambivalent and will among other things depend on the shape of the line $\pi^U \bar{\pi}$.

If the goal is to reach uniform pricing in European markets it is clear that facilitating arbitrage is the most powerful policy, since it moves pharmaceutical firms at unchanged price controls quickly towards their zero profit contour. This puts pressure on national authorities to lift price controls or to risk not having their market supplied by the company in question. Lifting price controls alone cannot eliminate market segmentation since, given the existing income differences within the EC and different demand structures, it will still be profitable to exploit the different price elasticities.

A welfare analysis in segmented markets raises the general question as to with which situation one wants to compare the current position. Since the welfare maximum with marginal cost pricing is not achievable one could use a constrained welfare maximum, e.g. with a zero profit constraint as shown by $W*$ in Figure 6.3. Yet this second-best optimum also leads to some degree of price discrimination, hence the equilibrium with uniform prices π^U is not even second best. The problem is then that the publicly announced goal of creating an internal market by eliminating market segmentation does not lead to a second-best situation as described by points along $W*\pi^A$ in Figure 6.3, not to speak of the first-best W^C which includes subsidies to firms. It is therefore not surprising that the policy initiatives of the European Commission discussed here have lead to welfare losses, or at best to ambivalent results.

REFERENCES

Bundesverband der Pharmazeutischen Industrie (BPI) (1990) 'Pharma Daten 1989', Frankfurt: BPI.
Commission of the European Communities (CEC) (1988a) 'The economics of 1992', *European Economy*, 35 (March) Brussels: European Commission.
    (1988b) 'The Cost of Non-Europe in the Pharmaceutical Industry', *Research on the Cost of Non-Europe, Basic Findings*, vol. 15, Brussels: European Commission.
Cooper, M.H. (1974) *European Pharmaceutical Prices*, London: Croom Helm.
Dunes, M.N. (1983) *Drugs and Money*, Copenhagen: WHO.
Eurim-Pharm Arzneimittel GmbH (1985) 'Arzneimittel-Parallel- und Reimport', Piding: Eurim-Pharm Arzneimittel GMBH.
EEC (1986) *Proposed Council Directive Relating to the Transparency of . . . Pricing of Medicinal Products . . .*, European Commission, Com (86) 765 Final, Table 1.
Hart, D. und N. Reich (1990) 'Integration und Recht des Arzneimittelmarktes und in der EG', **Bd 13**, Baden-Baden: Nomos Verlagsgesellschaft.
Health Economics (1982) Private communication.
Prognos (1981) Quoted in R. Chew, G. Telling-Smith and N. Wells (1985) *Pharmaceuticals in Seven Nations*, London: Office of Health Economics.
Sachverständigenrat für die Konzertierte Aktion im Gesundheitswesen (1987) 'Jahresgutachten 1987: Medizinische und ökonomische Orientierung', Baden-Baden: Nomos Verlagsgesellschaft.
Schmalensee, R. (1981) 'Output and welfare implications of monopolistic third-degree price discrimination', *American Economic Review*, 71.
Thier, U. (1990) 'Das Recht des EG-Arzneimittelmarktes und des freien Warenverkehrs', Europäische Hochschulschriften, **Reihe II, Bd. 951**, Frankfurt/M: Lang Verlag.
Varian, H.R. (1985) 'Price Discrimination and Social Welfare' *American Economic Review*, 75.

Discussion

DAMIEN NEVEN

The starting point of Gernot Klepper's Chapter 6 is the observations that price controls are frequent in the pharmaceutical industry and that parallel imports are seriously hindered by national registration procedures. As a result, markets are segmented and prices vary a great deal across countries. In addition it is asserted that price controls are used at the expense of foreign firms. The EC Commission is currently contemplating a directive which would simplify registration procedures and accordingly facilitate parallel imports. At the same time, the EC Commission is trying to ensure transparent price controls, short of banning them altogether.

Gernot Klepper wonders what will be the impact of these directives, in so far as they will indeed facilitate arbitrage. He uses a model where firms can discriminate across two countries; he then explicitly allows for price controls and arbitrage. He concludes that in the presence of arbitrage, the effect of price controls in one country may be to reduce price in both or merely in the country where control is imposed, depending on the technology available to arbitrageurs. Overall welfare effects are also ambiguous, both regarding the imposition of price controls and the costs of undertaking arbitrage.

At the outset, it is worth emphasising that the analysis undertaken by the author is innovative, in particular regarding his explicit treatment of arbitrage. Previous analysis of market integration has focused on the two alternative scenarios of a reduction in trade costs and the imposition of uniform prices. The latter scenario is unlikely to materialise given that the only constraint to price discrimination is arbitrage and uniform prices will prevail only when transaction costs are negligible. Hence, the explicit treatment of arbitrage, and the costs associated with it, is an important addition to our analysis of market integration and one that should prove particularly useful in providing reasonable upper bounds to our estimates of what the internal market can bring about in terms of welfare and price convergence.

The analysis of arbitrage that Klepper proposes is thus quite innovative. It seems, however, that the actual modelling of arbitrage could possibly be improved upon. Indeed, he considers that arbitrage activity can be represented by assuming that there is some 'representative firm' who faces increasing marginal costs of undertaking arbitrage. It is also assumed that this representative firm does not take into account that shifting quantities will raise price in the origin country and lower it in the destination country, whereas pharmaceuticals' producers are truly aware of their residual demand. Hence, it is assumed that pharmaceutical firms anticipate the effect that the representative arbitrageur has on prices whereas the representative arbitrageur does not himself take it into account. This assumption could be warranted if the supply function of this representative arbitrageur could be thought of as the supply function of a competitive industry. However, given that, as argued by Klepper, there are significant setup costs in undertaking arbitrage, it is unlikely that the arbitrage industry will approach perfect competition. In practice, most of the arbitrage also seems to be undertaken by a few large firms. On the whole, it might thus be worthwhile trying to model the arbitrage industry more carefully, assuming that firms have some market power, and recognise it. This exercise might give us more confidence in the results. Indeed, much of the analysis presented in this chapter seems to rest on the property of the arbitrageurs' supply function.

Throughout the chapter, Klepper takes a rather negative view of price controls, both in the absolute and in so far as they can be used to discriminate against foreign firms. Such an attitude might indeed be appropriate, but it might still be useful to consider more generally the rationale for price control before a definite judgement is reached.

As rightly emphasised by Klepper, the pharmaceutical industry is characterised by the presence of large investment in research and developments and a near-monopoly for drugs resulting from successful projects, as long as these drugs are protected by patents. From a public policy perspective, rents to innovative drugs will be granted so as to balance the need to provide incentives for research *ex ante* and the costs of insufficient dissemination *ex post*. The stream of rents awarded to drugs can be calibrated by the length of patents but also by restriction on the exercise of monopoly power during the period of protection; for a given level of rents (in present value), there is therefore a trade-off between price controls and the length of the patent. For instance, Germany has no price control but enforces short effective protection by encouraging vigorous competition from generics when patents have expired. At the opposite pole, competition from generics is weak in France, where strict price controls are enforced. The choice of instruments will affect the profile of the stream of rents over time and may thus depend on the discount rate that each country will deem appropriate. That is to say that price controls also have a *bona fide* purpose; one cannot simply rule them out as undesirable and a welfare analysis involving changes in price controls or arbitrage costs might usefully consider the overal horizon corresponding to the effective life of drugs and the market conditions after patents have expired.

To the extent that price controls are important in calibrating the flow of rents accruing to innovations, it seems that harmonisation, or at least some coordination, of price controls across countries might actually be appropriate. Indeed, national regulators acting independently might be tempted to free-ride on the rents that are awarded in foreign markets. Overall, uncoordinated actions will result in rents that are inadequate to encourage the appropriate amount of research.

Finally, the assertion that price controls are frequently used to discriminate against foreign producers might usefully be documented. Indeed, the motivation behind discriminatory controls is not entirely clear cut; national governments often have little to gain from such policies in terms of the protection of domestic firms because, as argued above, innovative drugs will often face little competition and *a fortiori* little domestic competition. Increasing consumer surplus does not seem to be a motivation either, given that firms will easily respond to discriminatory measures by relocating, which will give them the rights to higher prices. Providing incentives to relocation might still be a motivation to the extent that it provides some benefits which compensate for the high prices that it induces. Yet, as argued by Klepper, the actual production of pharmaceuticals is unlikely to generate much externality in terms of transfer of knowledge. Being highly capital-intensive, it is unlikely to help much in the labour market (assuming that the private cost of labour exceeds its social cost) but it is likely to generate some negative externalities to the environment. Overall, it is thus hard to find a valid motivation behind discriminatory price controls.

Part Four
Trade and industrial policy

7   Integration, trade policy and European footwear trade

L. ALAN WINTERS

1   Introduction

This chapter quantifies the impact on EC footwear trade of 5 events:
Spanish and Portuguese accession to the EC, the quantitative import
restrictions imposed on Korea and Taiwan in 1988, the removal of
barriers to intra-EC footwear trade under the '1992'[1] programme, the
change in trade policy implied by that programme, and the possible
opening of EC markets to Eastern European footwear exports. It does so
by means of a computable model of footwear production and trade,
calibrated to 1987. The model is partial equilibrium in that it considers
only the footwear sector, but it recognises substitution between 3 types of
footwear and 9 suppliers in 4 EC markets. Future research may expand
these dimensions, but they are already quite sufficient to illustrate the
phenomena of interest and to pose significant computing problems.

Footwear is not a major sector in the EC economy – it accounts for
about one-quarter of 1 per cent of GDP (ECU 7.7 billion in 1985,
Commission of the European Communities, 1988) and 0.8 per cent and
1.2 per cent of industrial value added and employment respectively
(Commission of the European Communities, 1990b). It is relatively open
to international trade, but the bulk of trade occurs between member states
(intra-EC trade). Extra-EC imports account for only about 15 per cent of
total consumption in value terms and 33 per cent in volume; extra-EC
exports exceed imports by 80 per cent in value and fall short by 40 per cent
in volume terms. The most striking feature of the sector is its distribution
across member countries – see Appendix, Table 7A.1; 4 countries are
strong net exporters and have around 2 per cent or more of industrial
employment in the sector – Italy, Greece, Spain and Portugal – while the
remainder are significant net importers, with employment shares of 1 per
cent or less, except for France at 1.6 per cent. Italy alone accounts for over
half of both intra- and extra-EC footwear exports.

175

Its extreme geographical distribution makes the footwear sector an interesting case-study for EC trade policy, but more important are the facts that footwear is expected by the Commission to be strongly affected by '1992' (Commission for the European Communities, 1990b) and that it has recently come under severe competitive pressure.

Footwear is also an attractive sector methodologically, for it combines a high frequency of trade policy shocks with tractability of economic modelling. As a simple product with competitive supply conditions and a small share of total expenditure, footwear avoids many of the difficulties of modelling large oligopolistic industries. It is true that such difficulties provide analytical interest, but the competitive model still has a lot to teach us and considerable practical relevance to the analysis of industrial decline under severe competitive pressure from developing countries. Footwear has also been subject to several bouts of trade restriction, but of a transparent and analytically tractable kind – voluntary export restraints (VERs) and bilateral quotas. Moreover, in the discussions of the EC's post-'1992' trade policy footwear has, along with motor vehicles, become something of a test case. The policies evolved for it in the late 1980s after extensive debate may, regrettably, form a precedent for other declining sectors.

The trade policies examined below are:

- The reduction to zero of tariffs on footwear trade between the EC-10 and Spain (EC tariffs with Portugal were zero already under the EC–EFTA free trade arrangements for manufactures).
- The effects of the bilateral quotas and VERs imposed on trade between Korea and Taiwan on the one hand and France and Italy on the other in 1988.
- The replacement of the latter by EC-wide VERs on Korea and Taiwan in 1990.
- The abolition of Article 115 restrictions on imports from East European suppliers, effectively changing the EC from 12 isolated and segmented markets into a single, although still restricted, market for East European exports.
- The abolition of the tariffs, quotas and VERs on East European exports, as has been negotiated under the recent Europe Agreements with Czechoslovakia, Hungary and Poland.

2   The structure of the model

Computable models should be as small and as simple as is consistent with answering the questions posed. In fact, the set of policies noted above

Table 7.1. *Classification and acronyms*

Suppliers				
High Income	(HI)	France	(FR)	
		Italy	(IT)	
		EC-North	(ECN)[a]	
Low Income	(LO)	EC-South	(ECS)[b]	
		Korea	(KOR)	
		Taiwan	(TAI)	
		Other Developing	(OD)	
Other	(OT)	Eastern Europe	(ST)	
		Other Industrial (OI)		

Markets	
France	(FR)
Italy	(IT)
EC-North	(ECN)[a]
EC-South	(ECS)[b]

Types of footwear	NIMEXE (1987) Codes
Leather (LTH)	6402.21–.59 less .40
Plastic, Rubber, Other (PL)	6401.41–.99 less .65 (plastic)
	6401.11–.39 (rubber)
	6402.99 ⎫
	6403 ⎬ (other)
	6404.90 ⎭
	6405.10–98
Textile (TXT)	6402.61–.69
Excluded Category: Slippers (SL)	6401.65
	6402.40, .60
	6404.10

Notes:
[a] Germany, UK, Denmark, Ireland, Belgium, Luxembourg and the Netherlands.
[b] Greece, Portugal, Spain.

imposes quite high demands on the dimensionality of the model and the classifications of data. At the minimum it is necessary to:

• Separate Spain and Portugal from the rest of the EC,[2]
• distinguish France and Italy as markets,
• distinguish Korea and Taiwan from other developing country suppliers,
• distinguish Eastern Europe, and
• distinguish leather footwear (which is extensively restrained from

Eastern Europe) from plastic and textile footwear (which figure promi-
nently in Korean and Taiwanese exports).

In addition, it was convenient to have the market and supplier classifications identical where they intersected, because I include domestic sales
among supplies. Table 7.1 describes the classification used in this chapter.
In fact, it is more pertinent to the Korean and Taiwanese exercises than
the East European one, because the vast bulk of EC imports from Eastern
Europe are concentrated on only one of our EC markets, namely,
EC-North.

The model is based on 1987 data for several reasons. First, 1987 was a
year of relatively undistorted trade: Eastern Europe and other state-
trading countries were restricted, but there were no major restraints on
imports from Korea, Taiwan or other developing countries. Second, it
was possible to obtain production and price data for EC member states
for that year – from Commission of the European Communities (1989a) –
while to generate this information for other years from published sources
would be quite complex. Third, in 1988 the EC trade classification was
extensively revised, making it very difficult to match data with 1987 and
meaning that at the start of this project data for 1988 were not available in
full detail.

Although footwear is a comparatively simple sector to model, it still
provides a number of dilemmas. The most important is the degree of
product differentiation and how to represent it computationally. The
NIMEXE classification of 1987 contains 48 headings for footwear, which
is far too many to model explicitly; among those referring to complete
shoes or boots the unit values of total imports into the EC range from
ECU 1.2 per pair for plastic injection-moulded shoes to ECU 45.8 per
pair for men's special plastic shoes.

For the purposes of the data analysis, I have followed Commission of the
European Communities (1989a) and aggregated these headings into 6
groups, basically according to the principal material used for the outer
sole of the footwear. This is far from being the only useful aggregation –
for example, leather and synthetic leather (plastic) dress shoes are argu-
ably better substitutes than are leather dress shoes and leather athletics
shoes – but it is by a long way the most practical. To keep the model
dimensions manageable, however, the computable model aggregates
further by combining plastic, rubber and other (mostly wood and cork)
footwear into 1 category. Of the 3, plastic is the most important for our
purposes, because rubber footwear tends to be rather specialised and has
relatively static supply and demand patterns, while sales of wooden
footwear are small. The only exception to classification by material is to

distinguish slippers regardless of material; slippers of different materials are likely to be highly substitutable and, because of their different construction and function, slippers and shoes of the same material are likely to be very poor substitutes. In fact the latter factors led the EC to reject appeals for safeguard protection for slippers in 1989 and has encouraged us to omit them from the modelling part of this study.

Consider now the geographical dimension. *A priori* one might expect demanders to show high elasticities of substitution between similar footwear from different sources, but the evidence is far from overwhelming. The coefficients of variation of the unit values of imports of each of my groups into 6 EC markets from 17 sources only once fall below 40 per cent, suggesting something less than perfect substitution between suppliers – see Appendix, Table 7A.2(A). This variation may reflect either discriminatory quantitative restrictions or differences in quality, and I have no formal means of telling which. I note, however, that the variation persists right down to trade-heading level, that it occurs across sets of suppliers facing no quantitative restrictions, and that in at least some cases suppliers subject to known trade restrictions have below-average unit values. I thus suspect substantial product heterogeneity and have, therefore, pursued the now traditional modelling route of distinguishing products by place of production.

Further evidence of the imperfect substitutability between suppliers comes from Winters and Brenton (1991) where estimated elasticities of substitution between different suppliers of footwear to the UK (including UK domestic suppliers) ranged from − 2.75 (men's leather footwear) to − 0.83 (textile footwear).

There is also a second, more troublesome, geographical dimension – markets. The coefficients of variation of unit values for each type/supplier measured across 6 EC markets also show substantial variation – see Appendix, Table 7A.2(B). This raises the possibility either that different parts of the EC have separate and segmented markets for footwear, or that they receive different products from the same set of supplying countries. Slight support for the latter view comes from de Melo and Winters (1990a, 1990b) in which models of export allocation are estimated for Korea and Taiwan: the elasticities of transformation between footwear for the USA and for other markets are 2.2 and almost 5 respectively.[3]

Differentiation by market as well as by place of production raises significant difficulties in modelling the effects of '1992'. Previous studies of the effects of removing Article 115 (which formally segments EC markets in some goods) have assumed that identical goods are supplied to different EC markets and that the observed differences in prices before

1992 reflect the barriers to trade within the EC – see, e.g. Winters (1988), Smith (1989) and Hamilton (1991). They then model the abolition of Article 115 as reducing or removing the barriers and hence harmonising prices. If, however, price differences reflect only product differences there is nothing left to model, for there are no barriers for '1992' to remove.

The notion that all price differences reflect quality differences seems too extreme a position intuitively and so below I attribute part of them to watertight national import restrictions (e.g. national quotas supported by Article 115) and explore the consequences of removing these. This results in the equalisation of each supplier's quota rents across markets, but continuing differences in final prices according to different qualities. Analytically this is akin to quality upgrading in the face of VERs on product aggregates. Under binding national quotas suppliers have no discretion over their export bundle – they export the maximum permitted to each market. When we move to a single EC quota, however, traders can redirect exports until the last unit to each market generates an equal contribution to profits (i.e. has an equal quota rent). It should be noted that under this arrangement abolishing Article 115 is not sufficient to ensure liberalisation, for there is no demand for Taiwan's 'French' shoes in Italy.[4]

Even after aggregating the basic data I have 108 distinct types of footwear which interact in different combinations in supply and demand. Hence it is necessary to model them hierarchically. In demand I treat each market independently determining, in order, demand by type of footwear, the split of each type across broad qualities (an intermediate hierarchy of suppliers), and finally, within qualities, the division between suppliers. In supply I currently have only 1 level, the supply by each supplier of each type of footwear – but I subsequently intend to combine the supply modules of different types into a single footwear sector, as in Takacs and Winters (1991).

I use Constant Elasticity of Substitution (CES) or Constant Elasticity of Transformation (CET) aggregations at all levels of the model. Writing $C(x_{jk};j)$ as the CES or CET aggregator of variable x_j across dimension j, and q_{mtkj} for sales in market m of type t of quality k supplied by country j, the model may be represented as follows, where a dot denotes aggregation over the corresponding subscript.

Demand

$$W_m \quad = C(q_{mt..};t) \tag{1}$$
$$q_{mt..} \quad = C(q_{mtk.};k) \tag{2}$$
$$q_{mtk.} \quad = C(q_{mtkj};j) \tag{3}$$

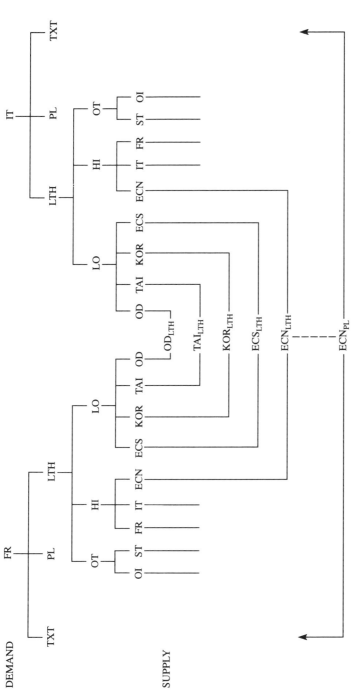

Figure 7.1 The hierarchies of supply and demand

Supply

$$Q_{.tkj} = C(q_{mtkj}; \mathrm{m}) \tag{4}$$

W_m is the sub-utility indicator for footwear in market m and $Q_{.tkj}$ the supply of footwear t by supplier kj. Figure 7.1 illustrates the relationships across two markets.

In addition to the equations above I allow the overall supply of footwear by country kj to expand as its price rises. Thus,

$$Q_{.tkj} = A P^{\eta}_{.tki} \tag{5}$$

where $P_{.tkj}$ is the appropriate unit cost function. Since I am modelling only supplies to the EC the elasticity of supply, η, will vary not only with the general flexibility of the supplying economy but also with the substitutability in production between footwear for the EC and for elsewhere, and with the EC share in the producer's total sales.

Further equations are incorporated in the model to reflect tariffs on footwear imports and the wedges of rent that VERs and bilateral quotas drive between consumer prices and supply prices (the minimum price necessary to bring forward the quantity supplied). It is argued elsewhere (Brenton and Winters, 1990) that UK restrictions on Polish and Czech footwear gave rise to a degree of non-price rationing – i.e. that the actual prices of imports did not rise sufficiently to cut demand back to the permitted quantity. Rationing provides no fundamental problems for this exercise. Neary and Roberts (1980) show that one models rationing as if trade occurred at the market-clearing price (their virtual price) but returns some or all of the rent from producers to consumers. With homothetic demand systems such as the CES, this extra expenditure is just spread across unconstrained supplies proportionately to their sales predicted using virtual prices.

All the results below refer to a compensated exercise in which the utility from consuming footwear is held constant and the effects of policy are calculated in terms of the cost of achieving that utility. Changes in the cost of footwear are borne in terms of the consumption of other goods (the numéraire) and are presented in terms of compensating variations. The changes in profits (producer surplus) reported are calculated by the linear approximation $\Delta p(q + 0.5\Delta q)$ where p and q are the supply price and quantity respectively.

3   Calibration

The model is written and calibrated using GAMS – see Brooke, Kendrick and Meeraus (1988). In each case calibration proceeds by selecting the elasticity of substitution from extraneous sources and then calculating the

Table 7.2. *Elasticities for base runs*
Elasticity of substitution between upper level suppliers

	LTH	PL	TXT
FR	3	3	3
IT	3	3	3
ECN	3	3	3
ECS	3	3	3

Elasticity of substitution within upper levels

	FR LTH	FR PL	FR TXT	IT LTH	IT PL	IT TXT
HI	2	1.5	1.2	2	1.5	1.2
LO	4	3.0	3.0	4	3.0	3.0
OT	2	1.5	1.2	2	1.5	1.2

	ECN LTH	ECN PL	ECN TXT	ECS LTH	ECS PL	ECS TXT
HI	2	1.5	1.2	2	1.5	1.2
LO	4	3.0	3.0	4	4.0	4.0
OT	2	1.5	1.2	2	1.5	1.2

Elasticity of substitution for top level

FR	1.5	ECN	1.5
IT	1.5	ECS	1.5

	Elasticity of substitution in CET for production				*Elasticity of supply of aggregate EC sales*		
	LTH	PL	TXT		LTH	PL	TXT
FR	5	5	5	FR	2	2	2
IT	5	5	5	IT	2	2	2
ECN	5	5	5	ECN	2	2	2
ECS	5	5	5	ECS	5	5	5
KOR	5	5	5	KOR	10	10	10
TAI	5	5	5	TAI	10	10	10
OD	5	5	5	OD	10	10	10
ST	5	5	5	ST	5	5	5
OI	5	5	5	OI	2	2	2

Table 7.3. *The main European quantitative restrictions on footwear imports, 1987*

France	Non-leather footwear from Taiwan
Italy	All footwear from state-trading countries:[a] Article 115
Germany	All except textile footwear from set A;[b] some exceptions for Romania
Benelux	Japanese rubber footwear; sports and rubber from state-trading countries; virtually all except textile from set A
Denmark	Slippers and non-leather sports shoes from Taiwan; all except textile sports shoes from set A
Ireland	Rubber, plastic, non-leather from Taiwan; all from Czecho-Slovakia; Article 115
UK	All from Asian state-trading countries (including China); some headings from set A (mostly leather – see Brenton and Winters, 1990) except for Romania; textile sports shoes; Article 115
Spain	All rubber, plastic and non-leather from non-state trading countries; all from state trading countries; Article 115
Portugal	Rubber and plastic from all countries for some shoe parts

Source: Commission of the European Communities (1989b)
Notes:
[a] State-trading countries include set A plus China.
[b] Set A of countries is those whose footwear trade with the EC is governed by Regulation 3420/83 (OJ L 346 8/12/1983): Albania, Bulgaria, Hungary, Poland, Romania, Czecho-Slovakia, USSR, German Democratic Republic, North Korea, Vietnam, Mongolia.

CES constants by applying the first order conditions to 1987's data. It is necessary to start the calibration at the lowest levels of the hierarchy in order to pass correct price and quantity aggregates up to the higher levels.

Table 7.2 reports the various elasticities in the initial runs. In general I have opted for fairly high levels of substitutability relative to previous econometric estimates, but there nonetheless remains a significant degree of geographical product differentiation.

The base data are given in Appendix Table 7A.3. The trade data are taken from the Eurostat *Foreign Trade Statistics* data base, measuring quantities in pairs (the EC's 'supplementary units') rather than weight. Domestic data are taken from Commission of the European Communities (1989a), where quantities are given in pairs and the basis of the prices is, frankly, somewhat vague. Where production was very low certain EC members did not report prices; in these cases I estimated them using trade statistics and other countries' domestic data. Tariff data were taken from the *Official Journal* – including details of Spanish accession – and for Spain from the official *Arancel de Importacion*.[5]

The major problem of calibration is the treatment of the trade restrictions existing in 1987. Apart from the UK – which is not separately identified here – we have no empirical work on which to base our estimates – so the values chosen are best viewed as parametric. Table 7.3 reports the principal quantitative restrictions operating on EC footwear imports in 1987 while Table 7.4 reports my translation of them into the framework of the model. I report the quota rents per pair that I assume wherever these are non-zero.[6] The translation requires a large degree of judgement, which has been guided by the following observations:

- wherever a binding VER is assumed, the actual level of trade is taken to define the limit
- small exceptions for Romania are ignored
- restrictions on the Asian state-trading countries are ignored because (a) countries such as Mongolia and Vietnam are not significant suppliers, (b) in 1987 China was much favoured in commercial diplomacy and, at least in the UK, her quotas had been recently increased and had anyway not been enforced, and (c) they are aggregated with a number of vigorous unconstrained exporters such as Thailand and Brazil
- national QRs not formally supported by Article 115 are nonetheless effective, because there is a threat of using the Article.

EC footwear imports have been subject to surveillance for several years but the view of the industry, corroborated by Winters (1990), is that this has had little effect. I therefore ignore it in estimating existing barriers.

Since the model is calibrated to 1987 I treat the various policy exercises as if they had occurred in 1987. For the VERs on Korea and Taiwan, which were imposed in 1988 and 1990, I scale back the permitted amounts to allow for the probable growth of consumption. Commission of the European Communities (1989b) suggests overall growth of around 2 per cent p.a. over the 1980s, although Commission of the European Communities (1990a) suggests slower growth: I reduce the limits by 1 per cent p.a. to be conservative.

Table 7.4. *Initial quota rent wedges, ECU per pair*

	FR LTH	FR PL	FR TXT	IT LTH	IT PL	IT TXT	ECN LTH	ECN PL	ECN TXT	ECS LTH	ECS PL	ECS TXT
FR												
IT												
ECN												
ECS												
KOR											1.000	1.000
TAI		0.740	0.916								0.500	0.500
OD											0.200	0.200
ST	2.150			1.280	1.413	1.466	1.94	2.100	2.561	7.010	2.118	3.163
OI											1.000	1.000

4   Spain and Portugal

The first shock I consider is the traditional customs union exercise of removing the tariffs on trade between Spain and the rest of the EC. These were below the two countries' mfn rates in 1987, while trade with Portugal already faced zero tariffs in 1987 and trade with Greece was basically free of tariffs following the latter's accession in 1981. Hence the aggregated tariffs assumed for EC-South (ECS) are not particularly high. The base tariffs are given in Appendix Table 7A.3(D). I define accession as the complete abolition of intra-EC tariffs and the universal application of the Common External Tariff (CET) at 1987 levels. The latter entails rates of 8 per cent on non-EC leather footwear and 20 per cent on other non-EC footwear. Naturally, given my aggregation, I can say nothing about trade between the countries of ECS: my results are as if accession applied to the whole of ECS.

Table 7.5(A) reports the principal effects of accession on trade flows, distinguishing between the first 9 EC members (EC-9) and the more recent accedents, ECS. While the consumption of footwear in EC-9 increases (the marginal valuation of 1.47 leather shoes exceeds that of 1.1 plastic plus 0.55 textile shoes in EC-9) and intra-bloc sales in EC-9 decrease, both indicating trade creation, there is also a large element of trade diversion as ECS displaces efficient developing country producers. Within ECS, external trade creation occurs in leather footwear because the external tariff falls, but similar effects are masked in the other commodities by the quantitative restrictions. In fact in the presence of QRs the usual normative prescriptions on potential trade effects are reversed: potential external creation raises quota rents (assumed here to accrue to the exporters) while trade diversion reduces them. Hence in this exercise the rents earned by non-EC suppliers of textile footwear to ECS rise slightly, and those to East European leather exporters rise by over ECU 2 per pair. All other rents fall as a result of accession.

The welfare effects of Southern accession are relatively small, see Table 7.5(B). EC consumers gain everywhere, but only modestly because neither the North nor the South is a major footwear supplier to the other. Profits fall in EC-9 but rise in ECS, while tariff revenues fall everywhere. If (rather inappropriately within the EC) we attribute tariff revenues to the countries whose imports are taxed, the final welfare effects are negligible in EC-9 and amount to about 4.2 per cent of expenditure on footwear in ECS. Clearly the EC as a whole (EC-12) gains from the enlargement.

Accession also strictly entails that the quantitative restrictions in Spain and Portugal be combined with those elsewhere in the EC. Ever optimistic, I assume that this would have entailed free trade in 1987 with all

Table 7.5. *The accession of Spain and Portugal*[a]

(A) Purchases of footwear (million pairs)

| | EC-9 | | | ECS | | | Total |
	LTH	PL	TXT	LTH	PL	TXT	(EC-12)
Changes in:[b]							
Total consumption	1.47	− 1.10	− 0.55	0.49	0.10	− 0.03	0.38
Supplies from:							
EC-9	− 2.57	− 0.69	− 0.23	0.25	0.31	0.13	− 2.81
ECS	5.40	0.68	0.62	− 0.32	− 0.21	− 0.16	6.02
Rest of World	− 1.35	− 1.09	− 0.94	0.56	0.00	0.00	− 2.82

(B) Economic welfare (million ECU)

	FR	IT	ECN	EC-9 (sub-total)	ECS	Total (EC-12)
Changes in:[b]						
Profits	− 4.6	− 10.3	− 8.4	− 23.3	11.6	− 11.7
Consumer welfare[c]	12.7	4.4	40.1	57.2	74.0	131.2
Tariff revenue	− 9.3	− 1.7	− 31.5	− 42.5	− 12.6	− 55.1
Total economic welfare	− 1.2	− 7.6	0.2	− 8.6	72.9	64.3

Source: Author's calculations.
Notes:
[a] Effects of tariff harmonisation with quantitative restrictions unchanged.
[b] Relative to calibrated base, 1987.
[c] Compensating variation.

partners except Eastern Europe. The quota rents assumed in ECS in Table 7.4 are crudely fixed at around 10–20 per cent of the unit value of trade and the existing levels of trade are rather small; hence the abolition of these QRs is not a major event. ECS imports of PL and TXT from non-EC suppliers rise by 2.6 and 1.2 million pairs respectively, but because the bulk of the increase is in very low-value footwear from other developing countries, ECS's gain from accession increases only to ECU 76 million.

This last simulation – with full Spanish and Portuguese accession – is now taken as the base for the next set of experiments.

5   Korea and Taiwan

This section considers the translation of the French and Italian VERs and quotas on Taiwan and Korea into EC-wide policies. This occurred in

Table 7.6. *Quantitative restrictions on Korea and Taiwan, quantities, million pairs per year*

		Actual[a] (1987) (A)	(B)	Restricted (Period)[b]
France	Korea	16.4	14.8	14.4 (1/7/88–30/6/89)
	Taiwan	13.0	10.6	14.2 (1988)
Italy	Korea	18.9	16.0	11.2 (1/3/88–31/12/88* 1.2)
	Taiwan	17.6	14.2	8.6 (1/3/88–31/12/88* 1.2)
EC	Korea	57.5	57.5	50.4 (1/7/90–21/12/90* 2)
	Taiwan	95.1	95.1	87.9 (1/7/90–31/12/90* 2)

Source: See text.
Notes:
[a] (A) based on legislation. (B) based on trade data.
[b] Reduced to allow for growth between 1987 and the policy date.

1990, and although not formally part of the '1992' process was clearly motivated in part by the Commission's embarrassment at having been forced into sanctioning new national trade policies in 1988 contrary to the spirit of '1992'.

I take trade policy as fixed in its 1987 form and consider (a) the addition of the VERs and quotas on imports into France and Italy and (b) the addition instead of the EC-wide VER.[7] As noted above I use the published limits for these two new policies, scaled back to allow for the growth in consumption between 1987 and 1990. In both cases the EC Commission argued that because of the difficulties of comparing their production and trade classifications for footwear, and because of the high substitutability between footwear types, restrictions had to be imposed on import of all footwear excluding slippers. Table 7.6 compares the actual (1987) quantities and the quantitative restrictions translated into 1987 terms. Two actual figures are quoted for the 1988 restrictions: column (A) is the total quoted in the preambles to the legislation *less* our data on slippers, while column (B) is based on our data, which almost exactly match those in Commission of the European Communities (1989a and 1989b). The differences are substantial and, at present, unexplained. I calibrate the model on column (B) – with one exception – but reduce the QR limits by the ratio of column (B) to column (A) to allow for the fact that the official coverage appears to exceed mine here.

The exception mentioned in the previous paragraph concerns France,

Table 7.7. *Quantitative restrictions on imports from Korea and Taiwan, effects on output and imports, million pairs*

	LTH	PL	TXT
Changes in output or in exports to the EC:[a]			
Policy:			
(A) French free trade			
EC-12	− 2.70	− 1.88	− 2.57
Korea and Taiwan	− 0.19	7.45	13.13
Rest of World	− 0.41	− 0.96	− 2.10
Total	− 3.30	4.61	8.46
(B) National quotas			
EC-12	2.49	0.50	0.57
Korea and Taiwan	− 1.71	− 5.60	− 8.37
Rest of World	0.28	1.43	1.66
Total	1.05	− 3.67	− 6.14
(C) EC-wide quotas			
EC-12	3.83	1.21	0.20
Korea and Taiwan	− 3.91	− 5.68	− 4.70
Rest of World	0.57	2.41	2.09
Total	0.49	− 2.05	− 2.41

Source: Author's calculations.
Note: [a] Relative to base with full Southern accession.

for which the Korean VER seems fairly loose while that for Taiwan allows for significant expansion. In fact, according to the legislation, both restrictions were still required because of the high potential growth rate of imports and the imminent expiry of France's existing QR on Taiwanese non-leather footwear.[8] I represent this view as entailing a potential shift in the supply of exports to France from Korea and Taiwan and model it below by reducing the CET parameters for Korea's and Taiwan's exports to France by 25 per cent and by removing the existing French QRs on Taiwan. The quota rents imputed to the existing QR are fixed at 20 per cent of the reported price. This is roughly the level necessary to bring the Taiwanese share of the French market up to the level of its share in Italy.

  The imposition of a single QR over several trade flows requires that the unit quota rents be equalised for each flow. For national restrictions this implies equality over types and for EC-wide restrictions equality over both types and markets. On the demand side this switches demand towards higher-value types (their relative prices to consumers rise less).

On the supply side, however, no such presumption exists, for in the initial position profit on the marginal unit is zero and the effect on rents of cutting output depends on the shape of the marginal cost schedule; this in turn depends on the elasticities in the supply module and on each market's importance to the exporters concerned.

The results of these experiments are given in Tables 7.7 and 7.8. The former reports the changes in output and exports for groups of suppliers. For the 4 EC producers this includes both domestic sales and intra-EC exports,[9] whereas for the non-EC suppliers it concerns only exports to the EC. Table 7.7(A) refers to the effects of the liberalisation of France's non-leather imports from Taiwan plus the increase in Korean and Taiwanese supply to France. French imports from Taiwan boom at the expense both of plastic and textile footwear imports from elsewhere and of the consumption of leather footwear. Turning to Table 7.8, where the first row of each block refers to French free trade, the strong effects on French trade are confirmed in blocks (E) and (F).[10] The earlier blocks show the consumer benefits of free trade to France (2.3 per cent of footwear consumption) and the spillover to other EC consumers as competition in France drives down producer prices in general. The latter effect, however, makes Italy and EC-South losers overall and also reduces net French benefits. Quota rents on state-traders' sales also fall slightly as demand is met by Taiwanese supplies.

The next exercise refers to the imposition of national restrictions on footwear imports by France and Italy on Korea and Taiwan. These are measured in the tables relative to the base run without the improved competitiveness and the liberalisation of Taiwan. To assess the effects of policy relative to the alternative of unrestricted French trade, then, one should subtract the values from the previous exercise. It is plain that the 1988 policy represented a significant tightening of restrictions in France and Italy. It reduced Korean and Taiwanese exports to the EC – see Table 7.8(E) and 7.8(F) – and increased output locally and in other exporters, see Table 7.7(B). It reduced consumer welfare throughout the EC, total welfare everywhere except the EC-South and drove up other suppliers' prices. The unit quota rents on French plastic and textile footwear from Taiwan increased relative to the base run and new rents were created on leather imports and for Italy. Total rents paid to Korea and Taiwan increased by ECU 28.6 million and ECU 16.8 million respectively – see the final columns of Table 7.8(G) and 7.8(H). Comparing the national quotas with unrestricted trade (by subtracting the first row from the second) reveals losses of welfare of 2.0 per cent of footwear expenditure in France, 0.7 per cent in Italy and 0.2 per cent in the rest of the EC.

The final simulation refers to the new EC-wide quota and VER on

Table 7.8. *Quantitative restrictions on imports from Korea and Taiwan, effects on welfare and trade*

	FR	IT	ECN	ECS	Total (EC-12)
Changes in:[a]					
Policy:					
(A) Profits, million ECU					
French free trade	− 18.4	− 12.7	− 3.7	− 2.2	− 36.9
National quotas	2.8	20.4	2.9	1.6	27.8
EC-wide quotas	− 5.3	17.4	12.7	4.3	29.1
(B) Consumer welfare, million ECU					
French free trade	64.4	3.8	10.4	0.4	78.9
National quotas	− 7.0	− 42.4	− 12.8	− 0.5	− 62.7
EC-wide quotas	26.2	− 23.7	− 70.4	− 3.6	− 71.5
(C) Tariff revenue, million ECU					
French free trade	6.6	− 0.0	− 0.2	0.0	6.4
National quotas	− 0.2	− 3.2	− 0.1	− 0.1	− 3.5
EC-wide quotas	3.5	− 1.6	− 4.6	− 0.7	− 3.3
(D) Total welfare, million ECU					
French free trade	52.5	− 8.9	6.6	− 1.8	48.4
National quotas	− 4.4	− 25.1	− 9.9	1.1	− 38.4
EC-wide quotas	24.4	− 7.9	− 62.2	0.0	− 45.7
(E) Imports of plastic shoes from Korea and Taiwan, million pairs					
French free trade	6.88	0.11	0.43	0.02	7.4
National quotas	− 0.01	− 5.18	− 0.39	− 0.02	− 5.6
EC-wide quotas	3.50	− 2.88	− 5.89	− 0.41	− 5.7
(F) Imports of textile shoes from Korea and Taiwan, million pairs					
French free trade	12.49	0.16	0.42	0.05	13.1
National quotas	0.29	− 8.01	− 0.60	− 0.05	− 8.4
EC-wide quotas	6.20	− 4.26	− 5.95	− 0.69	− 4.7
(G) Quota rents on Korea, per unit, ECU per pair total[b]					
National quotas	1.24	1.31	0	0	28.6
EC-wide quotas	0.63	0.63	0.63	0.63	31.8
(H) Quota rents on Taiwan, per unit, ECU per pair total[b]					
National quotas	1.41	1.21	0	0	16.8
EC-wide quotas	0.44	0.44	0.44	0.44	30.9

Source: Author's calculations.
Notes:
[a] Relative to base with full Southern accession.
[b] Change in total revenue relative to base run, million ECU.

Taiwan and Korea. This does not entail substantially greater protection than national QRs, but it shifts the burden of protecting French and Italian producers from consumers in those countries to consumers elsewhere – see Table 7.8(B). Total welfare costs increase from ECU 38 million to ECU 46 million, but those for EC-North increase from ECU 10 million to ECU 62 million – see Table 7.8(D). The extension of the quotas to EC-North reduces Taiwan's and Korea's exports of leather footwear and allows an increase in textile footwear exports relative to the national quotas – compare Tables 7.7(B) and 7.7(C) and see Table 7.8(F). This, coupled with their generally strong positions in the newly protected markets, makes EC-North and EC-South producers the major gainers from the EC-wide policy and also helps to offset losses to producers in France, whose main market is left more exposed by the switch to EC-wide quotas. The quota rents, while reduced in per unit terms, now of course apply to a far wider range of trade. They increase for both Korea and Taiwan relative to the national quotas exercise.

Table 7.8 suggests that the shift to EC-wide quotas probably benefited all groups of producers other than the French: EC producers' profits rise in total, Korean and Taiwanese rents increase, and returns to other foreign producers rise as both their prices and quantities sold increase.[11] Since tariff revenues also increase by ECU 3 million, it is plain that EC consumers potentially faced an overwhelming coalition of interests in the extension of trade restrictions of the whole EC market.

This exercise also highlights the unavoidable distributional frictions that will arise between countries in the operation of EC trade policy after '1992'. If restrictions must be imposed community-wide, regions with significant excess supply (e.g. Italy) will gain at the expense of net importing regions (ECN). Moreover, the complex interactions between markets – here types of footwear – make the effects difficult to predict without a full empirical model. The results also show, however, that whatever its distributional effects, trade restrictions entail substantial aggregate losses relative to free trade.

6   Eastern Europe

This section considers the abolition of Article 115 restrictions on supplies from Eastern Europe and the eventual abolition of all quantitative restrictions and tariffs on those supplies. For comparison it also considers briefly the complete liberalisation of EC footwear imports from all sources.

Table 7.4 reports relatively modest quota rents for East European suppliers – of the order of the price increases found in Winters (1990) excluding any non-price rationing. They are calculated to equate the supply prices of each type of footwear across markets to the following values in terms of ECU: LTH 8.00, PL 3.56 and TXT 2.84. For the last two these are the prices charged to France which are consequently unrestrained. For leather, however, I imputed a mild *de facto* restriction in France despite the absence of an entry in Table 7.3 because France reports both higher prices and a smaller 'ST' share than either EC-North or Italy.

Starting from a base with full Southern accession and EC-wide quotas on Korea and Taiwan, the first experiment was to combine the individual restrictions by market and type into a single QR on all East European exports to the EC fixed at the 1987 actual level, 39.14 million pairs. This results in a uniform rent of ECU 1.87 per pair but very little change in welfare or trade: a gain of ECU 6.1 million for EC-North (less than 0.1 per cent of footwear expenditure) and ECU 3.2 million for the EC as a whole. The effects are so slight because the existing quota rents are rather similar and because such a large proportion of existing Eastern European sales go to EC-North. Hence although proportionately large changes may occur in other flows, their effects on EC-North imports and total welfare are very small.

A more interesting exercise is to liberalise East European trade completely, as is due under the recent Europe Agreements with Czecho-Slovakia, Hungary and Poland. Tables 7.9 and 7.10 report four variants of this exercise – all based on the modest initial rents given in Table 7.4: (i) with the abolition of quantitative restrictions, (ii) with the abolition of all tariffs and QRs – I refer to this as 'full preferences', (iii) full preferences with the elasticity of supply in Eastern Europe increased to 40 to permit an increase in output at roughly current costs, and (iv) full preferences with a 25 per cent increase in East European output at current costs to reflect improvements in productivity. The last two exercises, with their essentially arbitrary positive shocks, reflect an optimism that the Eastern European countries can address their supply-side problems. They also presuppose that over the 10-year horizon for which this sort of exercise is legitimate, their comparative advantage remains in labour-intensive goods like footwear. I have argued elsewhere – CEPR (1990) and Hamilton and Winters (1992) – that Eastern European skill levels are such that at least parts of the region will progress well beyond that step on the ladder of comparative advantage. While there is little evidence to go on, however, I suspect that such advance will take at least a decade and that an expansion of labour-intensive production in the meantime will be a necessary condition for achieving it.

The abolition of QRs generates much more trade creation than trade diversion – see Table 7.9(A). This is because the liberalisation has major effects only on leather footwear, which account for 90 per cent of Eastern European sales in the EC and for which those suppliers compete mainly with EC local firms. ST exports to the EC rise by 41 per cent, 52 per cent and 103 per cent for LTH, PL and TXT respectively, while both local sales and those of the rest of the non-EC world fall by 1–1.5 per cent in each category. ST's share of the EC market rises from 3.4 per cent to 4.9 per cent. These increases in ST exports are impressive, but it must be noted that liberalisation entails the loss of quota rents which I assume

Table 7.9. *Liberalising imports from Eastern Europe and the world, effects on output and imports, million pairs*

	LTH	PL	TXT
(A) Abolishing QRs			
EC-12	− 8.08	− 2.04	− 0.98
E. Europe (ST)	12.87	2.21	3.36
Rest of World	− 1.05	− 1.82	− 1.81
Total	3.74	− 1.66	0.56
(B) Full preferences			
EC-12	− 11.36	− 2.95	− 1.39
E. Europe (ST)	18.42	4.05	5.18
Rest of World	− 1.48	− 2.65	− 2.52
Total	5.58	− 1.56	1.27
(C) Full preferences, eta = 40			
EC-12	− 16.18	− 4.14	− 1.96
E. Europe (ST)	27.62	5.96	7.99
Rest of World	− 2.14	− 3.70	− 3.51
Total	9.30	− 1.87	2.52
(D) Full preferences, dS = 25%			
EC-12	− 13.15	− 3.36	− 1.57
E. Europe (ST)	21.98	4.56	5.68
Rest of World	− 1.74	− 3.03	− 2.80
Total	7.09	− 1.83	1.32
(E) Complete liberalisation			
EC-12	− 32.69	− 13.24	− 8.76
E. Europe (ST)	16.11	3.72	4.22
Rest of World	10.84	58.26	48.55
Total	− 5.74	48.73	44.01

Source: Author's calculations.

Table 7.10. *Liberalising imports from Eastern Europe and the world, the effects on welfare and trade*

	FR	IT	ECN	ECS	Total (EC-12)
Changes in:[a]					
Policy:					
(A) Profits, million ECU					
Abolishing QRs	− 7.5	− 28.3	− 23.2	− 6.8	− 65.8
Full preferences	− 11.1	− 40.6	− 32.6	− 9.3	− 93.6
Full preferences, eta = 40	− 16.2	− 58.4	− 46.7	− 12.9	− 134.2
Full preferences, dS = 25%	− 12.9	− 47.0	− 37.8	− 10.6	− 108.4
Complete liberalisation	− 50.9	− 138.6	− 91.7	− 30.6	− 311.8
(B) Consumer welfare, million ECU					
Abolishing QRs	15.9	13.0	111.3	4.3	144.6
Full preferences	24.3	19.4	155.7	5.3	204.7
Full preferences, eta = 40	36.1	27.9	220.8	6.5	291.3
Full preferences, dS = 25%	28.4	22.4	179.6	5.7	236.0
Complete liberalisation	131.5	96.4	434.5	18.5	681.0
(C) Tariff revenue, million ECU					
Abolishing QRs	0.5	0.5	4.2	0.4	5.6
Full preferences	− 3.6	− 2.0	− 29.1	− 0.2	− 35.0
Full preferences, eta = 40	− 3.6	− 2.0	− 30.4	− 0.2	− 36.2
Full preferences, dS = 25%	− 3.6	− 2.0	− 29.6	− 0.2	− 35.4
Complete liberalisation	− 43.5	− 30.4	− 168.0	− 6.4	− 248.3
(D) Total welfare, million ECU					
Abolishing QRs	9.0	− 14.8	92.4	− 2.1	84.5
Full preferences	9.6	− 23.2	94.0	− 4.2	76.1
Full preferences, eta = 40	16.2	− 32.5	143.7	− 6.5	120.9
Full preferences, dS = 25%	11.9	− 26.7	112.2	− 5.1	92.3
Complete liberalisation	37.1	− 72.6	174.8	− 18.4	120.8
(E) Imports of leather shoes from ST, million pairs					
Abolishing QRs	1.22	0.29	10.94	0.41	12.87
Full preferences	1.75	0.46	15.72	0.49	18.42
Full preferences, eta = 40	2.63	0.74	23.62	0.62	27.62
Full preferences, dS = 25%	2.09	0.57	18.78	0.54	21.98
Complete liberalisation	1.55	0.42	13.65	0.49	16.11

Source: Author's calculations.
Note: [a] Relative to base with EC-wide quantitative restrictions on Korea and Taiwan and base restrictions on Eastern Europe.

accrue to exporters. Thus while ST's earnings from the EC increase from ECU 276 million to ECU 428 million through liberalisation, the rent component falls from ECU 78 million to zero. Hence such increases in revenue cannot be guaranteed to be welfare-improving.

Total consumption of plastic and textile footwear falls as leather becomes more competitive, with price declines observed for all suppliers. Table 7.10(E), which disaggregates the market for leather footwear, shows that the major effects of liberalisation occur in the EC-North, which takes 90 per cent of Eastern European sales.[12] Producers in Italy lose most sales absolutely, but proportionately ECN and OD producers feel the most pressure. The impact on ECN reflects the competition between ECN and ST producers in the ECN market, while that on OD reflects the assumed highly elastic supplies from developing countries, which means that the latter suffer their shocks more in quantities than in price. Korea and Taiwan's total exports are unchanged because they are constrained, but there is some reallocation of their sales towards PL and TXT and their quota rents fall by 0.06 and 0.05 ECU per pair.

Table 7.10 presents the welfare effects of removing QRs on Eastern European suppliers in the first line of each block. As noted previously, these are concentrated on the EC-North, with consumer gains of 1.6 per cent of total expenditure in footwear and net gains of 1.3 per cent. It is notable that in this set of exercises it is Italy and EC-South – the major suppliers of footwear to the rest of the EC – that suffer the welfare loses through reduced profits – see Table 7.10(A) – rather than France as in the previous exercise.

Table 7.9(B) and the second line of each bloc in Table 7.10 extend the exercise to full preferences for Eastern Europe by additionally removing all the tariffs they face. This situation will pertain under the Europe Agreements by 1997. The tariff reductions on plastic and textiles footwear exceed those on leather – see Appendix, Table 7A.3(D) – so that the incremental effects are slightly greater on the former. Nevertheless, the trade story remains much the same: ST exports increase by 58 per cent, 95 per cent and 159 per cent respectively, with approximately 2 per cent reductions in other suppliers' market sales, and the ST share increases to 5.7 per cent. A significant change occurs on welfare, however. The full preferences offer greater consumers' benefits than just abolishing QRs – see Table 7.10(B) – but they are more than offset by reductions in profits and, more significantly, tariff revenues – see Table 7.10(C). Because EC tariff revenue does not accrue directly to member states, the individual welfare effects are not reliable, but the total EC welfare benefits fall from ECU 85 million from abolishing QRs to ECU 76 million (about 0.55 per cent of total footwear expenditure) under full preferences. This is because the average price of East European exports rises by 2.6 per cent relative to the quotas-only liberalisation, and this is not offset by the marginal price reductions instituted by other producers as they lose demand. That is, given the less than infinite elasticities of supply, the EC's optimum tariff on East European exports is greater than zero.

Under the base elasticities, part of the benefit of freer EC markets is dissipated by increases in costs in Eastern Europe of 10–21 per cent. The two alternative exercises moderate this effect by either allowing for a stronger expansion in response to increased rewards of exporting or boosting output exogenously to reflect better economic organisation. The former case generates the larger benefits but neither changes the basic pattern of results much.

The final exercise in Tables 7.9 and 7.10 offers a standard of comparison for the liberalisation of imports from Eastern Europe. It is the complete liberalisation of tariffs and quotas on all footwear imports into the EC (using the original parameter values). Consumers, of course, benefit strongly from such a liberalisation – by 5 per cent of total footwear expenditure – but profits and tariff revenues fall significantly, leaving a net benefit of only 1 per cent of expenditure. Here again is an optimum tariff effect: although the prices of Taiwanese and Korean supplies fall as their rents are abolished, the (base-weighted) average supply price of non-EC imports (excluding rents) rises by 4.1 per cent as a result of the liberalisation. Table 7.9(E) shows that Eastern Europe's gains under complete liberalisation are not much smaller than those under preferential access – suggesting that they need not be overly concerned about maintaining their preferences; the major changes are the increases in imports of plastic and textile footwear – mainly from Korea and Taiwan. The latter effect means that compared with liberalising only ST imports, Italian and French profits are hit hardest by complete liberalisation – see Table 7.10(A).

The significance of the results in this section lies in their size. Very substantial gains in exports are available to East European producers if simultaneously they can take steps to correct their supply distortions and EC markets are opened. Given their small initial shares such changes do not imply huge changes in EC trade patterns. Nevertheless, as I have observed elsewhere (Winters, 1992), the opportunities to increase EC welfare via this route seem significantly larger than those available via 'traditional' 1992 routes. Perhaps this indicates a need to reorient political and economic attention.

7   Sensitivity

The final exercise is briefly to test the sensitivity of the model used to derive these results. In the Appendix, Table 7A.4 reports the changes in welfare relative to the 1987 base for a series of runs allowing full Southern accession and the abolition of all QRs. The runs consider alternative values of the initial policy wedges in Table 7.4, of all the demand-side elasticities of substitution, and of all the supply-side elasticities of transformation, both reported in Table 7.2. The results suggest a fair degree of robustness; the signs and relative sizes of the various effects are the same throughout. The values of the initial wedges appear to be fairly important to the results – suggesting that a high priority for future research in this and other sectors should be to establish a proper empirical basis to trade policy analysis by characterising existing policies more accurately. Variations in the elasticities, on the other hand, do not make much difference, more elastic demands and supplies tending to increase the absolute sizes of the effects only very slightly. It seems, then, that we may have some confidence in the qualitative results of the exercises above.

8   Conclusion

This chapter has modelled the effects of 3 major EC trade policies on the market for footwear. First it showed that while Spain and Portugal gain substantially from accession to the EC, the EC-9 suffers significant trade diversion and its welfare declines slightly. Second, it showed that, while the replacement of national with EC-wide quantitative restrictions against Korea and Taiwan in the spirit of '1992' did not greatly worsen protection, it did have significant distributional effects within the EC. Essentially it shifted the burden of supporting French and Italian producers from those countries' consumers to consumers elsewhere in the EC, lowering EC-12's consumer welfare by ECU 72 million and total welfare by ECU 46 million per year. Third, it showed that abolishing Article 115 restrictions on Eastern European suppliers would have virtually no effect, but that allowing them free access to EC markets would be potentially welfare-enhancing for both East and West Europe. Such a policy, however, would impose costs on Italy and Spain, the major EC footwear-producing countries.

Of course, footwear is hardly a commanding height of the European economy; but it is amenable to analysis and the results here suggest that, generalising to other larger sectors, significant amounts of economic welfare are at stake, especially between members of the EC. The most obvious examples are textiles and clothing and agriculture, but several other sectors suffer from trade restrictions of the sort described here, see GATT (1991). Moreover, the discussion over the period 1988–91 suggested that at least some commentators saw footwear as establishing a precedent or benchmark for policy in other sectors. '1992' affects the environment within which, and for which, trade policy is made, because it further decouples the costs and 'benefits' of protection. It would be a great improvement to EC policy-making practice, then, if the large but dispersed consumer losses of the sort identified in this exercise were formally identified and officially brought to bear against the specific and concentrated producer gains.

Appendix: additional data and results

Table 7A.1. *The EC footwear industry, 1985–7*

	Share in industrial employment (%)	Export–import ratios Extra-EC (%)	Intra-EC (%)	Shares in EC exports Extra-EC (%)	Intra-EC (%)
Belgium-Luxembourg	0.3	13	15	0.3	1.3
Denmark	0.3	54	41	1.6	0.8
West Germany	0.6	35	21	10.4	5.9
Greece	1.8	293	193	0.9	0.8
Spain	1.9	1406	1605	14.6	9.7
France	1.6	67	43	9.7	7.4
Ireland	0.6	26	15	0.3	0.3
Italy	2.8	915	3112	55.2	59.0
Netherlands	0.5	7	42	0.4	3.6
Portugal	3.9	1488	2516	3.8	7.9
UK	1.0	21	25	2.9	3.4

Source: Commission of the European Communities (1990b).

Table 7A.2. *Coefficients of variation, 1987, %*

(A) Across suppliers

	Leather	Plastic	Rubber	Textile	Other	Slippers
France	53	106	65	53	79	57
Italy	50	116	58	82	94	78
West Germany	45	81	63	51	111	48
United Kingdom	47	55	77	74	105	71
EC-North	40	52	66	48	53	59
EC-South	35	130	54	66	95	73
Total	49	80	48	53	57	54

(B) Across markets

	Leather	Plastic	Rubber	Textile	Other	Slippers
World	25	18	9	28	43	45
Intra-EC	23	19	16	22	12	34
Extra-EC	29	28	5	29	50	50
France	21	38	45	30	30	42
Italy	28	10	11	6	20	28
West Germany	6	16	27	30	74	9
United Kingdom	37	15	30	29	69	45
EC-North	23	35	47	40	41	49
EC-South	14	23	18	25	11	31
EFTA	18	36	31	33	12	27
Other Industrial	17	34	35	20	212	52
Korea	9	18	13	21	45	46
Taiwan	40	22	12	16	31	35
China	43	26	1	27	37	20
Thailand	34	15	9	20	15	25
Other Asia	39	22	34	18	21	36
Brazil	13	51	53	54	255	3
Other Developing	26	82	94	43	27	51
Eastern Europe	21	22	30	49	4	16

Table 7A.3. Basic data

(A) Value of sales by producer/market type/million ECU

	FR LTH	FR PL	FR TXT	IT LTH	IT PL	IT TXT	ECN LTH	ECN PL	ECN TXT	ECS LTH	ECS PL	ECS TXT
FR	1072.5	185.6	79.8	27.8	6.8	3.8	214.7	48.1	26.1	4.3	3.1	1.1
IT	565.8	136.7	33.6	1828.3	195.1	1.1	1809.0	212.6	42.4	18.7	16.0	4.8
ECN	97.1	16.9	18.2	32.7	5.0	4.5	2040.5	274.4	36.6	7.0	2.1	2.7
ECS	203.8	4.4	10.9	25.5	5.8	3.4	689.8	17.9	14.1	1270.2	235.5	62.0
KOR	18.0	8.3	49.0	17.3	5.8	40.6	75.3	14.9	77.1	10.8	0.6	2.2
TAI	10.7	14.3	24.8	11.4	10.4	21.5	115.2	106.2	110.9	5.2	2.0	5.2
OD	77.3	10.9	16.8	7.3	16.7	11.6	177.9	74.5	62.2	3.3	2.8	1.6
ST	28.0	5 0	2.6	10.6	5.1	0.8	272.8	10.0	11.8	2.6	0.6	0.1
OI	24.2	5 5	1.8	39.7	4.2	9.6	250.6	37.2	11.6	4.2	0.8	1.6
Total	2097.4	387.4	237.7	2000.7	254.4	97.0	5645.8	796.0	392.8	1326.2	263.5	81.3

Sub-totals

	FR	IT	ECN	ECS	LTH	PL	TXT	Grand Total
FR	1338.0	38.4	288.9	8.5	1319.4	243.5	110.9	1673.8
IT	736.1	2024.5	2064.0	39.5	4221.8	560.3	82.0	4864.1
ECN	132.2	42.2	2351.5	11.8	2177.3	298.4	62.0	2537.7
ECS	219.1	34.4	721.8	1567.7	2189.2	263.4	90.4	2543.0
KOR	75.2	63.7	167.4	13.6	121.4	29.5	169.0	319.9
TAI	49.8	43.3	332.4	12.4	142.6	132.9	162.4	437.9
OD	105.0	35.6	314.5	7.7	265.7	104.9	92.2	462.8
ST	35.6	16.5	294.6	3.3	314.0	20.6	15.4	350.0
OI	31.5	53.5	299.4	6.5	318.7	47.7	24.6	391.0
Total	2722.5	2352.2	6834.5	1671.0	11 070.1	1701.3	808.8	13 580.2

Table 7A.3. (cont.)

(B) Quantities by producer/market/type, million pairs

	FR LTH	FR PL	FR TXT	IT LTH	IT PL	IT TXT	ECN LTH	ECN PL	ECN TXT	ECS LTH	ECS PL	ECS TXT
FR	43.67	10.67	12.02	1.42	0.58	0.53	13.17	6.18	3.83	0.64	0.87	0.12
IT	36.97	25.89	5.97	90.46	9.10	0.18	122.03	38.59	6.36	1.24	4.52	0.86
ECN	5.44	3.55	3.77	1.34	1.05	0.91	106.53	36.23	6.74	0.49	0.77	0.30
ECS	15.01	0.84	3.81	1.45	1.12	0.83	60.56	3.42	4.42	38.67	32.42	16.33
KOR	1.98	1.76	10.95	1.79	1.69	12.54	7.85	2.86	14.83	0.99	0.09	0.34
TAI	1.30	3.87	5.42	0.90	6.28	7.07	14.13	27.94	25.03	0.52	0.77	1.55
OD	8.47	6.16	10.53	0.60	20.64	4.55	22.26	55.52	33.95	0.33	3.62	1.09
ST	2.75	1.40	0.93	1.14	1.02	0.20	27.45	1.77	2.18	0.17	0.10	0.02
OI	0.89	0.24	0.16	1.58	0.28	0.86	11.49	2.64	1.22	0.19	0.11	0.16
Total	116.48	54.38	53.46	100.67	41.76	27.67	385.49	175.16	98.56	43.25	43.28	20.78

Sub-totals

	FR	IT	ECN	ECS	LTH	PL	TXT	Grand Total
FR	66.36	2.52	23.18	1.63	58.90	18.30	16.50	93.70
IT	68.83	99.74	166.98	6.62	250.70	78.10	13.38	342.18
ECN	12.75	3.30	149.51	1.56	113.80	41.60	11.72	167.12
ECS	19.67	3.39	68.41	87.43	115.70	37.80	25.40	178.90
KOR	14.60	16.01	25.54	1.43	12.61	6.40	38.56	57.58
TAI	10.59	14.26	67.10	2.84	16.85	38.87	39.08	94.79
OD	25.15	25.80	111.73	5.04	31.66	85.95	50.11	167.72
ST	5.09	2.36	31.40	0.29	31.52	4.29	3.33	39.14
OI	1.28	2.72	15.36	0.46	14.14	3.27	2.40	19.81
Total	224.32	170.09	659.21	107.31	645.89	214.57	200.48	1160.94

(C) Prices (unit values), ECU per pair

	FR LTH	FR PL	FR TXT	IT LTH	IT PL	IT TXT	ECN LTH	ECN PL	ECN TXT	ECS LTH	ECS PL	ECS TXT
FR	24.56	17.40	6.64	19.65	11.66	7.27	16.30	7.78	6.81	6.69	3.53	9.36
IT	15.30	5.28	5.63	20.21	21.44	6.13	14.82	5.51	6.67	15.11	3.53	5.60
ECN	17.86	4.75	4.83	24.49	4.72	4.94	19.15	7.57	5.43	14.22	2.75	8.92
ECS	13.58	5.22	2.85	17.58	4.95	4.15	11.39	5.24	3.18	32.84	7.26	3.80
KOR	9.08	4.68	4.52	9.71	3.42	3.24	9.59	5.22	5.20	10.84	6.53	6.44
TAI	8.24	3.69	4.58	12.70	1.65	3.04	8.15	3.80	4.43	10.00	2.61	3.34
OD	9.13	1.77	1.60	12.11	0.81	2.55	7.99	1.34	1.83	9.91	0.79	1.44
ST	10.15	3.56	2.84	9.28	4.97	4.30	9.94	5.66	5.40	15.01	5.68	6.00
OI	27.31	23.35	11.30	25.18	14.96	11.16	21.81	14.08	9.51	22.01	7.26	9.62
Total	18.01	7.12	4.45	19.87	6.09	3.51	14.65	4.54	3.99	30.66	6.09	3.91

Sub-totals

	FR	IT	ECN	ECS	LTH	PL	TXT	Grand Total
FR	20.16	15.23	12.46	5.20	22.40	13.31	6.72	17.86
IT	10.69	20.30	12.36	5.97	16.84	7.17	6.13	14.22
ECN	10.36	12.80	15.73	7.54	19.13	7.17	5.29	15.18
ECS	11.14	10.15	10.55	17.93	18.92	6.97	3.56	14.21
KOR	5.15	3.98	6.55	9.51	9.63	4.61	4.38	5.56
TAI	4.70	3.04	4.95	4.35	8.46	3.42	4.16	4.62
OD	4.18	1.38	2.82	1.53	8.39	1.22	1.84	2.76
ST	7.00	7.00	9.38	11.17	9.96	4.81	4.62	8.94
OI	24.63	19.69	19.50	14.15	22.53	14.60	10.22	19.73
Total	12.14	13.83	10.37	15.57	17.14	5.41	4.03	11.70

H

Table 7A.3. (cont.)

(D) Tariffs, average values on international trade flows, 1987

	FR LTH	FR PL	FR TXT	IT LTH	IT PL	IT TXT	ECN LTH	ECN PL	ECN TXT	ECS LTH	ECS PL	ECS TXT
FR	0.00	0.00	0.00	0.00	0.00	0.00	0.00	0.00	0.00	0.10	0.07	0.10
IT	0.00	0.00	0.00	0.00	0.00	0.00	0.00	0.00	0.00	0.10	0.07	0.10
ECN	0.00	0.00	0.00	0.00	0.00	0.00	0.00	0.00	0.00	0.10	0.07	0.10
ECS	0.04	0.07	0.04	0.04	0.07	0.04	0.04	0.07	0.04	0.04	0.04	0.04
KOR	0.08	0.20	0.20	0.08	0.20	0.20	0.08	0.20	0.20	0.26	0.17	0.26
TAI	0.08	0.20	0.20	0.08	0.20	0.20	0.08	0.20	0.20	0.26	0.17	0.26
OD	0.08	0.20	0.20	0.08	0.20	0.20	0.08	0.20	0.20	0.26	0.17	0.26
ST	0.08	0.20	0.20	0.08	0.20	0.20	0.08	0.20	0.20	0.26	0.17	0.26
OI	0.08	0.20	0.20	0.08	0.20	0.20	0.08	0.20	0.20	0.26	0.17	0.26

(E) Extra-EC exports by EC producers

	Value (million ECU)			Quantity (million pairs)			Price (ECU per pair)		
	LTH	PL	TXT	LTH	PL	TXT	LTH	PL	TXT
FR	203.8	99.7	16.8	9.10	5.70	2.50	22.40	17.49	6.72
IT	1562.8	226.3	11.4	92.80	23.90	1.90	16.84	9.47	6.00
ECN	386.5	40.8	7.9	20.20	3.70	1.80	19.13	11.01	4.36
ECS	930.9	188.5	15.3	49.20	11.90	4.30	18.92	15.84	3.56
Total	3084.0	555.3	51.4	171.30	45.20	10.50	18.00	12.28	4.89

Table 7A.4. *Sensitivity analysis, welfare effects, million ECU*

Changes in parameter			Changes in welfare[a]				
			FR	IT	ECN	ECS	Total
Multipliers on:[b] initial							
rents	demand	supply					
1.0	1.0	1.0	57.1	− 30.8	87.0	60.0	173.3
0.5	1.0	1.0	45.2	− 20.9	39.2	60.0	123.5
1.5	1.0	1.0	72.3	− 44.6	153.6	60.0	241.2
1.0	2.0	1.0	74.3	− 51.7	107.3	60.0	189.9
1.0	0.4	1.0	44.7	− 13.2	72.2	60.0	163.7
1.0	1.0	1.5	64.1	− 30.0	85.3	60.0	179.4
1.0	1.0	0.5	47.0	− 32.7	90.6	60.0	164.9
1.0	0.4	0.5	40.7	− 15.1	72.8	60.0	158.4
1.0	2.0	0.5	54.1	− 51.7	113.7	60.0	176.1
1.0	2.0	2.0	92.3	− 53.3	103.5	60.0	202.6

Source: Author's calculations.
Notes:
[a] Relative to calibrated base, 1987.
[b] Relative to values in Table 7.2.

NOTES

Support for this research has been provided by the research funds of the School for Accounting, Banking and Economics, University of Wales, Bangor, and the School of Social Science, University of Birmingham. I am grateful to both. Thanks are also due to Tina Attwell and Maureen Hyde for typing, to Xiao Hua Wang for data preparation, and to Zhen Kun Wang, members of the IT92 programme and especially to Kym Anderson for comments.
1 I use the notation '1992' as shorthand for the general process of completing the internal market.
2 In fact we combine them with Greece to form the EC-South.
3 De Melo and Winters (1990b) estimates a Generalised Leontief allocation function which allows the elasticity of transformation to vary.
4 Of course analytically we can imagine Taiwan shipping 'Italian' shoes to France and then trans-shipping them – the process that Article 115 prevented. But given the way that we have to measure trade, that approach is non-operational, for all shoes delivered to France appear to be 'French' according to our data.
   An earlier version of this chapter suggested modelling the harmonisation of tastes as an additional alternative approach to modelling integration with heterogeneous goods. In the interests of economy, however, that is now left to a further occasion.

5 I am grateful to Amparo Roca for providing these data. Portuguese–EC trade was tariff-free in 1987 under the EC–EFTA arrangements.
6 The precise values chosen are discussed in the text below when they are relevant to the results.
7 These policies are Regulations 561/88 (OJ L 54, 1.3.88, p. 59) and 1857/88 (OJ L 166, 1.7.88, p. 6) for Italy and France respectively and 1735/90 (OJ L 161, 27.6.90, p. 12) for the EC-wide QR.
8 Moreover, the preamble to Regulation 1735/90 claims that the restriction did curtail imports (OJ L 161, 27.6.90, p. 12).
9 Changes in EC exports are ignored.
10 The small positive spillover in TAI exports to other EC markets results from an element of complementarity in the CET supply module. At any given price ratio the CET implies a preferred mix of exports across markets. If sales to France increase, the marginal costs of sales to elsewhere fall relatively, slightly stimulating sales.
11 Of course Korea and Taiwan lose sales which might offset their gains in rent. Without modelling all their production and their factor markets it is impossible to be sure – see de Melo and Winters (1990a) for a discussion of this issue in the context of the US restrictions on footwear imports.
12 Differentiation by place of production gives the model great conservatism in the sourcing of imports. The existing low shares for ST in IT and ECS are built into the taste parameters and can be overcome only by huge changes in relative prices.

REFERENCES

Brenton, P.A. and L.A. Winters (1990) 'Non-tariff barriers and rationing: UK footwear imports', *Discussion Paper*, **365**, London: CEPR.
Brooke, A., D. Kendrick and A. Meeraus (1988) *GAMS: User Reference Manual*, San Francisco: Scientific Press.
CEPR (1990) *Monitoring European Integration: The Impact of Eastern Europe*, London: CEPR.
Commission of the European Communities (1988) 'The economics of 1992', *The European Economy*, **35** (March) Brussels: European Commission.
  (1989a) 'Investigation into the trend of imports into the Community of footwear from South Korea and Taiwan', External Relations Directorate-General, I-C-2, Brussels: European Commission.
  (1989b) *The Community Footwear Industry*, SEC (89) 1901, Brussels: European Commission.
  (1990a) 'Regulation 1735/90', *Official Journal*, L 161, 27/6/90, pp. 12–20, Brussels: European Commission.
  (1990b) 'The impact of the internal market by industrial sector: the challenge for Member States', *The European Economy-Social Europe Special Edition 1990 EC*, Brussels: European Commission.
De Melo, J. and L.A. Winters (1990a) 'Do exporters gain from VERs?', *Discussion Paper*, **383**, London: CEPR; *European Economic Review*, .
  (1990b) 'Voluntary export restraints and resource allocation in exporting countries', *World Bank Economic Review*, **4**, pp. 209–33.
GATT (1991) *Trade Policy Review: The European Communities: Vols I and II*, Geneva: GATT.

Hamilton, C.B. (1991) 'European Community external protection and 1992': voluntary export restraints applied to Pacific Asia, *European Economic Review*, **35**, pp. 377–87.

Hamilton, C.B.and L.A. Winters (1992) 'Opening up trade in Eastern Europe', *Economic Policy*, **14**, pp. 78–116.

Neary, J.P. and K.W.S. Roberts (1980) 'The theory of household behaviour under rationing', *European Economic Review*, **13**, pp. 25–42.

Smith, A. (1989) 'The market for cars in the enlarged European Community', *Discussion Paper*, **360**, London: CEPR.

Takacs, W.E. and L.A. Winters (1991) 'Labour adjustment costs and British footwear protection', *Oxford Ecnomic Papers*, **43**, pp. 479–501.

Winters, L.A. (1988) 'Completing the European Internal Market: some notes on trade policy', *European Economic Review*, **32**, pp. 1477–99.

　(1990) 'Import surveillance as a strategic trade policy', *Discussion Paper*, **404**, London: CEPR.

　(1992) 'The policy and welfare implications of the trade consequences of "1992"', *American Economic Review, Papers and Proceedings*, **82**, pp. 104–8.

Winters, L.A. and P.A. Brenton (1991) 'Quantifying the economic effects of non-tariff barriers: the case of UK footwear', *Kyklos*, **44**, pp. 71–92.

Discussion

KYM ANDERSON

This is a very neat extension of the author's earlier analyses of footwear trade policy. It is useful both for its own sake (because European footwear protection levels are high) and as a case-study of the complexities involved in analysing economic integration. Many of those complexities are evident in the chapter despite the fact that the study assumes, as is appropriate for this product group, that the footwear sector is small so that straightforward partial equilibrium analysis can be used. Complexities arise here in part because there are several types of footwear (3 are identified) whose importance in production and consumption differ across the 4 EC and 5 non-EC countries/country groups identified in the chapter. They arise also because in the European integration setting there are several different types of trade policy issues that affect footwear markets. This chapter focuses mainly on 3 policy events: the accession of Spain and Portugal to the EC, the reform of France and Italy's quantitative import restrictions as part of the EC '1992' programme, and the EC's association accords with East European countries. Given the possibilities for substitution in production and consumption even with just 3 product groups and 9 country groups, not only the magnitude but even the direction of many of the effects of these policy changes cannot be determined *a priori*. Hence the need for an empirical model.

Section 2 of the paper describes in some detail the model used in the present study. It is the simplest model possible that captures all the key features necessary for analysing the partial equilibrium effects on the EC of EC footwear trade policies. It does, however, have scope for being extended to measure also more of the effects of those policies on the rest of the world.

The model is calibrated to 1987, at which time about 85 per cent of EC-12 footwear consumption in value terms was supplied by EC producers and the remainder by 5 outside countries/country groups each with a 3 per cent market share, namely, Korea, Taiwan, Other developing countries, Eastern Europe, and Other industrial countries. For the latter 2 groups leather footwear dominates, for Korea it is textile shoes that are most important, while for the other 2 plastic shoes are also significant. Since protection rates differ between these footwear types, and between EC-9 and the three more recent southern EC members, it is not surprising that even the direction of effects of integration initiatives is not predictable without a quantitative model.

For example, which domestic groups benefit from the accession of Spain and Portugal to the EC? The results suggest that both producers and consumers in those two acceding countries gain. Consumers gain because the newly adopted EC-wide tariffs are lower than those in place in Spain and Portugal prior to their accession, particularly for leather products. And footwear producers in those 2 countries gain because, despite lower external protection, they now have duty-free access to the huge EC-9 market. Taxpayers lose a little from reduced tariff revenue but the overall gain to these 2 economies is estimated to exceed ECU 70 million per year. Consumers/taxpayers in EC-9 gain but by less than EC-9 producers lose, so their economies are slightly worse off by the trade diversion caused by Spain and Portugal's accession – as are footwear producers in the Rest of the World (ROW). As it happens, the loss to EC-9 is much less than the gain to the new entrants, however, so in this case EC-12 as a whole is better off. The welfare of the ROW's net exporters of footwear would have been reduced a little by the cutback in the EC-12's net imports, while other countries that are net importers would be better off.

Unfortunately the model in its present form does not measure the size of the welfare effects on non-EC country groups, so we don't know whether the EC's gain is more or less than offset by the changes in welfare in

ROW. This is an obvious area for further modelling work. But, even in its present form, the model is able to estimate the effects of EC policy changes on the EC's external trade volume and its import quota rents. That makes it possible in some cases to infer whether non-EC producers are gainers or losers from European integration. Together with information on the distributional effects within the EC the model is thus able to shed light on the net benefits of different policy changes to pertinent interest groups.

Consider, for example, the second set of experiments in this chapter, on the conversion of French and Italian national import quotas to EC-wide quotas. As can be seen by examining the differences between the results for EC-wide quotas and those for national quotas in Table 7.8(A), the only producer groups to lose are the French and Italian (by ECU 11 million p.a.), and their loss is only one-fifth the gain to French and Italian consumers. Even the Korean and Taiwanese producers would appear to be no worse off if the EC-wide quota rents were transferred to them by way of VERs: while their rent per pair would drop, to less than half, the rent would apply to their exports to all of the EC which is more than twice their exports to just France and Italy (Table 7.8(G) and (H)). Moreover, ROW's exporters are made better off insofar as their exports to the EC expand with the conversion from national to EC-wide quotas (by 1.7 million pairs p.a. – compare sections (B) and (C) of Table 7.7). Thus even though the EC consumer losses from this policy change far outweigh the gains to EC producers, the latter's greater lobbying strength, with the support of overseas producers, has evidently been enough to ensure its implementation. That is, not only does the conversion to EC-wide quotas shift some of the burden of protection from French and Italian consumers to other EC consumers, but it also appears to help ROW's exporters at the expense of the EC. One wonders to what extent this would be true also for other commodity groups where national import quotas and VERs operate and will soon be converted to EC-wide quotas.

The chapter's third set of experiments concern the effects of liberalising EC footwear imports from Eastern Europe. Many readers will consider these the most important results, not least because this policy change is rather more prospective than historical, but also because it will have the largest impact on the EC of all the policy changes considered in the chapter. Net social welfare in the EC could be enhanced by as much as ECU 120 million p.a. by this policy change (far more than the gain from eliminating quota restrictions on Korean and Taiwanese imports), and East European exports would increase by between 18 and 28 million pairs of leather shoes p.a., an increase of more than 50 per cent of their former trade. Here again it is unfortunate that the model does not provide changes in welfare for non-EC countries: while there is an increase in East Europe's export earnings of ECU 160 million, the benefit of that is more or less offset by a loss of up to nearly half that in quota rent.

These results are compared in Table 7.10 with the effects of complete liberalisation of EC-12 footwear trade with all partners. The comparison shows that Eastern Europe would gain almost as much from EC total liberalisation as from the EC removing barriers to Eastern Europe's exporters alone. That is, should the EC choose to liberalise generally rather than preferentially – as it might following the Uruguay Round, for example – Eastern Europe would be just as well off.

To repeat, this is a very useful study. Even though the magnitude of the welfare effects of EC policies affecting footwear are relatively small (those affecting textiles and clothing, or agriculture, involve welfare losses 20 or 100 times as large – see Trela and Whalley, 1990 or Anderson and Tyers, 1991), this industry provides a further case-study of the wastefulness of present EC trade policies and of the scope for (hopefully) reducing that waste through Europe's integration initiatives.

REFERENCES

Anderson, K. and R. Tyers (1991) *Global Effects of Liberalizing Trade in Farm Products*, London: Harvester Wheatsheaf for the Trade Policy Research Centre.
Trela, I. and J. Whalley (1990) 'Internal Quota Allocation Schemes and the Costs of the MFA', University of Western Ontario, September, mimeo.

8 The long-run value of inflexibility

LARRY S. KARP and JEFFREY M. PERLOFF

1 Introduction

With the 'completion of the market' in 1992, EC strategic trade policies and economic adjustment policies will have greater impact on world trade. Current thinking about the effects of these policies based on existing trade models, which ignore dynamic adjustments of oligopolistic firms, is misleading. Using a dynamic model, we show that by increasing the costs of adjustment of domestic firms, governments may, surprisingly, increase domestic welfare. That is, the government can help domestic firms by 'hurting' them – making them less flexible. Moreover, the desirability of government actions and the size of government transfers depends on the degree of non-linearity of government policies.

Suppose, for example, that duopolists located in different countries sell in a third country. The firms play a non-cooperative game in quantities. For simplicity, further suppose that the home government can subsidise or tax its domestic firm without fear of retaliation from the foreign government. In a static model, if the home government uses the optimal investment *subsidy*, the domestic firm sells the Stackelberg leader level of output and home profits and welfare increase. In contrast, we show that in both repeated static models and dynamic models, if adjustment costs are convex enough, the optimal strategic policy is a *tax* and not a subsidy.

Many beliefs about the likely outcome of greater unity in the EC may thus be wrong. Consider two examples.

First, many non-Europeans worry that greater political and economic integration will enable the EC to use more aggressively export and R&D subsidies for national champions. The desirability of such a subsidy, however, depends on whether it is *specific* (proportional to the units of investment) or *ad valorem* (proportional to the value of investment) and on the convexity of investment costs. In our model, the optimal specific policy is a *subsidy* whatever the shape of the investment cost function. The

213

optimal *ad valorem* policy, however, is a *tax* if costs are sufficiently convex.

Many, if not most, actual subsidy programmes are *ad valorem* rather than specific. For example, national and regional governments frequently pay for a fraction of the *cost* (not the number of units) of R&D or other investments. Similarly, they may subsidise the interest rate. As a result, strategic subsidies may backfire.

Second, some EC interest groups and the British government worry that centralisation of EC decision-making will reduce competitiveness of European industries. An example of this concern in 1991 was the dispute over the proposed 'Social Charter', a set of labour laws that determine matters as diverse as rights of pregnant women, the length of the working week, and notification rules for plant closures. Advocates of the Social Charter regard it as a necessary and humane step toward harmonising working conditions across Europe. The British government's position is that these laws inhibit flexibility and harm affected industries. Again, in contrast to the conventional wisdom, we show that policies that raise the cost of adjustment may be beneficial.

Based on our analysis, we predict that more flexible European countries might be at a strategic *disadvantage* after the '1992' integration. For example, suppose that financial liberalisation enables the UK and Germany to offer banking services in Spain. If the UK firms are more flexible in the sense that they can adjust their services at lower cost (due to fewer government regulations and less social legislation), these firms might be at a strategic disadvantage. The strategic advantage of the German firms is that a lack of flexibility provides them with a credible commitment not to shrink. In section 2, we give an informal explanation of our basic point and describe the relation between this chapter and the previous literature. We present the formal model and the statement of results in section 3. In section 4, we discuss our simulation results. In section 5, we provide an alternative interpretation for our result based on the multiple targets used by governments in a dynamic game. In section 6, we argue that actual European policies are similar to those that we model. We conclude in section 7 by arguing that governments are unlikely to use strategic trade policies successfully.

2   The main idea

If a government uses a tax to *raise* a domestic firm's cost of adjustment, the firm may benefit in its strategic interactions with rivals. That is, a government may help the firm by 'hurting it'. The reason for this apparently paradoxical result is that as the cost of adjustment rises for the domestic firm, it is increasingly credible that the firm will not reduce its output in response to output increases by its rival. As a result, the domestic firm's equilibrium output is closer to that of a Stackelberg leader.

To discuss and illustrate this idea as simply as possible, we use a dynamic version of the standard static strategic trade model. In discussing both the static and dynamic models, we maintain four assumptions:

- A home firm and a foreign firm sell only in a third market
- No new firms can enter
- The duopolists play a non-cooperative game in quantities (e.g. output or investment levels)
- The home government uses a strategic tax or subsidy without fear of retaliation from the foreign government.

These assumptions are similar to those used by Spencer and Brander (1983) and others who use static models to study specific policies. Specific policies are linear in the sense that the value of the transfer (subsidy or tax) is proportional to the level of the firm's choice of an input or output. Other commonly observed policies are non-linear in the sense that the value of the transfer is not linearly related to the firm's decision variable. An *ad valorem* tax or subsidy, in which the transfer is proportional to the value, rather than to the level, of the firm's output or an input, is the simplest type of non-linear policy.

Linear and non-linear policies that subsidise investment may have very different welfare effects. We provide examples where the optimal specific policy is a subsidy and the optimal *ad valorem* policy is a tax. Although the examples are for restrictive functional forms, the underlying intuition holds more generally.

2.1   Static models

To make the contrast between our results and the standard results clear, we first characterise the two major results of the earlier static literature. First, a government that does not fear retaliation can use an export subsidy to shift oligopoly rents from foreign to domestic producers, thereby increasing domestic welfare. In this simple story, the firms initially play a Nash–Cournot game. One government acts before either of the firms and uses a subsidy to commit its firm to a large (Stackelberg leader) output. The other firm then chooses the Stackelberg follower output level. Some people argue, based on this result, that the use of export subsidies has desirable strategic effects. Other nations similarly fear that further integration could result in an increase in EC strategic power.

Second, whether a tax or subsidy is optimal depends on the environment: the choice variable of firms (e.g. prices or quantities) and the timing of moves (e.g. whether the government sets its policy before or after firms make their decisions).[1] For example, the government's optimal policy is a *subsidy* for oligopolistic firms playing a Nash–Cournot game, whereas the optimal policy is a *tax* for competitive firms. Indeed, the major application of these static models has been to determine the conditions under which the optimal policy is a tax or a subsidy. Because the optimality of a subsidy is not robust to changes in the nature of the game, one widely held conclusion is that even nationalists should reject the use of export subsidies based on the results of the static theory of strategic trade policy.

2.2   Dynamics

We show that, where the optimal policy is a subsidy in a static model, a tax may be superior in a dynamic model. In the dynamic model, the firms' levels of capital determine their payoff within a given period. The government is able to tax or subsidise domestic investment. By assumption, adjustment costs are convex, so that adjustment to the steady state does not occur instantaneously, implying that the dynamics are non-trivial.[2]

In the dynamic model, the optimal linear policy involves a subsidy to the domestic firm. For a given level of domestic investment, a linear policy affects the *level* of domestic adjustment costs. The explanation for the optimality of a subsidy is the same as for static models. By assumption firms' choice variables are 'strategic substitutes' (Bulow *et al.*, 1985). A subsidy induces the domestic firm to invest more, which discourages investment by the rival, thereby aiding the domestic firm.

A non-linear policy, such as an *ad valorem* tax or subsidy, has more complicated strategic effects. A non-linear policy affects both the *level* and the *curvature* (convexity) of adjustment or investment costs. The linear component of the policy – the part proportional to the change in investment – affects the level of costs. If the linear component is dominant, a subsidy is optimal. The non-linear component changes the curvature of adjustment costs. If the non-linear component is more important, a tax that raises the rate at which adjustment costs increase with further investment is optimal.

The desirable effect of such a tax is to decrease the flexibility of the domestic firm, which reduces the incentive of foreign firms to invest pre-emptively. In a dynamic investment game, firms have an incentive to invest in the current period partly to discourage future investments by their rivals. The incentive for pre-emptive investment is negatively related to the degree of flexibility of its rival. For example, if the rival's future investment level is fixed, there is no pre-emptive incentive. A policy that increases the curvature of domestic adjustment costs decreases the flexibility of the domestic firm and therefore decreases the incentive the rival has for pre-emptive investment. Thus, surprisingly, the decrease in flexibility from a non-linear adjustment tax is beneficial.

Against this benefit must be weighed the disadvantage of a higher level of costs from the tax (the linear component), which directly discourage domestic investment. Whether a tax or subsidy is optimal turns on the extent to which the policy affects the curvature relative to the level of domestic adjustment costs. An example makes this distinction precise.

3   The model

If a government uses a tax to *raise* a domestic firm's cost of adjustment, the firm may benefit in its strategic interactions with rivals. To present this idea as simply as possible, we use a dynamic version of a standard static strategic trade model. We maintain the same four assumptions as above except that, now, the dupolists play a non-cooperative *dynamic* game and the firms choose levels of investment rather than exports directly. For specificity, we assume that increasing capital lowers a firm's marginal cost, so that the firm increases its exports.

In period t, firm i ($= h$, for home, and f, for foreign) invests I_t^i so that its new capital stock in that period is $k_t^i = k_{t-1}^i + I_t^i$. For simplicity, there is no depreciation. In each period t, firm i's reduced-form profit function is $\pi^i(\mathbf{k}_t)$, where $\mathbf{k}_t = (k_t^h, k_t^f)$ is the vector of capital stocks. The use of a reduced-form profit function focuses the model on the dynamic investment decision.[3]

We assume that π^i is concave in k_t^i, and

$$\frac{\partial^2 \pi^i}{\partial k_t^i \partial k_t^j} < 0,$$

for $i \neq j$.[4] Given this inequality, k^i and k^j are strategic substitutes. In a static setting, it is optimal to subsidise domestic capital whether the government uses a specific or an *ad valorem* policy if this assumption holds.

3.1   Adjustment costs

In the absence of government intervention, firm i has a convex adjustment or investment cost of $v^i = v(I_t^i)$. Because of this convexity, adjustment to the steady state does not occur in a single period. Adjustment costs are 0 when there is no adjustment, $v(0) = 0$. Government actions

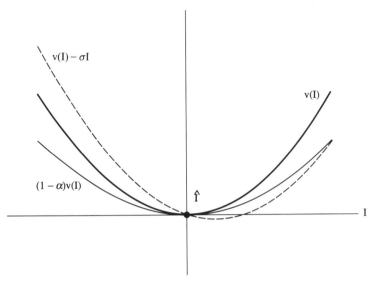

Figure 8.1   Adjustment costs (γ, a and σ positive)

may affect the firms' adjustment (i.e. investment) costs. Because the foreign government does not intervene, the foreign firm's adjustment costs are $v^f \equiv v(I_t^f)$.

The home government intervenes with an *ad valorem* subsidy (or tax), a, or a specific subsidy (or tax), σ. The government selects only the level of the given policy. We want to show that whether it is optimal to tax or subsidise depends on the type of policy used. Later we briefly consider which of the two policies results in a higher level of domestic welfare.

At the beginning of the game, the home government observes the initial level of capital, $\mathbf{k}_0$ and chooses a constant policy level, σ or a. If the home government uses a specific subsidy, $\sigma > 0$, the home firm's after-subsidy adjustment cost is $v^h = v(I^h) - \sigma I^h$. Note that if $\sigma > 0$ the government subsidises the home firm when it is growing ($I^h > 0$), and taxes it when it is shrinking. If the home government uses an *ad valorem* subsidy, $a > 0$, the home firm's adjustment cost is $v^h = (1 - a)v(I^h)$. If $a < 0$, it is a tax.

Whether the optimal level of a is positive or negative depends on the relative effects of the policy on the level and the curvature of adjustment costs. We can make this distinction precise using the following quadratic adjustment cost function:

$$v = \left(\gamma + \frac{\delta I}{2}\right)I \tag{1}$$

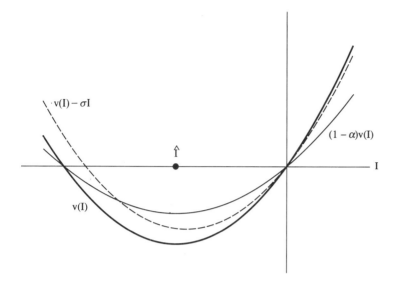

Figure 8.2   Adjustment costs ($\gamma = 0$, a and σ positive)

In Figure 8.1, we plot after-subsidy costs for three cases: (1) no subsidy; (2) a specific subsidy, $\sigma > 0$; and (3) an *ad valorem* subsidy, $a > 0$. Figure 8.2 is the same as Figure 8.1, except that $\gamma = 0$, so the cost function is symmetric around 0. If, in the absence of government intervention, adjustment costs are nearly symmetric around 0, Figure 8.2 is relevant, but if it is cheaper to shrink than to grow, Figure 8.1 is relevant.

Adjustment costs, $v(I)$, are minimised at $\hat{I}$. If k is a purchased input and there is free disposal, $v(I)$ is monotonic and $\hat{I} = -\infty$. If, on the other hand, k is a rented input, and the rental cost is included in the function π^i, $\hat{I} = 0$, as in Figure 8.2 For example, if k is human capital, there are positive adjustment costs involved in either increasing or decreasing the stock.

3.2   The equilibrium

We consider a Nash Markov Perfect Equilibrium.[5] In this equilibrium, each firm's strategy is a decision rule that gives current net investment, I_t^i, as a function of the state at t, $\mathbf{k}_{t-1}$. This function is firm i's best response to firm j's decision rule for all possible values of $\mathbf{k}_t$ and hence is perfect.

Firm i's objective is to maximise the present discounted value of its profits net of investment costs,

$$J^i(\mathbf{k}_{t-1}, t) = \sum_{s=t}^{T} \beta^{s-t} [\pi^i(\mathbf{k}_s) - v_s^i]$$

The endogenous function J^i gives the equilibrium payoff to agent i in the game. The solution to firm i's control problem is $\tilde{I}^i(\mathbf{k}_{t-1}, t)$, so $k^i_t = k^i_{t-1} + \tilde{I}^i(\mathbf{k}_{t-1}, t)$.[6] Due to the Markov assumption, the functions J^i and $\tilde{I}^i$ depend on $\mathbf{k}_{t-1}$, but not on the history of the game. The payoff functions and the decision rules depend on the government's policy, σ or a. We do not show this dependence where the meaning is clear.

At the beginning of the game, time 0, the government chooses a constant policy level to maximise domestic profits net of any transfer. At an arbitrary time t, given the state $\mathbf{k}_{t-1}$, the present discounted value of the government's payoff is

$$J^g(\mathbf{k}_{t-1}, t) \equiv \sum_{s=t}^{\tau} \beta^{s-t} [\pi^h(\mathbf{k}_s) - v(\tilde{I}^h(\mathbf{k}_{s-1}, s))]$$

where $\mathbf{k}_s$ is determined by the initial condition $\mathbf{k}_o$ and the firms' equilibrium decision rules, which depend on the government's choice of a or σ.

In the steady state, net investment, I, is zero. Because $v(0) = 0$, with either policy, the government transfer $[\sigma I$ or $av(I)]$ is 0 and the home firm's subsidy-inclusive adjustment cost is 0. Nonetheless, the policy affects the steady state because it affects the agents' behaviour outside the steady state. That is, the policy alters a firm's rational beliefs about what its rival's response would be if it were to move away from the steady state. A change in the level of the home government's policy alters these beliefs and hence the steady state.

A mechanical explanation is that the vector of equilibrium decision rules, $\tilde{\mathbf{I}}$, is a function of the government's policy variable, and therefore this variable affects the steady state, which is the solution to $\tilde{\mathbf{I}}(\mathbf{k}, \sigma) = \mathbf{0}$ or $\tilde{\mathbf{I}}(\mathbf{k}, a) = \mathbf{0}$. A government policy can thus be effective even if there is no transfer in equilibrium.

The specific tax, σ, affects the level of marginal adjustment costs. The *ad valorem* tax, a, affects both the level and slope of marginal adjustment costs. The relative magnitude of δ/γ provides a measure of the extent to which a alters both the curvature and the level or only the level of the firm's adjustment cost. If $\delta/\gamma \approx 0$, the effect of a on the curvature of costs relative to its effect on the level is negligible for any level of investment. Here, the optimal value of a is positive (a subsidy). However, when δ/γ is large, a has a non-negligible effect on the curvature of adjustment costs, and the optimal value is negative (a tax). In all our simulations, the optimal σ is a subsidy.

An increase in a specific subsidy ($\sigma > 0$) reduces the home firm's adjustment cost of becoming larger, but increases its cost of becoming smaller ($\sigma I < 0$ when $\sigma > 0$ and $I < 0$). The reduced cost of growth provides the home firm with an incentive to become large, while the increased cost of shrinking induces it to remain large. Capital is a strategic substitute in this model, so the foreign firm responds to this more aggressive behaviour by investing less. The home country welfare is increasing in k^h because marginal costs fall due to higher levels of capital. With a specific subsidy, the results from a dynamic model are the same as in a standard static model. A subsidy provides a way of establishing a credible domestic commitment to behave aggressively.

In contrast, the *ad valorem* policy changes the convexity of costs to the firm, which affects the incentive of the foreign firm to invest preemptively. Given the quadratic cost function in (1), if the government uses an *ad valorem* policy, the home firm's adjustment costs are: $v^h(I) = (1 - a) v(I) = (1 - a)(\gamma + \frac{1}{2}\delta I) I$. The *ad valorem* policy can be decomposed into a linear part, $- \gamma I$, and a non-linear part, $- \frac{1}{2}a\delta I^2$. When there is little convexity ($\delta \approx 0$), the *ad valorem* policy has essentially the same effect as a specific policy. If $\delta = 0$, the *ad valorem* and specific policy are equivalent. The direct effect of a subsidy on domestic investment causes the firm to grow large and is welfare improving.

Why might domestic welfare – and even the home firm's tax-inclusive profits – increase when an adjustment tax is used? Consider the limiting case where $\gamma = 0$ and hence $\hat{I} = 0$, so that an *ad valorem* tax raises adjustment costs for all levels (positive and negative) of investment. In a perfect Markov equilibrium, firm i knows that its rival will respond in future periods to an increase in k_t^i. When the firms' decision variables are strategic substitutes, firm j's equilibrium investment is a decreasing function of k^i. Firm i thus has a pre-emptive incentive to invest. The extent to which it is rational for firm j to respond depends on firm j's adjustment costs. If those costs are large (e.g. due to a social charter that inhibits flexibility or an adjustment or investment tax), firm i's pre-emptive incentive is diminished. Higher firm j's costs reduce firm i's equilibrium level of investment, which aids both firm and country j.[7]

It is thus credible that a domestic firm will remain large when a tax raises its convex adjustment costs. These same factors, however, make it costly to grow. One might therefore conclude that high adjustment costs increase domestic welfare if the home firm is initially large (so that it need credibly commit only not to shrink) and decrease welfare if the home firm is initially small.

3.3 How important is the initial condition?

To check this conjecture, we examined a repeated 1-period version of the game described above. We now summarise these results from Karp and Perloff (1991).

At the beginning of each period, all agents take the lagged value of **k** as given. First the government chooses the tax or subsidy, and then the firms choose their levels of investment. The lagged level of capital plus new investment equals the current level of capital, which is the initial condition for the next period. All agents maximise their payoffs in the current period, ignoring the future. Adjustment costs are quadratic and current profits are quadratic in **k**. Karp and Perloff (1991) gives the closed-form relationship between the equilibrium of this game and the initial condition $\mathbf{k}_{t-1}$.

If the initial value of **k** is close to the origin (so that the domestic firm is small), the government's optimal adjustment policy is a subsidy ($a > 0$), which encourages the home firm to expand. If the initial value of **k** is such that π^h is close to 0 (so that the combined home and foreign firms are large) it is optimal to tax domestic adjustment. This tax encourages the home firm to remain large. In either of these cases, the equilibrium level of $\mathbf{k}_t$ is the same as if the home firm were a Stackelberg leader, so the adjustment policy leads to a constrained first best. However, there is an intermediate range of $\mathbf{k}_{t-1}$ for which the adjustment policy cannot be used to reach the Stackelberg equilibrium. In this range, it is optimal to set $a = -\infty$ to prevent the domestic firm from becoming smaller.

Thus, in this repeated 1-period game, whether the optimal adjustment policy is a tax or subsidy depends on the initial condition (the lagged value of **k** in the 1-period model). The optimal linear policy, σ, on the other hand, is a subsidy for all initial conditions, and always leads to the Stackelberg equilibrium. In this sense the linear policy is more powerful; however, it requires a larger transfer from the government, and may be unattractive for that reason.

In contrast, as shown in section 4, in an infinite horizon dynamic model, the initial condition, $\mathbf{k}_0^h$, is relatively unimportant. For realistic discount rates, the present value of welfare depends on the steady state. As discussed above, increased adjustment costs decrease the pre-emptive incentive of the foreign firm, which shifts the steady state in a direction favourable to the home firm. In the steady state, actual adjustment costs are 0. Consequently, the home firm tends to benefit in the steady state from larger adjustment costs. The transitional effects of higher adjustment costs tend to harm the home firm. However, by moving very slowly toward the steady state, the adjustment costs can be kept small; and, if the discount rate is low (β is close to 1), these costs are more than offset by higher steady-state profits.

Thus, the welfare effects of an *ad valorem* adjustment tax, when the convexity of adjustment costs are important, are ambiguous. Using simulations, we illustrate the counter-intuitive result that *ad valorem* taxes may raise welfare in this game whatever the initial condition.

Table 8.1. *Optimal specific and* ad valorem *policies*

$\gamma = 0.2, \beta = 0.95, \mathbf{k}_0$

δ	a	σ
0.0001	1.99	4.2
0.1	0.95	4.0
0.2	− 0.08	4.0
0.5	− 1.7	3.6
1.0	− 1.7	3.4
2.0	− 1.5	3.2
3.0	− 1.4	3.0

4 Simulations

In our simulations, the cost of adjustment is quadratic ((1) above). Output is a linear function of capital, demand is linear, and production costs (net of adjustment) are linear. By appropriate choice of units we can write the price minus production cost, c, as

$$p_t - c = 1 - k^h - k^f \tag{2}$$

so the profit function, π, is quadratic:

$$\pi_t^i = (1 - k_t^i - k_t^j)k_t^i \tag{3}$$

We obtain the Nash Markov Perfect Equilibrium in a dynamic game using dynamic programming. The time horizon, T, is sufficiently large that the first-period decision rules and the value functions are insensitive to changes in T. We use these (approximately) stationary investment rules to determine the dynamics and the steady state. Similarly, the first-period value functions are approximations to the value functions of the infinite horizon problem. In this setting, the government commits to an adjustment policy at the initial time that remains fixed thereafter.

Simulations show that the optimal adjustment policy, a, is insensitive to the initial condition, $\mathbf{k}_0$. However, low initial levels of $\mathbf{k}_0$ encourage the use of somewhat smaller taxes (or larger subsidies), for the reasons described in section 3. Our reported simulations are for $\mathbf{k}_0 = \mathbf{0}$, where a subsidy is optimal for the static model.

The optimal *ad valorem* and unit taxes when γ (the linear part of adjustment costs) = 0.2, β (the discount factor) = 0.95, and $\mathbf{k}_0 = \mathbf{0}$ are shown in Table 8.1.

In these simulations, the optimal linear policy, σ, is always a subsidy, as in static models. Further, the optimal σ varies little with δ. For a given γ, δ measures the degree of convexity.

The optimal *ad valorem* policy, a, may be a tax or a subsidy and is much more sensitive to δ. If the degree of convexity is sufficiently small, the *ad valorem* policy is essentially a linear policy, so the optimal a is a subsidy. However, when costs are relatively convex ($\delta \geq 0.2$), the optimal *ad valorem* policy is a tax.

An *ad valorem* tax increases the home firm's tax-inclusive profits (as well as domestic welfare) when δ/γ is large. That is, the value to a firm of commitment from increased adjustment costs can offset the direct costs of the tax. Of course, an *ad valorem* tax that maximises the home firm's after-tax profits is smaller than the level that maximises social welfare.

The foreign firm suffers when the home government chooses an optimal *ad valorem* tax. The tax shifts the steady state in favour of the home firm and against the foreign firm. This result stands in sharp contrast to models in which the domestic industry behaves as a price-taker, either because it is perfectly competitive or because it plays a Bertrand game. Where firms are price-takers, it is optimal to use an export tax to force the domestic industry to restrict output and raise price. The tax unambiguously benefits rival exporters, who find their competition diminished.

The optimal (linear) unit subsidy results in a higher level of home welfare than the optimal *ad valorem* policy for the same parameter values. The reason for this difference is that the unit subsidy encourages the home firm to grow ($\sigma I > 0$ when $I > 0$), and discourages it from shrinking, thus discouraging the rival's investment. The *ad valorem* tax, on the other hand, is successful in discouraging pre-emptive investment by the rival, but does so by also making home investment more costly.[8]

Despite this advantage over the *ad valorem* tax, the unit subsidy may be inferior because it requires a larger transfer. This transfer may be costly for political reasons, or simply because there is a deadweight cost of raising government revenue.

In our simulations, the optimal unit subsidy results in a higher level of home welfare, but a much higher transfer, relative to the optimal *ad valorem* policy. Home welfare is 10 per cent greater under the optimal specific than the optimal *ad valorem* policy if $\delta = 0.1$, 7 per cent if $\delta = 1$, and 5 per cent if $\delta = 3$.

However, the transfers as a percentage of welfare are greater under the specific policy than under the *ad valorem* policy, as shown in Table 8.2. If $\delta = 0.1$, the optimal unit transfers are 85 per cent of domestic welfare, but only 3 per cent for the optimal *ad valorem* subsidy. For larger δ values, the optimal specific subsidy requires a large transfer from taxpayers to firms, whereas, under the optimal *ad valorem* tax, firms are taxed.

Table 8.2. *Present value of transfers from taxpayers to the home firm as % of domestic welfare*

	δ		
	0.1	1	3
Specific	85	75	68
Ad valorem	3	−7	−8

The specific policy thus gives the government more leverage, relative to the *ad valorem* policy, but it requires a much greater transfer. If transfers are costly or the government cares about the direction of the transfer the government may prefer the *ad valorem* policy.

5   Multiple targets

We now give an alternative explanation for our results based on the multiple targets of a government. This interpretation is useful in explaining why our results differ from those of Neary (1991) and thereby highlighting the importance of dynamics.

Using a static model in which firms choose prices, Neary compares the effects of specific and *ad valorem* taxes. Neary shows that the specific policy shifts the best-response function of only the domestic firm, whereas the *ad valorem* policy shifts the best-response functions of both firms, so it might appear that the two policies are not equivalent. However, in his model, the optimal specific and *ad valorem* policies are taxes on the domestic firm (because firms play a Bertrand game), and both policies lead to the same equilibrium level of sales.

Neary's results are different because he uses a static model in which the government has a single target. That target is to alter the domestic decision variable in order to induce a change in the foreign decision. The government moves the equilibrium from the non-cooperative Nash to the Stackelberg equilibrium with the home firm as leader. The government can use either instrument to reach this target. If, when the government used different instruments it reached different equilibria, the government could benefit from using both instruments. However, because either instrument alone is capable of achieving the constrained first best (the Stackelberg leader outcome) there is no gain to using both.

In our investment game with non-trivial dynamics, the government wants to achieve multiple targets – one for each period – using only one instrument, the tax or subsidy. Over time, the effect of a policy on firms' incentives – and thus on the government's target – varies due to previous investment.

Static models are not capable of capturing these reasons for the existence of multiple targets and thus miss an important explanation for the different effects of linear and non-linear policies. In our dynamic model, specific and *ad valorem* policies have different effects because of the multiplicity of government targets.

6   Industrial policies

Most developed countries use adjustment and non-linear industrial policies. Examples include adjustment assistance for declining industries, investment assistance for exports and for targeted expanding industries, and export marketing assistance.[9] Governments typically use these policies to help declining or rapidly growing (infant) firms or industries. We believe that all of these policies are more accurately modelled as *ad valorem* than as specific subsidies.

6.1   Adjustment assistance

Many OECD countries provide trade adjustment assistance and other aid to workers and firms in declining industries, such as textile and shipbuilding (Frank, 1977; Magaziner and Reich, 1982; Carliner, 1986). Moreover, all major developed countries provide aid that is independent of the cause of the industrial dislocation, such as general unemployment assistance programme and aid to distressed regions.

A (West) German programme designed specifically for trade adjustment assistance provided government guarantees and direct credits at reduced rates to small and medium-sized firms adversely affected by foreign competition. Its objective was to help the firms shift production into more competitive lines. Most of (West) Germany's economic adjustment programmes, however, were not trade-related and primarily provided incentives for industrial rationalisation and regional development by encouraging expanding firms to locate new plants in regions where declines in traditional industry were anticipated.

The British Industrial Reorganisation Corporation (1966–71) provided merger advice, counselling, and financial assistance for industries adversely affected by rising imports and other causes of dislocation. Most British assistance to declining industries and regions provides income maintenance and is not explicitly trade-related. Textiles, shipbuilding, and other declining industries have received substantial help through regional action or general labour market policies, such as the 1972 Industry Bill.[10] The 1965 Redundancy Payments Act allows firms to obtain partial reimbursement of severance pay. Such claims constitute about 70 per cent of the total costs of private firms' severance benefits.

Nearly all developed countries, except the United States, have programmes for warning workers of impending job terminations. Such policies raise the costs of adjustment by delaying plant closures. The current debate between Britain and other EC members over the Social Charter concerns similar labour policies: employment rights of pregnant women, the maximum working week, and plant closure laws. The British government opposes these laws because it believes that they harm industry by making firms less flexible.

6.2   Direct subsidies

Most developed countries provide investment assistance specifically to aid exports and R&D. In 1980, the annual level of interest rate subsidisation provided by the OECD nations through their official export credit programmes was about $4.0–$5.5 billion (Hufbauer and Erb, 1984). This support is often available only to the largest innovating firms in rapidly growing industries, such as electronics (e.g. Yamamura, 1986 on Japan).

Industrial policy proponents (e.g. Borrus, Tyson and Zysman, 1986) contend that Japan became a technological leader due to government support for emerging export industries, using low-interest loans, protection from imports, and R&D subsidies.[11] Similar claims are made about France, which has supported developing high-tech industries, including civilian aircraft, biotechnology, computers, machine tools, nuclear energy, semiconductors, and telecommunications equipment (Carliner, 1986). In some cases, several European governments coordinated support, such as for Concorde and Airbus.

7   Conclusions

Governments provide adjustment subsidies or taxes through industrial or investment programmes, as well as through less important marketing assistance programmes. Because these policies are non-linear, the conclusions from the standard static model are likely to be incorrect.

Our main result is that, even in simple dynamic models where oligopolistic firms face adjustment costs, raising adjustment costs – making firms less flexible – may benefit both those firms and the nation as a whole. That is, the widespread fears among politicians and firms that higher adjustment costs may put a firm at a strategic disadvantage may be false.

Policies that decrease an industry's flexibility, such as the proposed EC Social Charter, may have beneficial strategic effects.

For two reasons, however, we do not argue that the EC or any government should engage in adjustment policies or strategic trade policies. First, beggar thy neighbour policies are obviously unattractive and welfare-lowering from a world perspective. Second, even from a nationalistic perspective, such policies are difficult to apply successfully in the real world. In our simple model, all parties, including the home government, had full information and the home government did not fear retaliation by other governments. In the real world, where these conditions do not hold, the outcome of strategic policies is very difficult to predict.

It is well known that, even in static models, the sign of an optimal policy is sensitive to the order of moves or to nature of the game between firms and other factors that policy-makers are unlikely to know. We have shown that the sign of an optimal policy can also be sensitive to the degree of non-linearity of adjustment costs and the type of policy used. For example, the sign depends on whether the policy affects the level of marginal costs (as with a specific tax) or both the level and slope of marginal costs (as with an *ad valorem* tax).

Thus, a government intent on using these policies to achieve strategic advantage may find them counter-productive. The informational requirements for the successful strategic use of these policies is too great for them to be an attractive policy option, even in the absence of retaliation by competing countries. This view is widespread among economists but not among policy-makers and the public.

That non-linear policies have complex strategic effects also has an important implication for trade negotiations. Current negotiations use measures of government intervention, such as the Producer Subsidy Equivalents (PSE) or Aggregate Measures of Support (AMS). It is well known that these measures are imperfect. They suffer from the usual problems encountered when trying to summarise a complicated set of policies by means of a single statistic. However, most economists probably agree that both a PSE and an AMS at least 'get the sign right', in the sense that a reduction in either measure would benefit (or at least not harm) competing producers. Our simulation results illustrate that this belief may be wrong. A domestic adjustment tax can increase domestic welfare (and domestic profits) and decrease the rival's profits. Thus, a reduction in a PSE or AMS can harm a rival. Similarly, a policy may have no effect on the PSE or AMS, as is the case with an investment policy in the steady state, but still benefit a domestic firm and harm the foreign rival. Finally, a change from one type of policy to another may have a dramatic effect on the magnitude of the transfer (and thus on the PSE or AMS), but have a rather small effect on the amount of rent-shifting.

NOTES

We benefited from comments by Richard Baldwin, Harry Flam, Stanley Reynolds, and Alan Winters on an earlier draft. The usual disclaimer applies. Larry Karp thanks the CEPR for research funding.

1 Dixit (1984), Eaton and Grossman (1986), Gruenspecht (1988), Markusen and Venables (1988), Neary (1991), and others show that static strategic trade models are sensitive to the choice variable used by firms, the number of firms, barriers to entry, the exogeneity of costs, whether the firms or the government act first, and whether the foreign government intervenes. By analogy to their results, our simplifying assumptions are favourable to government intervention.

2 Models of adjustment costs have been widely used in theoretical work, and the practical importance of considering such costs is illustrated in a number of empirical studies including Pindyck and Rotemberg (1983) and Epstein and Denny (1983).

3 It is not necessary to specify whether firms choose quantities of exports or prices. In either case, their equilibrium decisions, and therefore their equilibrium flow of profits in a period, are a function of the current capital stocks. An alternative interpretation to our assumption that capital lowers marginal cost is that k determines capacity and firms always export at capacity.

4 Hereafter, time subscripts are suppressed when there is no danger of ambiguity.

5 Markov decision rules, which can be obtained by dynamic programming arguments, represent the natural extension of the standard 2-period model to many periods. They can thus be used to examine how the introduction of dynamics *alone* affects standard results. Alternatively, one might examine non-Markov sub-game perfect equilibria, which are dynamic and have more complex strategies. Welfare comparisons are not practical in such models, however, because there is a multiplicity of such equilibria supported by punishment strategies.

6 In solving the problem, we use a finite horizon that is sufficiently large to obtain a good approximation of an infinite horizon game. If the horizon is infinite, J^i and $\tilde{I}^i$ are stationary (independent of t).

7 Our intuition is based, in large part, on Reynolds' (1987, 1991) analysis of a symmetric linear–quadratic differential game with n identical firms and no government. Reynolds (1987) shows that as $\delta \to 0$ the steady state does not approach the static equilibrium. This surprising result is due to the pre-emptive incentive that exists in the dynamic game (but not in the static game). This incentive remains powerful even as adjustment costs become small. Reynolds (1991) also shows that as $\delta \to \infty$, the steady state of the dynamic game approaches the static equilibrium. The pre-emptive incentive vanishes as adjustment becomes very costly. In other words, the static equilibrium is likely to be close to the dynamic steady state precisely in those circumstances where dynamics are important (adjustment is slow).

8 We thank Harry Flam for this explanation for the reason why the optimal unit policy is more powerful than the optimal *ad valorem* policy.

9 In addition, most of the developed countries encourage exports by providing low-cost financing and insurance against political and commercial risks for overseas marketing (Magaziner and Reich, 1982). They also conduct market research, sponsor overseas trade shows, and provide exporters with the names of prospective foreign buyers, thereby lowering firms' transaction costs of finding new customers.

10 From 1959 to 1966, to encourage elimination of obsolete equipment in the textile industry, two-thirds of the costs in textiles were borne by the government. During the same period, the government paid one-quarter of the costs of re-equipping the industry.

11 See, however, Krugman (1984) for empirical evidence on the effects of targeted industrial policies of other countries on the United States and world markets.

REFERENCES

Borrus, Michael, Laura D'Andrea Tyson, and John Zysman (1986) 'Creating advantage: how government policies shape international trade in the semi-conductor industry', in Paul R. Krugman (ed.), *Strategic Trade Policy and the New International Economics*, Cambridge, MA: MIT Press.

Brander, James A. and Barbara J. Spencer (1985) 'Export subsidies and international market share rivalry', *The Journal of International Economics*, **18** (February) pp. 83–100.

Bulow, J.I., J.D. Geanakoplos and P.D. Klemperer (1985) 'Multimarket oligopoly: strategic substitutes and complements', *Journal of Political Economy*, **93**, pp. 488–511.

Carliner, Geoffrey (1986) 'Industrial policies for emerging industries', in Paul R. Krugman (ed.), *Strategic Trade Policy and the New International Economics*, Cambridge, MA: MIT Press.

Dixit, Avinash K. (1984) 'International trade policies for oligopolistic industries', *Economic Journal*, **94** (December) (Supplement), pp. 1–16.

Eaton, Jonathan and Gene M. Grossman (1986) 'Optimal trade and industrial policy under oligopoly', *Quarterly Journal of Economics*, **101** (May) pp. 383–406.

Epstein, Larry G. and Michael G.S. Denny (1983) 'The multivariate flexible accelerator model: its empirical restrictions and an application to US manufacturing', *Econometrica*, **51** (May) pp. 647–74.

Frank, Charles R., Jr (1977) *Foreign Trade and Domestic Aid*, Washington, D.C.: Brookings Institution.

Gruenspecht, H.K. (1988) 'Export subsidies for differentiated products', *Journal of International Economics* **24** (May) pp. 331–44.

Hufbauer, Gary Clyde, and Joanna Shelton Erb (1984) *Subsidies in International Trade*, Washington, D.C.: Institute for International Economics.

Karp, Larry S. and Jeffrey M. Perloff (1991) 'Helping by Hurting: Industrial Policy as an Alternative to Trade Policy', University of California, Berkeley, Giannini Foundation Working Paper.

Krugman, Paul R. (1984) 'The U.S. Response to Industrial Targeting', *Brookings Papers on Economic Activity*, **1**, pp. 77–121.

Magaziner, Ira and Robert Reich (1982) *Minding America's Business: The Decline and Rise of the American Economy*, New York: Harcourt Brace Jovanovich.

Markusen, J.R. and A.J. Venables (1988) 'Trade policy with increasing returns and imperfect competition: contradictory results from competing assumptions', *Journal of International Economics*, **24**, pp. 299–316.
Neary, J. Peter (1991) 'Export subsidies and price competition', in E. Helpman and A. Razin (eds), *International Trade and Industrial Policy*, Cambridge MA: MIT Press.
Pindyck, Robert S. and Julio J. Rotemberg (1983) 'Dynamic factor demands and the effects of energy price shocks', *American Economic Review*, **73** (December) pp. 1066–79.
Reynolds, Stanley S. (1987) 'Capacity preemption and commitment in an infinite horizon model', *International Economic Review*, **28** (February) pp. 69–88.
 (1991) 'Dynamic oligopoly with capacity adjustment costs', *Journal of Economic Dynamics and Control*, **15**, pp. 491–514.
Richardson, J. David (1974) 'Trade adjustment assistance under the United States Trade Act of 1974: an analytical examination and worker survey', in J. Bhagwati (ed.), *Import Competition and Response*, Chicago: University of Chicago Press.
Spencer, Barbara J. and James A. Brander (1983) 'International R & D rivalry and industrial strategy', *Review of Economic Studies*, **50** (October) pp. 707–22.
Yamamura, Kozo (1986) 'Caveat Emptor: The Industrial Policy of Japan', in Paul R. Krugman (ed.), *Strategic Trade Policy and the New International Economics*, Cambridge, MA: MIT Press.

Discussion

HARRY FLAM

Larry Karp and Jeff Perloff's Chapter 8 should not be seen as a new case for strategic trade or industrial policy but as additional theoretical evidence that the basis of such policies is fragile – as the authors themselves stress. Brander and Spencer (1985) showed that a subsidy that lowers marginal costs raises profits and welfare of the national champion when two firms play Cournot–Nash in a third market in a one-shot game. We now know that this outcome depends on the assumptions about market conduct, entry barriers, the order in which the government and the firm act, foreign government action, and the exogeneity of costs. Chapter 8 demonstrates that a non-linear tax on negative investment can improve welfare in the Brander–Spencer basic framework even when quantity is the strategic variable and even if the tax applies to positive investment as well.

In Karp and Perloff's model firms do not decide on quantity directly, but on the capital stock (capacity). Output is a positive, linear function of the capital stock, and production cost is a negative function. The cost of investment and disinvestment is assumed to be a convex function. It may therefore be optimal not to carry out a change in the capital stock in one period, but to spread the change over several periods. Firms maximise profits by deciding on the quantity of investment or disinvestment, taking as given the rival's past-period capital stock, which is assumed to be the only payoff relevant condition given by history. These Markov strategies give rise to a Nash Markov perfect equilibrium, i.e. a closed-loop Nash equilibrium is reached from an initial state.

The capital stocks of the two firms are strategic substitutes, i.e. an increase of the capital stock of one firm leads to a decrease of the capital stock of the other. A government can exploit this fact in two ways. It can subsidise investment to make its firm act more aggressively, thereby helping it to capture a greater share of the market and of profits. It can also tax negative investment to make its firm act less defensively, thereby preventing the rival firm from acting as aggressively. No transfers in the form of subsidies or taxes will take place in equilibrium, but the mere fact that such policies exist makes the policy equilibrium different from the no-policy equilibrium, and raises profits and welfare for the active country.

A symmetric tax on changes of the capital stock such as an *ad valorem* tax makes it costly to be aggressive as well as defensive. The main – and interesting – point of the chapter is that the defensive effect can be stronger than the negative offensive effect, so that a tax becomes the optimal policy and not a subsidy. This actually constitutes the proof of a theorem by Leon Trotsky, organiser of the Red Army. He proposed that it should be twice as costly in expectational terms to retreat as to advance, presumably because he realised that this would enhance his soldiers' fighting spirit and diminish that of the enemy. Trotsky's equivalent of the disinvestment tax was a bullet from a political officer. The greater the convexity of the adjustment cost in Karp and Perloff's model, the more likely is the optimality of the *ad valorem* tax. (Trotsky's cost function was obviously quite convex.) Initial conditions have (almost) no effect when the number of periods is made very large, as in the simulations.

Another point that the chapter makes is that the optimal linear policy, such as a specific subsidy or tax per unit of investment, is always a subsidy. I question this conclusion. The specification of the linear subsidy as

$$v(I) - \sigma I$$

means that it is a subsidy when investment is positive, but a *tax* when investment is negative. This is in a sense the best of both worlds: the firm is given an incentive both to be aggressive and not to be defensive. The *ad valorem* policy, on the other hand, is always symmetric: a tax (subsidy) makes both positive and negative investment more (less) costly. The proper specification of the specific policy in the present context is to make it symmetric also, by making it dependent on the *absolute* quantity:

$$v(I) - \sigma |I|$$

The comparison of linear and non-linear policies as it stands in the chapter is misleading. With symmetric specification, in which a specific subsidy is a subsidy regardless of whether the investment is positive or negative, one may find that some parameter values call for a specific tax and not a subsidy. In other words, the different results for the two types of policies could be a function of the specification of the linear policy, and not of whether the policy is linear or non-linear.

When I state that the proper specification of the linear policy should be such that it taxes or subsidises regardless of the direction of investment, I overlook the empirical facts of investment and disinvestment policies. Real-world policies are designed either for expanding *or* for contracting industries or regions or even firms, and do not usually cover both expansion and contraction. Karp and Perloff's sample of actual policies underlines this point. Industries or regions are usually classified explicitly or implicitly as having or not having future potential. In the former case, subsidies are given to R&D and perhaps to production costs. Any contraction or loss of competitiveness is met with more subsidies to encourage a return to expansion. The history of Airbus is a case in point. In the latter case, policies are typically designed either to speed up the reallocation of resources to other activities, or to slow down such reallocation to prevent sudden and large increases in unemployment and other social costs, or both, but *not* to encourage expansion.

The empirical facts thus call for considering one- instead of two-directional policies. One-directional policies have unambiguous effects in the present framework. For example, a tax on investment is always bad and a tax on disinvestment always good. A government bent on promoting national champions can choose between an investment subsidy or a disinvestment tax. This is a useful insight because it should serve to make the French minister for trade and industry and other policy-makers of the same persuasion think twice before introducing strategic trade and industrial policies and to appreciate the fact that the case for strategic trade and industrial policies is based on simplification and special assumptions. One should insist that they use a tax on disinvestment instead of a subsidy on investment since the subsidy will benefit foreign buyers during the transition to the new equilibrium. That should make the minister and others think again.

REFERENCES

Brander, James A. and Barbara J. Spencer (1985) 'Export subsidies and international market share rivalry', *The Journal of International Economics*, **18** (February) pp. 83–100.

Part Five
Empirical evidence

9 Macroeconomic import functions with imperfect competition: an application to EC trade

JOAQUIM OLIVEIRA-MARTINS and JOËL
TOUJAS-BERNATE

1 Introduction

Macroeconomic trade equations – defined at a global or at a sectoral level – usually consider industries as a homogeneous aggregate. Even if products are assumed to be differentiated by place of production (the usual Armington hypothesis) within each particular grouping of goods there is, implicitly, homogeneity among individual components. This may be a serious drawback as estimates of trade equations with usual price variables cannot capture a key element of imperfect competition suggested by trade theory, namely, that industries should be modelled as a group of heterogeneous firms. This chapter explores a means of introducing at a macro level the impact of the heterogeneity existing at the firm level.

The first part of the chapter analyses the consequences of assuming the supply-side hypothesis of oligopolistic competition with symmetric firms in the usual trade equations framework. Norman (1990), develops this point in a CGE framework, but here we focus on demand-side aspects. The oligopolistic model suggests that, in a given market, prices and the number of products (or firms) competing are joint determinants of market shares. Traditional equations can be generalised to incorporate both effects in a tractable way. Bismut and Oliveira-Martins (1987), and Oliveira-Martins (1989) developed this approach with CES trade functions, and this chapter extends it to the more flexible Translog system which seems more appropriate for modelling market shares over a long period (1963–87).

The empirical test of this model is conducted for the 4 major European countries, France, Germany, the UK and Italy, and for 3 industries with quite different market structures: textiles and leather, chemical products and electrical machinery. Following Winters (1984), we do not impose the stringent separability hypothesis between domestic and foreign sources of domestic demand. Accordingly, in each market, 3 types of producers are identified: National, Other EC and All Other. The empirical analysis

237

J

begins with an assessment of the statistical long-term relationship – measured by a cointegration technique – between market shares and relative prices. It turns out that in a significant number of cases there is no evidence of the existence of such a relationship, corroborating the fact that other supply-side variables should be taken into account. The system of market shares is then estimated using as the explanatory variable a 'composite price index' embodying prices and an activity variable as a proxy for the number of firms.

The estimates of the demand system enable us to calculate the key substitution parameters characterising the degree of product differentiation among aggregate producers. Finally, we use this set of parameters to simulate the consequences of the '1992' integration process. The integration of European markets is sometimes predicted to lead to the homogenisation of tastes across countries; this implies a hypothetical change in the underlying parameters of the utility function that can be compared with the actual estimates.

2   Macro trade functions and imperfect competition

In the spirit of monopolistic competition models, each aggregate regional producer offers a bundle of differentiated products (or varieties) supplied by a given number of heterogeneous but symmetric firms.[1] Each firm produces only 1 product which makes the number of products equal to the number of firms. In order to focus on the demand equation we treat the price and the number of 'representative' firms within an industry as predetermined.

As a starting point, we assume that a given national market is supplied by two aggregate producers (for example, domestic and foreign producers) referred to as N and E. For convenience, we define the ratio between the market share of each producer, V_{NE}:

$$V_{NE} = \frac{\sum_{i=1}^{n_N} p_{N_i} \cdot q_{N_i}}{\sum_{i=1}^{n_E} p_{E_i} \cdot q_{E_i}} \tag{1}$$

Where n_N and n_E are, respectively, the number of firms of the aggregate producers N and E. With symmetry, the ratio V will be equal to $(n_N \cdot p_N \cdot q_N / n_E \cdot p_E \cdot q_E)$, where p_N and q_N are the price and output of the representative firm in N, and similarly for E.

Models of international trade with monopolistic competition usually assume Dixit–Stiglitz CES preferences (see the survey by Helpman, 1990). In that case, with rational behaviour, the ratio between the market shares of the two aggregate producers is given by:

$$V_{NE} = \frac{n_N \cdot p_N \cdot q_N}{n_E \cdot p_E \cdot q_E} = c \cdot \left[\frac{n_N}{n_E}\right] \cdot \left[\frac{p_N}{p_E}\right]^{(1-\sigma)} \qquad (2)$$

where $\sigma > 1$ is the elasticity of substitution between each pair of products and c is a constant depending on the parameters of the CES utility function. This equation says that the ratio V is determined by relative prices between N and E and by the relative number of firms. As Norman (1990) observes, this result is quite different from the traditional Armingtonian equation. Indeed, when perfect competition is assumed on the supply side,[2] the term n_N/n_E, that can be viewed as an imperfect competition effect, will not appear in the equation. If the 'true' model is the imperfect competition one, an econometric estimate of V using only relative prices as the explanatory variable will suffer a specification bias. Indeed, available data are generally based on weighted averages of individual prices, and therefore they cannot capture the valuation of product diversity as in the case of a CES aggregate.[3]

It is very likely, then, that supply-side effects have been underestimated by empirical work on trade equations, as noted by Goldstein and Khan (1985). There have been attempts at introducing non-price competitiveness effects in trade equations (e.g. Barker, 1977; Geracci and Prewo, 1982) but generally without an explicit link to trade theory, and indeed the practice of introducing time trends to trade equations can be interpreted as an attempt to proxy missing supply-side effects. All these heuristic approaches can be improved upon, taking account of our recent understanding of how imperfect competition interacts with trade flows. Along these lines, the imperfect competition model suggests that one should construct a 'composite price index', encompassing the ratio (n_N/n_E) that combines both price and non-price effects.

The market share equation (2) can be suitable for estimates if consumers perceive differences among varieties but are unable to perceive a global difference between the bundles offered by aggregate producers N and E. However, as trade equations are usually estimated at a broad level of aggregation, it seems more convenient to allow for different degrees of differentiation within and outside each group. To this end, Bismut and Oliveira-Martins (1987) used a 2-level CES function with an intra-firm layer and an aggregate producer layer, with 3 elasticity parameters characterising the substitution possibilities. Their market share ratio V is then given by:

$$V_{NE} = c \frac{n_N^{\beta_N}}{n_E^{\beta_E}} \left[\frac{p_N}{p_E}\right]^{(1-\sigma)} \qquad (3)$$

where $\beta_N = (1 - \sigma)/(1 - \sigma_N)$, and $\beta_E = (1 - \sigma)/(1 - \sigma_E)$.

σ_N and σ_E, (> 1) are the elasticities of substitution inside each group. The parameter σ which characterises the substitutability between the two bundles of products is required only to be positive. Compared with equation (2) the 2-level system has the same price elasticities but the 'product elasticities' β_N and β_E can now be different from 1. Whereas in the previous model increasing product variety by one producer always increased market shares, in equation (3) its effects depend on the elasticity of substitution between the 2 bundles of differentiated products. For a very low degree of substitution ($\sigma < 1$) the entry of new firms can have an adverse effect on the ratio V. Also, one should expect (but not necessarily) that the upper level elasticity σ is lower than the intra-varieties' elasticities of substitution.[4] As the equation (3) is embodied in equation (2) it would be possible to choose between the 2 models by testing the hypothesis $\beta_N = \beta_E = 1$.

In order to carry out an econometric estimation with more than 2 bundles of products, the generalisation of equation (3) would entail severe restrictions on the parameters. Deaton and Muellbauer (1980) suggest two options:

(i) Assume that the overall substitution between each pair of differentiated product bundles is the same. This is equivalent to assuming strong separability among all aggregate sources of domestic demands.

(ii) Or, assume weak separability among groups of products. This hypothesis will lead to a nested framework in which groups of products are in their turn gathered together in broader groups over several layers. A structure of this type would be very similar to the nesting used in applied general equilibrium models.

The second is less restrictive than the first, but requires a careful choice of the separability hypothesis embodied in the nesting. Indeed, the price effects can be radically different according to the separability assumptions. Empirical work has consistently reported that, as far as price effects are concerned, separability between foreign and domestic sources is rejected by the data (see Winters, 1984, 1985).

Moreover, over a large period it also seems quite restrictive to assume that the overall substitution effects remain constant. Accordingly, it seems best to abandon the search for simple and constant elasticities of substitution and adopt instead a more flexible demand system. Among the many candidates, we chose the Translog functional form. The main advantage of the Translog system is that it allows for variable own – and cross-effects within a tractable form. The AIDS model (see Brenton and Winters, 1991), could also be a possible alternative, but it would be somewhat more complex to handle, namely when dealing with the composite prices defined below.

Consider the Translog indirect utility function (introduced by Christensen, Jorgenson and Lau, 1975):

$$- \log U = a_0 + \sum_i a_i \log(\Pi_i/Y) + \tfrac{1}{2} \sum_i \sum_j \beta_{ij} \log(\Pi_i/Y) \log(\Pi_j/Y) \quad (4)$$

where $[\Pi_i]$ is the vector of prices and Y total income. In our experiment, we assume rational behaviour implying constraints on the parameters:

$$\sum_j \beta_{ij} = 0, \quad \beta_{ij} = \beta_{ji} \quad \text{and} \quad \sum_i a_i = 1$$

These constraints imply homogeneity of degree 1 with respect to income. By using the logarithmic form of Roy's identity one gets the market share w_i of producer i:

$$w_i = a_i + \sum_j \beta_{ij} \log(\Pi_j) \quad (5)$$

According to the argument above, the price vector $[\Pi_j]$ should be defined over a bundle of differentiated products, incorporating both a pure price effect and a 'variety' effect. As in the Dixit–Stiglitz approach, we assume a CES functional form for the composite price index:[5]

$$\Pi_j = \left[\sum_{k=1}^{n_j} p_k^{(1 - \sigma_j)} \right]^{\frac{1}{(1 - \sigma_j)}} \quad (6)$$

where σ_i is the intra-group elasticity of substitution. Moreover, with intra-group symmetry (hence each product has the same price P_j) the composite price index for source j will be:

$$\Pi_j = n_j^{1/(1 - \sigma_j)} \cdot P_j \quad (7)$$

It can be noted that, if the first level Translog system is homothetic, by introducing the CES second level, we are possibly introducing other income type effects via the number of firms (or the number of products). This is an important point given the imperfect competition features embodied in this system.[6]

We recall the usual direct (ϵ_{ii}) and cross-price (ϵ_{ji}) elasticities between groups of product derived from the Translog parameters:

$$\epsilon_{ii} = (\beta_{ii} + w_i^2 - w_i)/w_i \quad (8)$$

$$\epsilon_{ji} = (\beta_{ji} + w_j \cdot w_i)/w_j \quad (9)$$

This demand system can be used to characterise the degree of substitution among different bundles of products. The direct (Hicksian) or the Allen elasticities of substitution are not very appealing in the n-

commodity case, but there is an alternative measure that can be interpreted in terms of the curvature of indifference surfaces, thus measuring the ease of substitution – the so-called Morishima partial elasticity of substitution M_{ij}. It can be defined (see, Blackorby and Russel, 1981, 1989) as:

$$M_{ij} = \epsilon_{ji} - \epsilon_{ii} \qquad (10a)$$

by using (8) and (9) one gets:

$$M_{ij} = \beta_{ji}/w_j - \beta_{ii}/w_i + 1 \qquad (10b)$$

M_{ij} is asymmetric since it refers only to the situation in which the composite price of group i varies. Hence, the possibilities of substitutability between groups i and j will be different if only the price of group j varies.[7] This measure, however, has the appealing property of being a straightforward generalisation of the 2-group case by relating clearly the impact of relative prices over the market share ratio V_{ij}. Indeed, by taking the logarithmic derivatives of market shares w_i and w_j with respect to the relative composite price and comparing with (10b), one gets:

$$\frac{\partial \log(w_i/w_j)}{\partial \log(\Pi_i/\Pi_j)} = 1 - M_{ij} \qquad (11)$$

We have now set up the base framework of a macroeconomic import system with imperfect competition. We now turn to the data sources and the empirical estimates.

3   Empirical implementation

3.1   The data

For France, Germany, the UK and Italy, data were collected for trade and output variables for National, Other EC and All Other producers, on an annual basis covering the period 1963–88 (except for production data in Italy which cover 1967–88); 3 industrial sectors were chosen: textiles and leather, chemical products and electrical goods.

Trade data (values and unit values) were derived from the EC Volimex data base.[8] Unfortunately, the production data were not available from an unique source. The primary source was the EC sectoral BDS data base.[9] As there are many missing data concerning production, this base has to be completed with other sources – in order of preference, the OECD IAI data base, the Statistical Office of the European Communities (SOEC) Industrial Statistics, and the UNIDO's Industrial Statistics. Data for France before 1970 were derived from a particular source, the Propage data base.[10] Appendix 1 (p. 259) summarises the data collecting process. Domestic demand is derived by using the usual identity:

$$P^d D + P^x X = P^q Q + P^m M \qquad (12)$$

where D is demand, X exports, Q domestic production, M imports, with their respective prices (based on 1980).

3.2   A proxy for the product differentiation effect

As data for the number of firms do not exist for a sufficiently long time period, the variables corresponding to the number of firms must be replaced by proxies. Nonetheless, some information for France, Germany and the UK is available in the SOEC Industrial Statistics. The latter can be used to qualify the proxies we derived from industrial activity indexes in the UNIDO Industrial Statistics data base.

These indexes were constructed in two steps. First, an aggregate index for each of the major trading partners of the Volimex classification was calculated: individual EC countries; the USA; Japan; Australia/New Zealand/South Africa; rest of OECD; and the dynamic Asean economies (Singapore, South Korea, Hong Kong, Taiwan and Malaysia). Second, the group was weighted together into our aggregates by their import market share in the base year 1980 for each market/sector we consider (4 markets × 3 products).

The rationale behind the proxy relationship is grounded on the monopolistic competition model. Therefore the proxy will capture the product differentiation effects better when the market structure is fragmented, i.e. when the number of firms grows in parallel with output expansion of the industry. We used the available data from the SOEC Industrial Statistics to test the relationship between the activity index (I_N) and the number of firms (n_N) in each of the 3 sectors, for national producers. The results of the pooled regressions are shown in Table 9.1.[11]

The results indicate, as far as the main European producers are concerned, that the proxy should perform much better for textiles and leather and electrical goods' industries than for the chemical sector. Indeed, in the latter sector the negative correlation between the activity index and the number of firms suggests that the market should be closer to a segmented rather than a fragmented structure. In this case, the proxy cannot be consistent with the underlying hypothesis of oligopolistic competition with symmetric firms and free entry.

Table 9.1. *Results of pooled regressions*

Textiles and leather:

$$\log n_N = 1.283 \log I_N \qquad R^2 = 0.65 \text{ See} = 0.088 \text{ ndf} = 36$$
$$(7.84) \qquad\qquad \text{period: 1975–87}$$

Chemical products:

$$\log n_N = -0.302 \log I_N \qquad R^2 = 0.22 \text{ See} = 0.062 \text{ ndf} = 36$$
$$(-2.87) \qquad\qquad \text{period: 1975–87}$$

Electrical goods:

$$\log n_N = 0.672 \log I_N \qquad R^2 = 0.69 \text{ See} = 0.053 \text{ ndf} = 36$$
$$(8.50) \qquad\qquad \text{period: 1975–87}$$

Note: All variables are defined as deviations from their country sample means. Student-t are in parenthesis.
See = standard error of the regression; ndf = number of degrees of freedom.

3.3   Market shares and relative prices: is there a long-term relation?

This section conducts a preliminary test on our data. Before estimating our extended model it seemed interesting to assess whether or not a long-term relation exists between market shares and relative prices. If not, this possibly reveals that a more general model may be required by the data. The stationarity and cointegration tests described in this section can be viewed as an analysis of this question.

Intuitively, cointegration among a set of variables implies that there exist fundamental economic forces which make the variables move stochastically together over time. Johansen (1988) and Johansen and Juselius (1990) provided a unified approach based on a maximum likelihood procedure for estimation and test in the context of a multivariate system.[11]

We applied this procedure to test whether our sample was comparable with the following simple (often used) long-run empirical relation between market share and relative prices:

$$\log(q_i/D) = a \cdot \log(p_i/P) + b \qquad (13)$$

where q_i is the demand for product i in a given market, p_i is its respective price, D is total demand and P is the price index of total demand. Variable q_i is equal to $(Q - X)$ for domestic producers and equal to imports for foreign producers. Table 9.2 applies Johansen's procedure to the 2-dimensional vector composed of market shares and relative prices taken in logarithms. We assume an autoregressive process of order 2 and that series can be integrated up to order 1. Moreover, we also assume that there are no deterministic trends in the series. When the dimension of the

Table 9.2. *Tests for the dimension and the structure of the cointegration space between the logarithms of market share and price competitiveness*

Sample: 1963–88, except for Italy: 1967–88

Market	Producer/ sector	Domestic	European	Non-European
France	Textiles	0	0	0
	Chemicals	1*	1[a]	1[a]
	Electrical	1*	0	1*
Germany	Textiles	1[a]	1[b]	0
	Chemicals	0	1[a]	0
	Electrical	0	1[b]	0
Italy	Textiles	0	1*	0
	Chemicals	1[a]	1*	0
	Electrical	0	0	0
UK	Textiles	0	1*	1[a]
	Chemicals	0	0	0
	Electrical	0	0	0

Note: The numbers indicate the dimension of the cointegration space.
[a] The tests on the structure of the cointegration space indicate that price competitiveness is stationary while market share is not.
[b] The tests on the structure of the cointegration space indicate that market share is stationary while relative price is not.
* The hypothesis of cointegration between market shares and relative prices is not rejected.

cointegration space is different from zero, we test whether the vector(s) which spans this space embody(ies) one of the 2 variables. In this way the stationarity of the series can be tested.

Over the 36 instances (4 markets × 3 sectors × 3 producers), the dimension of the cointegration space was found to be zero in 22 cases (61 per cent). In this group, market share and relative prices are integrated but not cointegrated, and the existence of a long-run relation between the two series is rejected by the data. For the remaining 14 cases, the dimension of the cointegration space is 1. The tests on the structure of the cointegration space show that in 8 of these, the stationarity of only 1 of the 2 variables is accepted. In only 6 cases (14 per cent) was a cointegration relation found. This happens in France, for domestic producers in chemical and electrical products, and for the non-European producers for electrical products; in Italy, for European producers in textiles and chemical products, and in the UK, for European producers in textiles.

These results require two caveats, however. First, the small size of our sample makes the tests very weak. Second, there is a strict inconsistency in a bounded variable like a market share generating a non-stationary time series.[13] That we found this occasionally can only reflect our finite sample size. In spite of these limitations we conclude that equation (13) is rejected by the sample in the majority of cases we studied.

It would also be difficult to continue this road and extend the dimensionality of the cointegration test without imposing non-linear constraints or relations among the variables, hence the need for a structural modelling approach of demand systems.

3.4   Estimation and results with the nested Translog–CES demand system

The estimation of the Translog–CES market share equations defined above was carried out for each of the 12 markets (4 countries × 3 products). As was defined above, in each market 3 producers are identified: Domestic, Other European and Non-European. The system was estimated simultaneously by a maximum likelihood technique.[14] Given our limited data set, the restrictions of homogeneity and symmetry were imposed *a priori*. The adding-up constraint is fulfilled by dropping the equation for the foreign producers, but as is well known the maximum likelihood estimates are independent of the choice of the equation which is dropped from the system.[15] Based on Anderson and Blundell (1982), the only dynamic form which seemed tractable in our framework was a very simple partial adjustment process with a common adjustment speed (λ) across all suppliers. Preliminary estimates, not reported here, showed that the dynamic model tended to perform much better than the static model with respect to residual autocorrelation. By combining equations (5) and (7) with a proxy for the number of firms and a partial adjustment process one finally gets the system of equations to be estimated:

$$\Delta w_i = \lambda \cdot \left(a_i + \sum_j \beta_{ij} \cdot [\log(P_j) + 1/(1 - \sigma_j) \cdot \log(I_j)] - L w_i \right) + u_i \quad (14)$$

where I_j is a proxy for the number of firms (in our case, an activity index), (i, j) stands for National (N), Other European (E) and Non-European (F) producers, L for the lag operator and u_i is a normally distributed random term. The first aim was to estimate the full system in a systematic way, but it turned out that because of convergence problems, it was necessary to adopt a specific estimation strategy[16] and to add more structure to the system. In general, the near-collinearity between activity indexes makes it difficult to estimate the second level CES elasticities of substitution freely. In that case it was necessary to add more structure to the system by

Table 9.3. *Comparison between the homogeneous and the differentiated product model*

Sector/country	Textiles	Chemicals	Electricals
France	12.4**	3.4	9.6**
Germany	3.4	6.2*	0.4
UK	10.2**	10.4**	5.2*
Italy	1.6	0.2	13.2**

Note: log-likelihood ratio (LR) test. The test statistic follows a $\chi^2(2)$ for France and a $\chi^2(1)$ for the other countries.
* The homogeneous product model is rejected at the 5 per cent level.
** The homogeneous product model is rejected at the 1 per cent level.

imposing the equality of some of the σ_j parameters across the 3 producers. For Germany, the UK and Italy is was required to impose equality of the 3 elasticities. For France, it was possible to obtain a more general form by imposing only the equality of 2 σ_j.[17] In addition, in very few cases, the adjustment speed λ was also constrained in order to ease the convergence process.[18]

For each market the nested Translog–CES model can be compared with the 1 level system where varieties are implicitly supposed to be homogeneous ($\sigma = \infty$). Table 9.3 gives the results of LR test between the two models.[19] Tables 9.4–9.7 show the parameter estimates.

Several inferences can be drawn from the results. In 7 out of 12 cases the model embodying product differentiation effects significantly increases the likelihood of the sample (see Table 9.3). In the electrical goods' sector the composite price effect also appears to be more significant than in the other sectors. On the other hand, the extended model works better in France and in the UK than in the other 2 countries. Parameter σ_j is significant and tends to be greater than 1 in the majority of the cases, which is compatible with the oligopolistic competition hypothesis. Perhaps one could expect to find greater values for these parameters[20] and it is possible that our high level of aggregation and weak proxy for the variety have biased our results. However, it should be noted that the effect of expanding the variety of products over market shares reduce very quickly with increases in this elasticity.[21] Our estimates thus imply quite a high impact of the non-price effects. Under the assumption that our proxy reflects the number of products, this can also be interpreted as a high valuation of the variety embodied in the preferences. The value of this intra-variety elasticity of substitution can be crucial for the assessment of

Table 9.4. *Estimates for the French market, 1965–87*

Sector/parameters	Textiles	Chemicals	Electrical
Estimates with homogeneous products ($\sigma_j = \infty$):			
β_{NN}	− 0.177	− 0.15	− 0.213
	(− 14.3)	(− 3.9)	(− 9.9)
β_{NE}	0.091	0.11	0.08
	(10.6)	(3.7)	(5.9)
β_{NF}	0.085	0.040	0.133
	(8.3)	(2.8)	(12.3)
β_{EE}	− 0.117	− 0.037	0.007
	(− 3.7)	(− 0.9)	(0.5)
β_{EF}	0.026	− 0.073	− 0.087
	(0.7)	(− 1.4)	(− 9.4)
β_{FF}	− 0.111	0.033	− 0.046
	(− 2.6)	(0.6)	(− 5.0)
λ	0.334	0.157	0.5
	(3.0)	(2.2)	[a]
LL	177.7	177.2	156.1
Estimates with differentiated products (σ_j estimated):			
β_{NN}	− 0.031	− 0.008	− 0.147
	(− 2.0)	(− 0.2)	(− 6.6)
β_{NE}	− 0.017	0.005	0.082
	(− 1.1)	(0.2)	(8.9)
β_{NF}	0.048	0.003	0.066
	(4.3)	(0.2)	(2.9)
β_{EE}	0.063	− 0.004	0.011
	(2.5)	(− 0.02)	(0.7)
β_{EF}	− 0.046	− 0.001	− 0.092
	(− 3.1)	(− 0.2)	(− 6.5)
β_{FF}	− 0.002	− 0.002	0.026
	(− 0.4)	(− 0.2)	(1.2)
λ	0.659	0.431	0.5
	(4.6)	(3.4)	[a]
σ_N	1.371	1.016	3.79
	(14.5)	(12.0)	(1.5)
σ_E	1.181	1.016	1.604
	(22.2)	[a]	(8.6)
σ_F	1.181	1.044	3.79
	[a]	(4.4)	[a]
LL	183.9	178.9	160.9

Note: Student-t are in parentheses. *LL*: log of likelihood function.
N = National, E = Other European, F = Non-European.
[a] The parameter was constrained.

Table 9.5. *Estimates for the German market, 1965–87*

Sector/parameters	Textiles	Chemicals	Electrical
Estimates with homogeneous products ($\sigma_j = \infty$):			
β_{NN}	− 0.422	− 0.125	− 0.203
	(− 5.8)	(− 2.2)	(− 0.9)
β_{NE}	0.160	0.048	− 0.154
	(3.1)	(0.8)	(− 0.6)
β_{NF}	0.263	0.077	0.357
	(3.0)	(1.3)	(1.1)
β_{EE}	0.048	− 0.084	0.122
	(0.5)	(− 0.5)	(0.6)
β_{EF}	− 0.208	0.035	0.031
	(− 1.7)	(0.2)	(0.2)
β_{FF}	− 0.055	− 0.112	− 0.389
	(− 0.3)	(− 0.7)	(− 0.9)
λ	0.098	0.066	0.030
	(1.9)	(1.0)	(0.9)
LL	170.5	181.7	182.6
Estimates with differentiated products (σ_j estimated):			
β_{NN}	− 0.125	− 0.003	− 0.067
	(− 1.9)	(− 0.1)	(− 1.7)
β_{NE}	0.049	0.000	0.013
	(1.8)	(0.1)	(0.9)
β_{NF}	0.077	0.003	0.054
	(1.5)	(0.1)	(1.6)
β_{EE}	− 0.033	0.002	0.000
	(− 0.7)	(0.1)	(0.0)
β_{EF}	− 0.016	− 0.002	− 0.013
	(− 0.5)	(− 0.1)	(− 1.5)
β_{FF}	− 0.061	− 0.001	− 0.041
	(− 1.6)	(− 0.1)	(− 1.6)
λ	0.264	0.145	0.213
	(2.8)	(2.3)	(2.7)
$\sigma_N = \sigma_E = \sigma_F$	1.466	1.005	1.275
	(3.8)	(18.5)	(6.3)
LL	172.2	184.8	182.8

Note: Student-t are in parentheses. *LL*: log of likelihood function.
N = National, E = Other European, F = Non-European.

Table 9.6. *Estimates for the UK market, 1965–87*

Sector/parameters	Textiles	Chemicals	Electrical
Estimates with homogeneous products ($\sigma_j = \infty$):			
β_{NN}	− 0.160	− 0.045	− 0.203
	(− 3.5)	(− 3.1)	(− 5.3)
β_{NE}	0.070	0.048	0.079
	(3.5)	(4.8)	(5.4)
β_{NF}	0.091	− 0.003	0.124
	(2.1)	(− 0.6)	(4.8)
β_{EE}	− 0.314	− 0.019	− 0.002
	(− 1.5)	(− 0.4)	(− 0.1)
β_{EF}	0.245	− 0.029	− 0.077
	(1.1)	(− 0.7)	(− 3.3)
β_{FF}	− 0.335	0.032	− 0.047
	(− 1.3)	(0.8)	(− 1.8)
λ	0.136	0.535	0.205
	(1.9)	(3.9)	(2.4)
LL	153.7	133.1	152.7
Estimates with differentiated products (σ_j estimated):			
β_{NN}	0.100	0.016	− 0.121
	(1.6)	(0.6)	(− 4.4)
β_{NE}	− 0.055	− 0.010	0.037
	(− 1.9)	(0.6)	(2.7)
β_{NF}	− 0.044	− 0.006	0.084
	(− 1.3)	(− 0.6)	(5.3)
β_{EE}	0.027	0.001	0.029
	(1.8)	(0.3)	(1.4)
β_{EF}	0.028	0.009	− 0.066
	(1.3)	(0.7)	(− 3.6)
β_{FF}	0.016	− 0.003	− 0.018
	(1.1)	(− 0.9)	(− 1.3)
λ	0.354	0.608	0.300
	(4.7)	(4.8)	(3.2)
$\sigma_N = \sigma_E = \sigma_F$	0.824	0.976	1.788
	(10.1)	(3.9)	(4.9)
LL	158.8	138.3	155.3

Note: Student-*t* are in parentheses. *LL*: log of likelihood function.
N = National, E = Other European, F = Non-European.

Table 9.7. *Estimates for the Italian market, 1969–87*

Sector/parameters	Textiles	Chemicals	Electrical
Estimates with homogeneous products ($\sigma_j = \infty$):			
β_{NN}	− 0.034	− 0.067	− 0.050
	(− 6.6)	(− 2.1)	(− 2.9)
β_{NE}	0.014	0.035	0.023
	(4.7)	(1.4)	(2.0)
β_{NF}	0.020	0.031	0.027
	(6.8)	(3.0)	(3.9)
β_{EE}	0.017	0.030	0.030
	(1.1)	(0.4)	(1.2)
β_{EF}	− 0.031	− 0.065	− 0.053
	(− 1.8)	(− 1.0)	(− 2.4)
β_{FF}	0.011	0.033	0.026
	(0.6)	(0.6)	(1.3)
λ	0.420	0.2	0.462
	(3.3)	[a]	(3.5)
LL	158.2	128.6	120.2
Estimates with differentiated products (σ_j estimated):			
β_{NN}	− 0.035	− 0.046	0.060
	(− 5.4)	(− 1.1)	(3.8)
β_{NE}	0.009	0.014	− 0.038
	(1.5)	(0.4)	(− 3.7)
β_{NF}	0.026	0.032	− 0.023
	(3.8)	(1.9)	(− 3.6)
β_{EE}	0.020	0.043	0.024
	(1.2)	(0.6)	(3.4)
β_{EF}	− 0.030	− 0.057	0.014
	(− 1.7)	(− 0.9)	(3.6)
β_{FF}	0.003	0.025	0.009
	(0.2)	(0.5)	(3.4)
λ	0.349	0.2	0.725
	(2.6)	[a]	(5.5)
$\sigma_N = \sigma_E = \sigma_F$	1.848	1.451	0.938
	(1.9)	(1.6)	(87.0)
LL	159.0	128.7	126.8

Note: Student-*t* are in parentheses. *LL*: log of likelihood function.
N = National, E = Other European, F = Non-European.
[a] The parameter was constrained.

welfare effects of market integration in applied GE models (see Burniaux and Waelbroeck, 1992). With high values of σ_j the variation of the number of products has a small impact on welfare; typically, the benefits from market integration coming from firm specialisation will not be outweighed by the decrease in the number of products. For lower values of this elasticity the variety effect may dominate the sign of welfare gains.

In brief, in a significant number of cases, the broad picture seems to be consistent with the extended model incorporating both price and nonprice effects. But one must bear in mind that the very simple symmetric market structure which underlies the proxy for product differentiation represents only one source of non-price effects.

4   Simulation of the effects of the '1992' market integration

4.1   Substitutability parameters characterising the competition in each market

Using the previous estimate it is possible to calculate all the substitution parameters characterising the competition in each market. As discussed above, we report Morishima partial elasticities of substitution M_{ij} derived from equation (10b), given the estimates of coefficients β_{ij}. The M_{ij} are not constant over the period and are asymmetric; each measures the impact of a change of producer i price over the market share ratio between i and j, all other prices are kept constant but all quantities adjust to their optimal levels. The point estimates of this parameter for the year 1987 are shown in Table 9.8. From equation (11) above, 1 minus the Morishima elasticity can be interpreted as the impact of relative prices over the corresponding market share ratio; hence, a value of M_{ij} greater than 1 indicates that a decrease in relative prices induces a market share gain. Given this appealing interpretation, it turns out to be easier to design an alternative hypothesis on the value of these parameters rather than on the values of the coefficients β_{ij}.

4.2   Price and non-price effects

The composite price index (7) enables us to simulate shocks either to relative prices or to aggregate producer output, the latter supposed to proxy the creation of new products. Since both operate via the composite price the 2 shocks are qualitatively equivalent, the numerical equivalence depending on the value of the estimated intra-variety elasticity of substitution σ_i. The lower this parameter, the higher the relative impact of non-price effects. As noted above, our system embodies quite a strong

Table 9.8. *Matrix of partial elasticities of substitution, 1987*

Model with differentiated products

	France			Germany			UK			Italy		
Textiles	–	0.971	1.403	–	1.459	1.549	–	0.560	0.597	–	1.150	1.332
	0.687	–	0.372	1.233	–	1.068	0.774	–	1.017	0.771	–	0.426
	1.089	0.805	–	1.387	1.158	–	0.841	1.054	–	0.998	0.607	–
Chemicals	–	1.030	1.042	–	1.004	1.034	–	0.935	0.921	–	1.124	1.389
	1.022	–	1.004	0.990	–	0.971	0.980	–	1.077	0.875	–	0.295
	1.024	1.016	–	1.014	1.000	–	1.018	1.063	–	0.808	0.560	–
Electrical	–	1.631	1.632	–	1.201	1.398	–	1.422	1.539	–	0.739	0.718
	1.077	–	0.392	1.019	–	0.927	0.905	–	0.585	0.835	–	1.009
	0.948	0.398	–	1.307	1.125	–	1.219	0.702	–	0.890	0.988	–

Note: For each market (country × product), producers (ij) are ranked in the following order: National N, Other European E and Non-European F. For example, the first line corresponds to the Morishima partial substitution elasticities M_{NE} and M_{NF}.

impact of output growth differential over market shares. For example, with an intra-variety elasticity of substitution equal to 2, an 11 per cent growth in the number of products (or firms) would lead to a decrease of the composite price index of 10 per cent; with an elasticity of 1.5, only a 5.4 per cent shock would be required to achieve the same shock over the composite price.

4.3   The effects of market integration

The purpose of this exercise is two fold. First, it illustrates the impact of a price shock on market shares when preferences remain unchanged. Secondly, it aims to explore the impact of a particular homogenisation of tastes over European markets after the '1992' integration process. As an illustrative case, we assumed a counterfactual shock of a 10 per cent decrease on the composite price of the National producers in each market. Two scenarios were considered:

- *Differentiated tastes:* This is the base case using the estimated parameters, differentiated by producer and market.
- *Homogenisation of tastes:* In this scenario, we assume that the substitutability effects among the 3 aggregate producers are the same in all markets. As we are dealing with the impact at the level of the composite price index, the design of each scenario relies upon the value of the Morishima elasticities of substitution. The values of the Morishima elasticity are assumed to be a cross-country average of the estimated elasticities used in the first scenario. This can be viewed as a possible homogenisation of tastes across European countries. Whereby their behaviour with regard to the substitution between home, European and foreign goods become more similar. The values of the average Morishima elasticities are given in Table 9.9. Given these values and the observed market shares it is possible to derive the parameters β_{ij} of the demand system which corresponds to this change in preferences (see Appendix 2, pp. 259–60). The impact on market shares can then be calculated straightforwardly.

The results of these simulations sector by sector are shown in Tables 9.10–9.12. The responsiveness of market shares is higher for the textiles and electrical goods than for the chemicals products. Depending on the value of the partial elasticity of substitution, the price decrease can have a positive or an adverse effect on National producers' market share and on the competitive position of the Other European and Foreign producers. However, as is common in econometric work on trade equations, the impacts on market shares are rather low.

Table 9.9. *Matrix of average partial elasticities of substitution, 1987*

Model with differentiated products

Textiles	–	1.035	1.220
	0.866	–	0.721
	1.079	0.906	–
Chemicals	–	1.023	1.097
	0.967	–	0.837
	0.966	0.910	–
Electrical	–	1.248	1.322
	0.959	–	0.728
	1.091	0.803	–

Note: See note to Table 9.8.

In the first scenario, for the textiles industry in France, the Foreign producers lose market share whereas the share of the Other European producers increases slightly (for the latter producer the Morishima elasticity M_{NE} is lower than 1); in Germany and Italy, National producers record market share gains over the 2 other producers. For the UK there is an adverse effect for the National producers (the Morishima elasticities are both lower than 1).

In the chemicals sector, the effects are typically very low. The Italian market is an exception, as there is a sizeable market share loss for the foreign producers.

The highest impacts are in the electrical goods industry. In France, National producers have a 2.5 per cent increase of their market share in comparison with a 4.2 per cent market share loss for each other producer. The same pattern applies for Germany and the UK. In Italy, the price decrease has a negative impact on the market share of National producers.

The effect of a homogenisation of tastes across European markets is shown in the third column of Tables 9.10–9.12. As we assume the same elasticities in all markets the results are naturally less contrasted than in the previous scenario. The magnitude of the market share deviations also tends to be lower than in the preceding case, because there is a compensation between negative and positive effects across countries. Except for the textile industry, the decrease of national producers' price induces a uniform market share loss for the other producers. In all sectors, the market share of foreign producers falls by around 2 per cent relative to the base shares. The losses for the other European producers are higher for

Table 9.10. *Results of the simulations, textiles and leather*

Simulation of a − 10 per cent shock on the National producers' composite price index

Market/producer	(Shares of total demand in 1987) Base shares (%)	(Deviations from base shares) Differentiated tastes	Homogenisation of tastes
France			
National	64.5	0.33	0.25
Other European	21.9	0.18	0.01
Non-European	13.5	− 0.50	− 0.26
Germany			
National	45.9	1.32	0.34
Other European	26.2	− 0.52	0.10
Non-European	27.9	− 0.81	− 0.44
UK			
National	62.1	− 1.06	0.30
Other European	19.7	0.58	0.03
Non-European	18.2	0.46	− 0.33
Italy			
National	82.7	0.37	0.26
Other European	8.3	− 0.09	− 0.01
Non-European	9.0	− 0.27	− 0.19

the electrical goods than for the other sectors. For chemicals, they are very small. For the textiles sector, the European producers benefit from a low substitutability with national products and show market share gains.

5   Summary and conclusions

In this chapter we have estimated a demand system for domestic, European and foreign products in the 4 main European markets, allowing for both price and non-price determinants of market shares. Non-price effects are related to a supply-side hypothesis of oligopolistic competition with a large number of firms, in which price and product differentiation effects are channelled through a composite price index. Some advantages of this model can be put forward compared with the usual import demand equations, namely that it is a flexible demand system which does not

Table 9.11. *Results of the simulations, chemical products*

Simulation of a − 10 per cent shock on the National producers' composite price index

Market/producer	(Shares of total demand in 1987) Base shares (%)	(Deviations from base shares) Differentiated tastes	Homogenisation of tastes
France			
National	59.9	0.08	0.11
Other European	29.6	− 0.05	− 0.02
Non-European	10.5	− 0.03	− 0.09
Germany			
National	69.1	0.03	0.10
Other European	20.8	0.00	− 0.02
Non-European	10.1	− 0.03	− 0.08
UK			
National	63.8	− 0.17	0.11
Other European	25.1	0.11	− 0.02
Non-European	11.1	0.06	− 0.09
Italy			
National	60.7	0.49	0.11
Other European	29.1	− 0.15	− 0.02
Non-European	10.2	− 0.34	− 0.09

impose the habitual separability over national and foreign sources of domestic demand. The composite price index can capture secular shifts in market shares, via changes in import penetration, that usually have to be treated non-theoretically through the introduction of deterministic trends.

The empirical implementation of this model requires the use of a proxy for the number of representative firms in a given industry. We used a weighted index of industrial activity of each aggregate producer present in each market. A better approximation of this variable could eventually be constructed by using microeconomic data at the firm level, but through lack of available data this was not possible at this stage. Before the estimation of the demand system a test of the long-term relationship between relative prices and market shares was performed by means of a cointegration technique. This confirmed that in a significant number of cases such a relation does not exist, which suggests that the usual model

Table 9.12. *Results of the simulations, electrical goods*

Simulation of a − 10 per cent shock on the National producers' composite price index

Market/producer	(Shares of total demand in 1987) Base shares (%)	(Deviations from base shares) Differentiated tastes	Homogenisation of tastes
France			
National	62.8	1.55	0.70
Other European	20.7	− 0.86	− 0.31
Non-European	16.6	− 0.70	− 0.38
Germany			
National	69.8	0.70	0.65
Other European	12.4	− 0.14	− 0.21
Non-European	17.9	− 0.57	− 0.44
UK			
National	56.0	1.28	0.76
Other European	18.0	− 0.39	− 0.23
Non-European	26.0	− 0.88	− 0.53
Italy			
National	65.5	− 0.63	0.65
Other European	22.4	0.40	− 0.36
Non-European	12.1	0.24	− 0.29

based exclusively on pure price effects should be ruled out in favour of a more general one.

The results show that the composite price indexes – incorporating product differentiation – may perform better in explaining market shares than relative prices alone. Secondly, we obtained plausible and significant estimates of the intra-variety elasticity of substitution. As very often in the literature on trade equations, the estimates of price effects over market shares are on average rather moderate. However, one must note that the non-price effects intervene with a much higher elasticity. Finally, we attempted two simulations related to the '1992' market integration effects. We showed that a counterfactual decrease of 10 per cent on domestic producers' price has a differentiated, but rather moderate, impact across markets. In the hypothetical case that a homogenisation of tastes would lead to the same average elasticities in all countries, these effects could even be lower.

Appendix 1:   Sources of the data

The production data used in this chapter were derived from the reconciliation of several sources, summarised in Table 9A.1.

For the base year 1980, the production value was derived from the input–output table of the OSCE. Trade and production data were reconciled by using the correspondences between the Nace–Clio classification and the CITI industrial products' list described in Table 9A.2.

Table 9A.1. *Primary sources for production data*

Country	Data type	BDS[a]	OECD[b]	UNIDO[c]	SOEC[d]	INSEE[e]
France	Value	1970–87				1963–9
	Volume	1970–87				1963–9
Germany	Value	1960–88				
	Volume			1963–80	1980–7	
Italy	Value				1980	
	Volume		1980–8	1963–9		
	Price		1970–88	1967–9		
UK	Value	1970–88		1963–9		
	Volume			1963–9		
	Price		1970–88			

Note: The figures indicate the period for when the data source was used.
[a] Banque de Données Sectorielles, EC-DG II.
[b] OECD, IAI data base.
[c] UN, Industrial Statistics.
[d] Statistical Office of European Communities, Industrial Statistics.
[e] Institut de la Statistique et des Etudes Economiques (INSEE), Propage Model data base.

Table 9A.2. *Correspondences between the CITI, Nace–Clio and BDS classifications*

Sectors	CITI	Nace–Clio	BDS
Textiles and leather	321 + 322 + 323 + 324	43 + 44 + 45	14
Chemical products	351 + 352	25 + 26	17
Electrical goods	383	34	11

Appendix 2:   Derivation of the parameters of the demand system from the Morishima elasticities

Given the values of the Morishima elasticities (M_{ij}) and the constraints on the demand system, it is possible to derive the parameters of the Translog function. Indeed, from equation (10b) in the text we have:

$$M_{ij} = \beta_{ji}/w_j - \beta_{ii}/w_i + 1 \qquad (A1)$$

$$M_{ik} = \beta_{ki}/w_k - \beta_{ii}/w_i + 1 \qquad (A2)$$

The homogeneity and symmetry constraints imply that, $\beta_{ii} + \beta_{ji} + \beta_{ki} = 0$. By using this relation and rearranging (A1) and (A2) we get:

$$\beta_{ji} \cdot (w_i + w_j) + \beta_{ik} \cdot w_j = w_i \cdot w_j \cdot (M_{ij} - 1) \qquad (A1')$$

$$\beta_{ji} \cdot w_k + \beta_{ik} \cdot (w_i + w_k) = w_i \cdot w_k \cdot (M_{ik} - 1) \qquad (A2')$$

Finally, by using the adding-up condition $w_i + w_j + w_k = 1$, and solving the above system we find that:

$$\beta_{ji} = w_j \cdot w_k \cdot (1 - M_{ik}) - w_j \cdot (1 - w_j) \cdot (1 - M_{ij}), \quad \text{for } i \neq j$$

and by symmetry $\beta_{ji} = \beta_{ij}$.

NOTES

We received helpful comments from the participants of the CEPR, IT'92 Workshop (London), of the EEA 1991 Annual Conference (Cambridge), and of the CEPR Conference 'Trade Flows and Trade Policy after "1992"' (Paris). In particular, we would like to thank L.A. Winters, P. Brenton and R. Faini. We also wish to thank M. Christian Dewaleyne from the EC-DG II, who authorised the access and provided the information on the Volimex and BDS data bases. The views expressed in this chapter are those of the authors and should not be attributed either to the OECD or INSEE.

1 Following the mainstream of this literature, in this chapter only a symmetric market structure will be considered. A recent work by Abd-el-Rahman (1991) incorporates empirical information on intra-firm heterogeneity together with trade data in order to explain the overall composition of trade.
2 Actually, perfect competition in the supply side was not an explicit assumption in the original paper by Armington (1969). He derived only a demand system with imperfect substitutes. Afterwards, the so-called Keynesian approach of trade flows made this hypothesis explicit by assuming an infinite elastic supply.
3 This is a well-known problem in price index theory. See, for example, Lloyd (1975) for a discussion of the bias arising from a Laspeyres approximation of a 2 level CES price index.
4 As shown by Sato (1967), inside a group, say N, the Allen partial elasticity of substitution equals:

$$A_{ij} = \sigma + \frac{1}{w_N} \cdot (\sigma_N - \sigma) \quad \text{for } i, j \in N, \, i \neq j$$

where w_N is the market share of aggregate producer N. When σ is higher than σ_N the varieties are complementary and a monopolistic competition equilibrium will be unstable.

5 Note that this Translog–CES system is a nested structure which is different from the more general CES–Translog system proposed by Pollack, Sickles and Wales (1984); the latter combines both a CES and a Translog function at the same level.

6 See Krugman (1989) for a discussion of the relation between income elasticities and growth in the context of a monopolistic competition model of international trade.

7 In this case all relative prices Π_j/Π_k, $k \neq i$ would vary, whereas they remain constant in the previous case.

8 This data base contains bilateral trade flows for each OECD country and a world breakdown of 30 groups of countries at the Nace–Clio disaggregation level (25 products), for the period 1963–88.

9 This data base contains value added (value and volume), production (value and volume), investment and employment for the 12 EC countries at an aggregation of Nace–Clio level.

10 This data base can be provided by the INSEE, Paris, upon request.

11 In order to take into account the cross-country differentials, we estimated a fixed effects model (or the so-called 'within estimator') over the pooled data of France, Germany and the UK for the period 1975–87. Because of a break in the statistical coverage of the number of firms for Italy, this country was removed from the sample.

12 Johansen's approach can be summarised as follows. Consider a p-dimensional Gaussian autoregressive vector:

$$X_t = \sum_{t=1}^{k+1} \pi_t X_{t-i} + e_t$$

with non-singular covariance matrix. By reparameterising the process in first differences, we get:

$$\Delta X_t = \sum_{i=1}^{k} \Gamma_i \Delta X_{t-i} + \Gamma_{k+1} X_{t-k-1} + e_t$$

The rank of Γ_{k+1} gives the dimension of the cointegration space. Under the null hypothesis that this dimension is equal to r, this matrix can be decomposed into $\Gamma_{k+1} = \alpha\beta'$ where a and β' are p.r. full rank matrices. The dimension of the cointegration space can then be determined sequentially, by analysing the canonical correlations between levels and first differences corrected for lagged differences. The determination of this dimension is based on a likelihood ratio statistic with a known asymptotic distribution. Given this dimension, Johansen's procedure allows for testing a hypothesis on the structure of the cointegration space, e.g. that this space contains or is contained in another space. The test statistic is distributed as chi-squared. In particular, it can be tested if some series are stationary or not.

13 Note that as the estimates were made in logs, the market share variable is only bounded upwards.

14 We used the non-linear least squares procedure of the software TSP 4.1a.

15 See Italianer (1986) for an exhaustive review of simultaneous systems of equations techniques applied for import allocation models.

16 As very often when estimating non-linear systems, the initialisation point is crucial to get convergence of the maximisation procedure. To overcome this problem, we adopted a linear iterative procedure over two sub-sets of parameters; this procedure performed quite well to supply initial estimates. More information on these technical aspects can be supplied by the authors upon request.
17 The choice of the constrained elasticity was based on the likelihood of the estimates.
18 The value was chosen according to a grid search over the range $[0, 1]$.
19 The null hypothesis corresponds to the homogeneous product model where $1/(1 - \sigma)$ is constrained to be zero.
20 Namely, when they are compared with the equivalent parameters calibrated in AGE imperfect competition models (e.g., Gasiorek, Smith and Venables, 1992).
21 The elasticity of the market share of producer i with respect to the number of products of producer j is given by $\beta_{ij}/((1 - \sigma_j) \cdot w_i)$.

REFERENCES

Abd-el-Rahman, K. (1991) 'Firms' competitive and national comparative advantages as joint determinants of trade composition', *Weltwirtschaftliches Archiv*, **127(1)**.
Anderson, G.J. and R.W. Blundell (1982) 'Estimation and hypothesis testing in dynamic singular equation system', *Econometrica*, **50(6)**, pp. 1559–71.
Armington, P. (1969) 'A theory of demand for products distinguished by place of production', *IMF Staff Papers*, **16(1)** (May).
Barker, T. (1977) 'International trade and economic growth: an alternative to the neo-classical approach', *Cambridge Journal of Economics*, **1**, pp. 153–72.
Bismut, C. and J. Oliveira-Martins (1987) 'Price competitiveness, market shares and product differentiation', *Working paper*, **CEPII 87–07**.
Blackorby, C. and R.P. Russel (1981) 'The Morishima elasticity of substitution: symmetry, constancy, separability, and its relationship with Hicks and Allen elasticities', *Review of Economic Studies*, **48**, pp. 147–58.
(1989) 'Will the elasticity of substitution please stand up? (A Comparison of the Allen/Uzawa and Morishima elasticities)', *American Economic Review*, **79(4)**, pp. 882–8.
Brenton, P. and L.A. Winters (1991) 'Estimating trade functions for exploring the effects of 1992', Chapter 10 in this volume.
Burniaux, J.-M. and J. Waelbroeck (1992) 'European integration and product specialisation', Université Libre de Bruxelles, mimeo.
Christensen, L.R., D.W. Jorgenson and L.J. Lau (1975) 'Transcendental logarithmic utility functions', *American Economic Review*, **65**, pp. 367–83.
Deaton, A. and J. Muellbauer (1980) *Economics and Consumer Behaviour*, Cambridge: Cambridge University Press.
Gasiorek, M., A. Smith and A. Venables (1992) '1992: trade and welfare – a general equilibrium model', Chapter 2 in this volume.
Geracci, V.J. and W. Prewo (1982) 'An empirical demand and supply model of multilateral trade', *The Review of Economics and Statistics* (August), pp. 432–41.

Goldstein, M. and M. Khan (1985) 'Income and price effects in foreign trade', in R.J. Jones and P. Kenen (eds), *Handbook of International Economics*, Amsterdam: North-Holland.

Helpman, E. (1990) 'Monopolistic competition in trade theory', *Special Papers in International Finance*, **16** (June), Princeton University.

Italianer, A. (1986) *Theory and Practice of International Trade Linkage Models*, Dordrecht: Martinus Nijhoff Publishers.

Johansen, S. (1988) 'Statistical analysis of cointegration vectors', *Jouranl of Economic Dynamics and Control*, **12**, pp. 231–54.

Johansen, S. and K. Juselius (1990) 'Maximum likelihood estimation and inference on co-integration – with applications to the demand of money', *Oxford Bulletin of Economics and Statistics*, **52**, pp. 169–210.

Krugman, P. (1989) 'Differences in income elasticities and trends in real exchange rates', *European Economic Review*, **33**, pp. 1031–54.

Lloyd, P.J. (1975) 'Substitution effects and biases in nontrue price indices', *American Economic Review*, **65**, pp. 301–13.

Norman, V. (1990) 'Assessing trade and welfare effects of trade liberalisation: a comparison of alternative approaches to CGE modelling with imperfect competition', *European Economic Review*, **34**, pp. 725–51.

Oliveira-Martins, J. (1989) 'Export behavior with differentiated products', in M. Dagenais and P.-A. Muet (eds), *International Trade Modelling*, New York: Chapman & Hall.

Pollack, R.A., R.C. Sickles and T.J. Wales (1984) 'The CES–Translog: specification and estimation of a new cost function', *Review of Economics and Statistics*, **664**, pp. 602–7.

Sato, K. (1967) 'A two-level constant elasticity-of-substitution production function', *Review of Economic Studies*, **34**, pp. 201–18.

Winters, L.A. (1984) 'Separability and the specification of foreign trade functions', *Journal of International Economics*, **17**, pp. 239–63.

(1985) 'Separability and the modelling of international economic integration', *European Economic Review*, **27**, pp. 335–53.

Discussion

LARS-HENDRIK RÖLLER

Chapter 9 by Oliveira-Martins and Toujas-Bernate estimates a model of macroeconomic trade equations introducing monopolistic competition on the supply side for three European manufacturing industries. As they state in the introductory section 1, the focus of the chapter is on the demand side, which is much more developed than the supply side. They expand on earlier models of this kind by allowing for translogarithmic trade functions, which introduces a certain amount of flexibility on the demand side, at the expense of fewer degrees of freedom and a rather complicated and highly non-linear econometric estimation. Using this model, they perform several very interesting simulation exercises, quantifying the effects of European integration.

The chapter is indeed a valuable contribution in the area of imperfect competition and trade. Given my personal bias and the fact that the supply side is comparatively less developed, I will concentrate my remarks on the modelling of market power.

The central equation (2), on which the empirical implementation is based, is a rather underdeveloped model of the supply side. This is especially so since the chapter claims to be a model of imperfect competition (as the title states), without paying much detail to the modelling of strategic interactions, either static or dynamic. On the other hand, the chapter is obviously a step in the right direction by introducing the term n_N/n_E through the model of monopolistic competition. Later in the chapter, the authors choose a somewhat different specification (14) in their empirical estimation of the textile, chemical, and electrical industries, namely one in which the change in market share of one producer is related to the level of the prices and the activity index of all other producers. However, they rely substantially on specification (2) when constructing their composite price index. Let me make a few suggestions and state a few problems with an equation such as (2), which postulates that relative market shares are a function of relative prices and the relative number of firms alone.

First, suppose $n_N = n_E$, that is the number of firms are identical. In this case, the model basically reduces to that of perfect competition. This seems to be true even when there is only one aggregate producer, that is $n_N = n_E = 1$. Conversely, imperfect competition is inferred even if the number of firms, or equivalently the number of products, is large but asymmetric (these conditions are indeed empirically rather plausible).

A second potential problem is the fact that prices, and possibly even the number of firms, are assumed to be exogenous. However, one could easily argue that firms set prices, in addition to other instruments, strategically and therefore endogenously. Consequently, the endogeneity introduces a simultaneity bias. A solution might be to specify a structural model of competition along the lines of the 'new empirical industrial organisation' literature (see Bresnahan, 1989, for a survey). A model of this kind would ideally eliminate the simultaneity bias, as well as taking into account strategic interactions more directly. Alternatively, an instrumental variable model could be employed.

Third, just as the authors show that there is some evidence for the inclusion of the number of firms (or number of products) through their proxy of activity, it can easily be argued that there are other important variables that affect market share. Consequently, the same argument put forward by the authors about misspecification bias (see also below) could be evoked. Let me elaborate this point briefly using the example of the pharmaceutical industry (CITI code 352), which is included in the present study. As is well known for the pharmaceutical industry, price competition is not the only source of competition. Product competition, marketing and R&D expenditure are equally important in this industry (see Thomas, 1990). Moreover, various types of government regulations, such as drug approval, pre-clinical testing, and laboratory practices affect market shares substantially, especially amongst producers from different regulatory regimes. To model market shares it would be important to incorporate these effects in some form. This would undoubtedly require one to build an industry-specific model, rather than pooling various heterogeneous industries.

Finally, for the sake of argument, assume that the true model is indeed one of imperfect competition as described by equation (2). The authors state that if the true model is one of imperfect competition, econometric estimates of V using only relative prices as an explanatory variable will suffer from specification bias. As already mentioned above, this might not be the case whenever the number of firms is rather symmetric. Thus no bias might occur in this case, even though the underlying model is one of imperfect competition. Even in the asymmetric case, the bias would be in the estimation of parameter c, and not in predicting V, if the ratio n_N/n_E is constant over the sample. This would presumably not upset many of the policy conclusions and simulations. In fact the bias would be n_N/n_E. One way of checking for this bias might be to re-estimate the inverted model. If the results are not robust, this would be evidence of a misspecification problem.

To conclude, let me reiterate that I find this chapter to be a step in the right direction. My preference for future research would be towards a more structural approach of imperfect competition, ideally at the industry level. This would imply estimation of first order conditions of a well-defined strategic situation. However, given the inherent degree of complexity this introduces on the supply side, it is not clear that the flexible demand specification chosen in this chapter is possible to maintain. Unless the data are very rich, we are thus left with this trade-off.

REFERENCES

Bresnahan, T.F. (1989) 'Empirical Studies of Industries with Market Power', Chapter 17 in R. Schmalensee and R.D. Willig (eds), *Handbook of Industrial Organization*, vol. 2, Amsterdam: North-Holland.

Thomas, L.G. (1990) 'Regulation and Firm Size: FDA Impacts on Innovation', *RAND Journal of Economics*, **21(4)** (Winter).

10 Bilateral trade elasticities for exploring the effects of '1992'

PAUL A. BRENTON and L. ALAN WINTERS

1 Introduction

The principal means by which the economic effects of the creation of the Single European Market will be felt is through changes in international trade flows. Thus, crucial to any quantitative assessment of the '1992' programme are estimates of international trade elasticities. Existing studies (e.g. CEC, 1988), however, have used elasticities from a range of previous studies[1] based upon different methodological approaches and data samples, and often more than 20 years old. When disaggregate analysis is undertaken aggregate elasticities have to be applied across a number of more detailed product groups.

 The project from which this chapter is derived seeks to estimate the key parameters of purchasing behaviour for each of the 4 major EC countries (France, West Germany, Italy and the UK). A recent sample (1970–87) of relatively detailed production and trade data is used to estimate a model of the allocation of expenditure across both domestic and import suppliers. The resulting estimates are then used to calculate the changes in welfare arising from some simple price-reduction scenarios of '1992'.

 Initial results for West Germany using a theoretically consistent model of demand, the Almost Ideal Demand System, applied to data for 70 manufacturing industries are presented in Brenton and Winters (1992b). These suggest that for nearly all the industries and suppliers uncompensated own-price elasticities of demand are relatively low: the vast majority were found to lie between -0.5 and -1.5. In addition, expenditure elasticities for domestic supplies were found to be consistently greater than those of import suppliers and often in excess of unity. Thus, when we simulated the effects of a 2.5 per cent fall in the price of imports from other EC countries together with a 1 per cent fall in the price of extra-EC imports, we actually recorded an increase in the quantity of domestic sales

266

in most industries. The strength of the income effect outweighed the effects of the adverse relative price change.

In this chapter we seek to assess whether this conclusion of relatively low price elasticities is robust; specifically whether it pertains to other countries using the same model of demand, and whether it still holds if we use a much more restrictive functional form of the demand equations, the constant elasticity of substitution (CES) model. CES functions have long been used to model international trade flows – see, for example, Armington (1969). We concentrate on a sub-set of 15 of our industries and consider demand in Italy as well as in West Germany. We commence by briefly reviewing our initial specification of the demand equations which sought to apply the theoretically most appropriate approach to the estimation of the trade allocation model.

2   The model of demand

We adopt the assumption traditionally made in studies of bilateral trade flows that products are differentiated by their place of production and that the prices of all supplies can be treated as given over the ranges of variation of relevance to this type of exercise. However, in contrast to common practice we do not impose separability between imports and home supplies. The restrictiveness of such an approach has been highlighted by, and its empirical validity rejected by, Winters (1984) and Brenton (1989). The cost of rejecting separability, however, is that non-separable models require the collection of data on domestic sales and their prices – data which are less plentiful than those on imports and which consequently severely restrict the level of disaggregation of the exercise we can conduct.

Since one of the principal aims of the project is to provide a set of estimated parameters for use in other simulation models we specify relationships for the purpose of obtaining 'plausible' estimates of price elasticities rather than for a general exploration of price responses. Ideally, estimates of such parameters should be derived from the theoretically most appropriate approach to the estimation of the trade allocation model. Hence we apply a general but well-specified model of demand – the Almost Ideal Demand System of Deaton and Muellbauer (1980). This allows the restrictions on behaviour suggested by consumer demand theory to be imposed by constraining the relevant parameter values. With regard to the plausibility issue discussed above we impose these restrictions irrespective of any evidence that the data rejects them. This ensures consistency with utility maximisation, and provides our measures of welfare change with a secure theoretical underpinning. Additionally, it conserves degrees of freedom in estimation. On the other hand, being a flexible functional form the Almost Ideal Demand System provides a second order approximation to any underlying utility function and thereby avoids imposing further undue restrictions.

The Almost Ideal Demand System is defined by

$$w_i = \alpha_i + \beta_i \log(c/P) + \sum_j \gamma_{ij} \log p_j + u_i \tag{1}$$

where

$$\log P = \alpha_0 + \sum_k \alpha_k \log p_k + 1/2 \sum_j \sum_k \gamma_{kj} \log p_k \log p_j, \tag{2}$$

and where w_i is the budget share of the ith supplier, c is total expenditure for the relevant industry, p_j the price of supplies from source j, and a_i, β_i and γ_{ij} are parameters.

Adding-up requires that

$$\sum_i \alpha_i = 1; \quad \sum_i \beta_i = \sum_i \gamma_{ij} = \sum_i u_i = 0 \tag{3}$$

which will automatically be satisfied since the budget shares sum to unity. Homogeneity will be satisfied if

$$\sum_j \gamma_{ij} = 0 \tag{4}$$

and symmetry when

$$\gamma_{ij} = \gamma_{ji} \tag{5}$$

Negativity, however, is difficult to impose parametrically since the Slutsky matrix of compensated price derivatives, defined by

$$S_{ij} = \frac{1}{w_i} \left[\gamma_{ij} + \beta_i \beta_j \log\left(\frac{c}{P}\right) - w_i \delta_{ij} + w_i w_j \right] \tag{6}$$

(where δ_{ij} is the Kronecker delta) involves data as well as parameters. Our approach to this problem is to test for negativity by checking the Slutsky matrix at all data points for positive eigenvalues, and then, if there is rejection, to impose a series of increasingly restrictive conditions on the price coefficient matrix, $\Gamma = [\gamma_{ij}]$, until the Slutsky matrix becomes negative semi-definite.[2]

Our set of trade data identifies 16 individual or country group suppliers of imports (each member of the EC, Japan, North America, Comecon, Non-EC Western Europe, the NICs, the Rest of the World (ROW)). Given our limited time series of data and the large number of parameters generated by flexible functional forms we are forced to include a heirarchical element in the allocation model to allow for the geographical dimension. Brenton and Winters (1992a) discuss this issue and show that

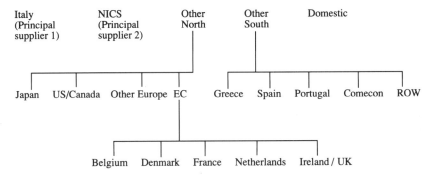

Figure 10.1 Typical hierarchy for estimation

if both precise aggregation between levels of the hierarchy and fairly general substitution possibilities at the upper level are required then the Almost Ideal Demand System for the lower-level groups must be homothetic. This can be imposed in equation (1) by setting $\beta_i = 0$, for all i.

We attempt to meet homotheticity by means of a careful grouping of suppliers according to the similarity of the income elasticities of demand that they face. Operationally we assume that the latter are associated with the suppliers' *per capita* income. Thus at the highest level of the hierarchy we allow for five sources of supply: domestic sales, the two principal suppliers of imports and two aggregate groups defined as 'rich' and 'poor'. The lower levels then define the allocation over the 'poor' group (Greece, Portugal, Spain, Comecon, NICs, ROW) and the 'rich' countries. Within the latter group we further identify the allocation between 'rich' EC suppliers. Figure 10.1 shows a typical hierarchy.

3   Estimation and extensions

Following the substitution of equation (2) into equation (1) we can estimate the Almost Ideal Demand System using maximum likelihood methods.[3] As is well known, however, the adding-up property of demand systems implies singularity of the error variance–covariance matrix, Ω. This can be treated either by dropping one of the equations or, as we prefer, by estimating $\Omega + ii'$ rather than Ω, where i is an n-dimensional vector with each element equal to $1/n^{\frac{1}{2}}$.

Previous experience suggests that this approach of freely estimating the error variance-covariance matrix can absorb much of the sample information and may even preclude convergence. Superior fit and more plausible parameter estimates may often be obtained by imposing suitable restrictions upon Ω. One possibility, due to Deaton (1975), is to set

K

$\Omega = \sigma^2(I - ii')$, where as before, i is a vector with n elements of $1/n^{\frac{1}{2}}$. This imposes homoscedasticity between shares and, when adjusted for singularity in the manner described above, reduces Ω to I and so estimation amounts to OLS with across-equation constraints. Throughout, we estimate the demand system under both forms of the variance-covariance matrix and prefer the latter restriction if it avoids convergence difficulties or materially improves the degree of fit or the extent of autocorrelation relative to the full variance-covariance matrix.

Poor estimation results, primarily in terms of low R^2s and significant amounts of autocorrelation, led us first to introduce time trends into the model, where because of adding-up the trend coefficients must sum to zero, and second to consider introducing dynamic effects into the estimating equations. Ideally, the latter would entail estimating a full autoregressive scheme on the vector of shares w, but our limited number of observations prevents this. Instead we are obliged to use the rather restrictive approach of adding the term $\lambda L w_i$ to each equation, where L is the lag operator and the dynamic parameter, λ, is common to all suppliers. There is no position intermediate to full autoregression or this common parameter form which preserves adding-up.[4]

4   The '1992' experiments

The hierarchies for estimation vary between industries according to the principal import suppliers. In analysing the implications of our results for '1992', on the other hand, we concentrate on a country breakdown which is consistent across industries. For each of two hypothetical experiments which attempt to capture the effects of '1992' on prices we calculate:

(1)   The proportionate changes in the volume of sales from:
    domestic suppliers – DOM
    EC-North (excluding the home country) – ECN
    EC-South (Greece, Portugal and Spain) – ECS
    Other Industrial Countries – OICS
    The Newly Industrialised Countries – NICS
    Rest of the World – ROW.
(2)   The compensating variation of the price changes.

The two experiments reflect conservative estimates of the effects of '1992'. First we consider

    (a) price of intra-EC imports   – 2.5%
        price of extra-EC imports   – 1%

The reduction of 2.5 per cent in the costs of intra-EC trade derives from Pelkmans and Winters (1988); it is crude, but has not, so far as we are aware, been bettered except for specific cases. The simultaneous reduction of 1 per cent in the costs of extra-EC imports reflects the fact that several '1992' measures benefit third-country suppliers – for example, freer physical movement within the EC and the harmonisation of standards. Second the case above is supplemented by a 2.5 per cent cost reduction within the EC due, perhaps, to the reduction of X-inefficiency or increased economies of scale. Thus,

    (b) price of domestic supplies   − 2.5%
           price of intra-EC imports   − 5%
           price of extra-EC imports   − 1%

All our exercises are partial equilibrium, taking total expenditure on the product concerned as exogenous. Given the level of disaggregation, this is not inappropriate. It does, however, imply that our estimated trade responses will be smaller than the expected actual responses, since any growth of income deriving from '1992' will further affect demand via each product's income elasticity. In both of our hypothetical cases the changes due to '1992' are estimated relative to a base year of 1987, the final year of our sample. It must be noted that significant changes in prices or expenditure shares between 1987 and 1992 would render our summary results misleading.

5   The data

To estimate the trade allocation model we require data on the value and price of imports and domestic sales (domestic production *less* exports). Within the constraint of having an acceptable number of observations we seek to apply the model to the most detailed industry data available. Trade data can be readily obtained at a highly disaggregated level, so that the level of specificity of the product is determined by the availability of domestic production and price data. For this study the longest available time series of detailed production values for the large EC countries was that according to the 4-digit level of the International Standard Industrial Classification (ISIC). These data have been collected by the OECD and cover the period 1970–85. Data according to the more detailed 3-digit level of the NACE classification of the EC are available only from 1975. We use the OECD data but to increase the number of observations we convert NACE 3-digit data for 1986 and 1987 to the ISIC 4-digit industries.

The price of imports is generally not available on a bilateral basis nor at disaggregate commodity levels, and so in common with previous studies we use unit values (value per tonne) to proxy the price of traded goods. We thus require both the value and volume of imports from each major source for the period 1970–87. We have obtained import data, again from the OECD, for each source, together with export data for the domestic country, at the 5-digit level of the Standard International Trade Classification (SITC). The data were already converted from Revision 2 to Revision 1 of the SITC by the OECD; the data were then converted from the commodity classification (SITC) to the industry classification (ISIC) using a detailed conversion table provided by the OECD. Prior to aggregation we incorporate tariffs into the import value data using data published by the EC.[5]

The volume of domestic production is not available so that we are unable to use unit values to proxy domestic prices. We are thus forced to use producer and wholesale prices. For West Germany detailed wholesale prices are available for our sample period, but their reclassification from the West German Commodity Classification for Production Statistics (GP) to the ISIC is roundabout, via the West German SYPRO and then the NACE, and in a few cases the concordance is only approximate. For Italy, producer prices according to the NACE classification were provided by the Italian Statistical Office (ISTAT) and converted to the ISIC.

6   Results from applying the Almost Ideal Demand System

A broad summary of the results for applying the Almost Ideal Demand System to West German 4-digit data is presented in Brenton and Winters (1992b). Table 10.1 provides a very simple overview of the principal features of those results. In general the uncompensated own-price elasticities were clustered about unity with a tendency for the elasticities for domestic sales to be slightly in excess of 1 whilst the price responsiveness of imports was on average (across industries) a little lower. There was, however, a more marked difference in expenditure elasticities between imports and domestic supplies, with most imports being necessities (a few were inferior), while products supplied domestically in West Germany were luxuries.[6] As Brenton and Winters (1992b) note, the final estimating equations are often characterised by the presence of significant trend effects and dynamic adjustment. Despite the latter, significant autocorrelation remained a problem for the majority of estimated share equations at the upper level of the hierarchy. In addition, to achieve negativity it was often found necessary to impose the most extreme constraint upon the price parameter matrix, that is $\Gamma = 0$.

The implications of these parameter estimates are shown in our simulations of '1992'. In both the exercises the changes due to '1992' are estimated relative to a base year of 1987, the last year of our sample. Table 10.1 shows the change in quantity for each of our identified suppliers

Table 10.1. *Summary of results from Almost Ideal Demand System applied to 70 West German manufacturing industries*

1 Uncompensated own-price elasticity averaged across industries and suppliers of imports

	Intra-EC suppliers	Extra-EC suppliers	Domestic supplies
	0.835	0.969	1.061
	(0.317)*	(0.347)	(0.250)

2 Proportion of the total number of price elasticities falling in the relevant range

$0 < e < 1$	77	61	23
$1 < e < 2$	23	37	77
$2 < e$	0	2	0

3 Expenditure elasticities averaged across industries and all suppliers of imports

	Imports	Domestic
	0.334	1.368
	(0.968)	(0.554)

4 Proportion of the total number of expenditure elasticities falling in the relevant range

$e < 1$	85	13
$1 < e$	15	87

5 1992 experiments: average change in quantity (income for cv)

	ECN	ECS	OICS	NICS	ROW	DOM	CV
Ex. (a)	1.99	2.34	0.58	0.89	0.75	0.45	− 0.71
Ex. (b)	3.13	4.37	− 0.80	− 0.33	− 0.44	3.49	− 2.73

* The numbers in brackets are standard deviations.

again averaged across industries. For exercise (a), despite an adverse relative price change, the quantity of domestic sales actually increases due to the strength of the income effect. With the price of the major supplier (domestic) unchanged the effect on welfare is relatively modest – 0.7 per

Table 10.2. *Summary of results from Almost Ideal Demand System applied to 15 Italian manufacturing industries*

1 Uncompensated own-price elasticity averaged across industries and suppliers of imports

	Intra-EC suppliers	Extra-EC suppliers	Domestic supplies
	0.943	0.967	1.101
	(0.329)	(0.502)	(0.141)

2 Proportion of the total number of price elasticities falling in the relevant range

$0 < e < 1$	66	53	13
$1 < e < 2$	33	40	87
$2 < e$	0	7	0

3 Expenditure elasticities averaged across industries and all suppliers of imports

	Imports	Domestic
	0.419	1.108
	(1.230)	(0.122)

4 Proportion of the total number of expenditure elasticities falling in the relevant range

$e < 1$	80	7
$1 < e$	20	93

5 1992 experiments: average change in quantity (income for cv)

	ECN	ECS	OICS	NICS	ROW	DOM	CV
Ex. (a)	2.32	1.65	1.58	0.45	1.02	0.02	− 0.47
Ex. (b)	3.82	2.13	0.20	− 0.38	− 0.04	2.84	− 2.68

cent of base year sales. Under exercise (b), domestic together with intra-EC suppliers experience an improvement in competitiveness, and as a result there is a decline in sales for countries in the rest of the world. The welfare effect is now much larger, on average 2.7 per cent.

Table 10.2 shows the summary results from applying the Almost Ideal

Demand System to data for 15 Italian industries (the actual industries chosen are shown in the Appendix on p. 281). Although we cannot make too much of averages from such a small sample, these results suggest similar conclusions to those from using the West German data; estimated responsiveness to changes in prices is low and domestically supplied products tend to be treated as luxuries and imports as necessities.

7   An alternative demand system

Despite their theoretical attractions, flexible functional forms can be very demanding of the data. Hence we now use a more restrictive functional form, the CES model, to assess the robustness of the Almost Ideal Demand System results. It might be noted that it is the CES model which is most commonly employed in simulation models.

CES functions are highly restrictive: being separable and linearly homogeneous they allow for only limited substitution possibilities and impose unitary expenditure elasticities. However, previous experience suggests that by concentrating all price responses into the estimation of a single parameter, the CES model may produce better defined results from noisy data sets such as those used in this study.

The CES demand equations are derived from a sub-utility function defined by

$$U = \left[\sum_{i=1}^{n} \alpha_i q_i^{\delta} \right]^{1/\delta} \tag{7}$$

which is maximised subject to

$$C = \sum_{i=1}^{n} p_i q_i$$

where U is the sub-utility level, q_i is the quantity purchased from the ith supplier of the good and α and δ are parameters. Standard manipulations produce the demand functions

$$q_i = \alpha^{\sigma} \left(\frac{p_i}{P^*} \right)^{\sigma} U \tag{8}$$

where $\sigma \equiv -1/(1 + \delta) < 0$

and $P^* = \left[\sum_j a_i^{-\sigma} p_i^{(1+\sigma)} \right]^{1/(1+\sigma)}$

σ being the elasticity of substitution. Following Hickman and Lau (1973) we obtain our basic estimating equations as

$$s_i = a_i p_i^{\sigma} P^{-1} + \epsilon_i \tag{9}$$

where $a_i = \alpha_i^{-\sigma}$,

$$s_i = q_i / \sum_{j=1''}^{n} qj,$$

$$P = \sum_{j=1}^{n} a_j p_j^{\sigma}$$

As with the Almost Ideal Demand System we allow for dynamic adjustment and for trends. The dynamic adjustment is handled in the same way as previously by estimating a common parameter on the lagged dependent variable. With regard to trends we allow the share parameters, a_i to evolve through time such that

$$a_{jt} = a_j^0 \exp(\sigma \gamma_j t) \approx a_j^0 [1 + \sigma \gamma_j t] \tag{10}$$

where t is set to zero in the base year and adding-up requires that $\Sigma_j a_j^0 \gamma_j = 0$. The dynamic parameter and the trend effects are excluded if they are not (jointly for the trends) statistically significant. Finally, the same considerations of the variance-covariance matrix as discussed above apply to the estimation of the CES. Estimation is thus undertaken with both a restricted and free variance-covariance matrix.

We apply the CES model to the sub-set of 15 manufacturing industries using both West German and Italian data and using the same hierarchy as used before with the Almost Ideal Demand System. Prices are passed to higher levels using the correct CES aggregator

$$p = \left[\sum_j a_j p_j^{(1+\sigma)} \right]^{1/(1+\sigma)} \tag{11}$$

where the a_j may vary through time.

In general the explanatory power of the CES model is high, with more than 65 per cent of the equations estimated at the upper level of the hierarchy having R^2s in excess of 0.8, and 45 per cent exhibiting an R^2 greater than 0.9. The results also show, however, the prevalence of autocorrelation, even after allowing for dynamic adjustment. Approximately 70 per cent of the estimated equations have significant values of the Lagrange Multiplier test statistic at the 10 per cent level and over 90 per cent of the equations have significant autocorrelation at the 5 per cent level.

The first column of Table 10A.1, in the Appendix, presents the estimated elasticities of substitution for West Germany and Italy for each of the 15 industries together with its associated standard error. Most of the estimates are very well defined and the majority lie in the range between -0.5 and -1.5.[7] Only one of the estimated elasticities is greater than 2 in absolute magnitude.

Table 10.3. *Summary of results from CES Demand System applied to 15 West German and Italian manufacturing industries*

1 Uncompensated own-price elasticity averaged across industries and suppliers of imports

	Intra-EC suppliers	Extra-EC suppliers	Domestic supplies
Germany	1.009	1.027	0.945
	(0.416)	(0.452)	(0.248)
Italy	1.076	1.026	1.170
	(0.365)	(0.361)	(0.579)

2 1992 experiments: average change in quantity (income for cv)

	ECN	ECS	OICS	NICS	ROW	DOM	CV
Germany							
Ex. (a)	1.81	1.27	0.21	0.22	0.24	− 0.68	− 0.75
Ex. (b)	2.48	1.70	− 1.49	− 0.99	− 1.71	− 0.22	− 2.68
Italy							
Ex. (a)	2.02	1.67	0.35	0.20	0.27	− 0.92	− 0.69
Ex. (b)	2.57	2.30	− 2.07	− 0.85	− 1.94	− 0.36	− 2.84

These relatively low values for the elasticity of substitution imply small price elasticities. Table 10.3 summarises, as averages across industries, the values of the price elasticities derived from the CES model. For each of the broad groups of suppliers for both the West German and Italian markets the average value of the price elasticity is very close to unity.

The implications of these results in terms of the estimated effects of '1992' are shown in the second part of Table 10.3. For exercise (a), all suppliers of imports increase their quantities at the expense of domestic suppliers. Under exercise (b), domestic suppliers still suffer a decline, albeit smaller, in the quantity of their sales, but there is now some trade diversion from non-EC suppliers of imports. The estimated effect on welfare is very similar to that predicted using the results from the Almost Ideal Demand System – approximately 0.7 per cent of base sales for exercise (a) and 2.8 per cent for exercise (b).

There are, however, well-known reasons why our estimates may be biased – see, for example, Orcutt (1950). Amongst these is the assumption that prices are exogenous. In an attempt to illustrate any possible bias from failure to take account of simultaneity between prices and quantities we undertook instrumental estimation at all levels of the hierarchy.[8]

The estimates of the elasticities of substitution from the instrumental exercise are presented in the second column of Table 10A.1, in the Appendix (blank entries reflect failure to achieve satisfactory convergence), and show no tendency for systematic increase over the previous estimates. This is despite the change in the method of estimation leading to important changes in the nature of the demand system. In particular, significant time trends are far less prevalent under instrumental estimation. For example, at the highest level of the hierarchy trends were jointly significant for 25 of the 30 initially estimated CES demand systems. This number declines to 16 when instrumental estimation is used.

Finally in an attempt to reduce the extent of autocorrelation in the estimated share equations, and so improve the efficiency of the estimates, we applied a first differenced form of the CES model at each level of the hierarchy, whereby

$$\Delta s_i = a_i \left[\frac{p_{it}^{\sigma}}{P_t} - \frac{p_{it-1}^{\sigma}}{P_{t-1}} \right] + u_i \tag{12}$$

and where a_i are again allowed to vary through time if the trend coefficients are significant. The resulting estimates of the elasticity of substitution are shown in the third column of Table 10A.1, in the Appendix. There is a slight tendency for some of the elasticities to be greater in magnitude than those obtained from the previous CES estimates, although these changes are not sufficient to alter the general tenor of our results. However, although some of the autocorrelation is removed, it is significant in less than 50 per cent of the estimated equations, the explanatory power of the first differenced model is very low. Only 37 per cent of the equations have R^2 values in excess of 0.3. In addition the estimated point elasticities are in general not as well defined.

The results from estimating the CES model thus suggest that the magnitude of the price elasticity of demand is not sensitive to our choice of functional form for the demand equation. Relatively low values for the elasticity of substitution are consistently found, regardless of whether the model is estimated in levels or differenced form or if instrumental variables' techniques are used. There is, of course, a wide range of alternative demand systems that could be investigated. However, we have applied both a flexible functional form and a system which imposes much structure upon the data, so we conjecture that the use of intermediate demand systems, semi-flexible functional forms, would not lead to a radical overhaul of the basic features of these results.

8   Implications and conclusions

There are plainly a number of further estimation exercises which we could conduct on these data, and it is possible that they would change the flavour of the results significantly. However, two studies applying different data and using slightly differing methodologies produce similar results to those found here. Lachler (1985) uses simple linear functional forms to estimate the elasticity of substitution between domestic supplies and aggregate imports in West Germany. Estimation is undertaken for 23 industrial sectors using import price indices rather than the unit values used here. The average elasticity from the most restrictive model is 1.2.

Reinert and Sheills (1991) estimate CES demand systems for the allocation of US expenditure over domestic goods and imports from Mexico, Canada and ROW. Of the 77 sectors analysed the elasticity of substitution exceeded 2 in magnitude in only 8 cases. The unweighted average elasticity across sectors was 1.49. The use of a simple Cobb–Douglas price aggregator and adjustment for simultaneity and serial correlation did not change the nature of the estimates.

Thus all the evidence we have collected so far is pushing us towards the conclusion that international trade flows are less price sensitive than has been presumed over recent years – in particular, less sensitive than assumed in most exercises on '1992'. If this turns out to be the case in the final analysis, it will have significant consequences for the way in which the implications of '1992' are discussed.

Most significantly, lower price elasticities imply that the removal of price-defined distortions will have much less effect on trade flows than previously assumed. Hence reducing border formalities, for example, will have smaller direct effects and, hence, indirect effects as well. This suggests that both the internal and external trade effects of '1992' may be smaller than forecast. On the other hand, where trade frictions are defined in terms of quantities – e.g. in public procurement, in which there are very tight implicit quotas, or Article 115 – lower elasticities imply greater effects – that is, larger price and rent effects for a given quantitative change.

The distinction that should be drawn here is less one of how the barrier is legally defined and operated (if it is at all), but of how economists choose to measure its effects. For example, by comparing a restricted with an unrestricted market, one might argue that an Article 115 action has prevented imports in the former from growing by x per cent, or alternatively that it has driven the prices of imports up by y per cent. In the first instance the implied price change would be (x/ϵ) per cent, where ϵ is the elasticity of demand, and the estimated rent and deadweight loss (x/ϵ) per cent and $(x^2/2\epsilon)$ per cent of the initial value. In the alternative case the two estimated losses would be y per cent and $\frac{1}{2}y^2\epsilon$ per cent. Although we tend to think in terms of price wedges, these are quite frequently calculated by applying an assumed elasticity to an estimated quantity effect – e.g. it is assumed that the restriction reduces the imported market share from a per cent to b per cent. Any uncertainty about the elasticity is immediately transferred to these wedges.

If we are right about the elasticities and a significant number of barriers are defined on quantities, it follows that the important dimension of '1992' for the rest of the world is not so much its effects on the volume of trade but those on price. That is, reducing the assumed elasticities will, if anything, reduce estimates of trade diversion (and allied effects) but increase those of rent transfers forgone. Relatedly, if rents to QRs are larger than anticipated, further research on who receives them – exporters (as is usually assumed), consumers (as in Winters and Brenton, 1991, where a VER induces rationing) or no-one (if there is rent-seeking) – should receive a higher priority.

Lower estimates of price elasticities mean that substantial changes in relative prices would be necessary to generate significant changes in trade shares. Since the data suggest, however, that changes in shares are not associated with major terms of trade disturbances our results suggest the need for an alternative explanation – possibly along the lines of Krugman (1989) or Oliveira-Martins and Toujas-Bernate (1992). This in turn complicates predictions of the effects of '1992', for it becomes necessary to plot how the associated policy changes impact on factors determining non-price competitiveness. An implication of this is that more than just removing intra-EC trade barriers will be necessary to overturn the strong domestic-share biases observed in our current data.

Appendix

Table 10.A1: Estimates of the elasticity of substitution

	Basic CES	Instrumental estimate	Differenced model
ISIC 3140 – Tobacco manufactures			
Italy	− 0.804 (0.161)	− 1.661 (0.842)	− 1.197 (0.258)
Germany	− 0.692 (0.090)	− 0.608 (0.201)	− 1.137 (0.286)
ISIC 3240 – Manufacture of footwear			
Italy	− 0.791 (0.122)	− 0.800 (0.255)	− 1.129 (0.856)
Germany	− 1.136 (0.200)	− 0.368 (0.068)	− 0.348 (0.083)
ISIC 3320 – Manufacture of furniture & fixtures, except of metal			
Italy	− 0.690 (0.055)	− 0.855 (0.196)	− 2.149 (0.315)
Germany	− 1.911 (0.309)	− 5.277 (1.800)	− 1.834 (2.133)
ISIC 3411 – Manufacture of pulp, paper & paperboard			
Italy	− 0.818 (0.103)	− 0.883 (0.091)	− 1.322 (0.200)
Germany	− 0.372 (0.124)	− 0.236 (0.111)	− 2.890 (0.420)
ISIC 355 (3551 + 3559) – Tyre & tube industries & rubber prod.			
Italy	− 0.997 (0.126)	− 0.430 (0.137)	− 1.822 (0.322)
Germany	− 1.610 (0.148)	− 1.722 (0.226)	− 0.583 (0.076)
ISIC 3620 – Manufacture of glass & glass products			
Italy	− 0.692 (0.059)	− 1.064 (0.133)	− 0.812 (0.259)

	Basic CES	Instrumental estimate	Differenced model
Germany	− 0.607	− 0.390	− 0.528
	(0.052)	(0.106)	(0.064)

ISIC 3692 – Manufacture of cement, lime & plaster

	Basic CES	Instrumental estimate	Differenced model
Italy	− 0.683	− 0.703	− 2.474
	(0.108)	(0.153)	(0.340)
Germany	− 0.347	− 0.628	− 1.161
	(0.080)	(1.767)	(0.945)

ISIC 3811 – Manufacture of cutlery, hand tools & general hardware

	Basic CES	Instrumental estimate	Differenced model
Italy	− 0.951	− 0.996	− 1.131
	(0.101)	(0.158)	(0.228)
Germany	− 0.772	− 1.440	− 0.635
	(0.185)	(0.439)	(0.099)

ISIC 3824 – Manufacture of special ind. mach. & equipment . . .

	Basic CES	Instrumental estimate	Differenced model
Italy	− 0.710	− 0.719	− 0.902
	(0.105)	(0.285)	(0.203)
Germany	− 1.129	− 0.329	− 0.599
	(0.179)	(0.126)	(0.126)

ISIC 3825 – Manufacture of office, computing & accounting mach.

	Basic CES	Instrumental estimate	Differenced model
Italy	− 1.478	− 0.776	− 0.941
	(0.335)	(0.154)	(0.134)
Germany	− 1.412	− 0.561	− 1.028
	(0.381)	(0.312)	(0.113)

ISIC 3832 – Manufacture of radio, television . . .

	Basic CES	Instrumental estimate	Differenced model
Italy	− 0.935	− 0.675	− 1.122
	(0.050)	(0.122)	(0.121)
Germany	− 1.198	− 2.606	− 0.700
	(0.199)	(0.951)	(0.131)

ISIC 3833 – Manufacture of elec. appliances & housewares

	Basic CES	Instrumental estimate	Differenced model
Italy	− 1.241	− 1.163	− 1.550
	(0.104)	(0.184)	(0.331)

	Basic CES	Instrumental estimate	Differenced model
Germany	− 0.951	− 0.531	− 0.733
	(0.061)	(0.200)	(0.184)

ISIC 3843 – Manufacture of motor vehicles

Italy	− 1.496	− 1.403	− 1.711
	(0.180)	(0.429)	(0.179)
Germany	− 1.599		
	(0.619)		

ISIC 3844 – Manufacture of motorcycles & bicycles

Italy	− 1.640	− 0.930	− 0.933
	(0.456)	(0.238)	(0.136)
Germany	− 0.956	− 0.945	− 1.084
	(0.147)	(0.206)	(0.295)

ISIC 3851 – Manufacture of professional, scientific . . . equipment n.e.s.

Italy	− 3.613	− 0.712	− 1.384
	(1.296)	(0.124)	(0.106)
Germany	− 0.670	− 0.349	− 0.647
	(0.153)	(0.092)	(0.264)

NOTES

This chapter results from research on the ESRC-funded project 'The Implications of "1992" for the International Trade Relations of the EC' (grant no. R00023 1932). We are grateful to Riccardo Faini and to participants of both the CEPR programme and the International Economics Study Group for comments and to Maureen Hyde for typing.
1 Stern *et al.* (1976) provide a compendium of such elasticities.
2 The restrictions, which are described in more detail in Brenton and Winters (1992a) are:
  (A) $\Gamma = -FF'$ where F is a lower triangular matrix of dimension $(n-1)*(n-1)$
  (B) $\Gamma = (g'\,i)^{-1}gg' - \hat{g}$ where g is a $(n \times 1)$ vector of coefficients
  (C) as (B) but with $g = \eta w$ where w is a vector of budget shares and η a parameter
  (D) as (C), but with $\eta = 1$
  (E) $\Gamma = 0$.
3 All equations are estimated by NLFIML – see Deaton (1981).
4 Experimentation with a first differenced version of the Almost Ideal Demand System did not prove a successful solution to these problems.
5 Further details are available in Brenton and Winters (1992a).
6 The price elasticities were derived by simulating the effect of a 1 per cent change

in the prices charged by suppliers in each broad group (intra-EC, extra-EC and domestic), measuring responses at all levels of the hierarchy. The expenditure elasticities are derived directly from the estimated parameters at the highest level of the hierarchy due to homotheticity at lower levels.

7 Note, however, that by analogy with the linear model autocorrelation means that the estimated standard errors are downward biased.

8 The instruments used for the domestic price were an index of industrial production, the producer price for industrial production, an aggregate import price index, and a time trend. The same instruments were used for import prices but with the exporters' aggregate export price index substituted for the import price index. Comecon prices were not instrumented due both to the paucity of data and to the nature of supply conditions in those countries. The data were obtained from *International Financial Statistics* (IFS) and the World Bank data base. For ROW we use the IFS aggregates 'developing countries' where available and 'non-oil developing countries' otherwise and use GDP at constant prices and a GDP deflator instead of the index of industrial production and its associated price index, which were unavailable. These variables also had to be used for Hong Kong. Taiwanese data were collected from the *Taiwan Statistical Data Book*.

REFERENCES

Armington, P.S. (1969) 'A theory of demand for products distinguished by place of production', *IMF Staff Papers*, **16**, pp. 159–76.

Brenton, P.A. (1989) 'The allocation approach to trade modelling: some tests of separability between imports and domestic production and between different imported commodity groups', *Weltwirtschaftliches Archiv*, **125**, pp. 230–51.

Brenton, P.A. and L.A. Winters (1992a) 'Estimating trade functions for exploring 1992', *Discussion Paper*, **717**, London: CEPR.

(1992b) 'Estimating the international trade effects of "1992": West Germany', *Journal of Common Market Studies*, **30(2)** (June).

European Communities (CEC) (1988) 'The economics of 1992', *The European Economy*, **35** (March) Brussels: European Commission.

Deaton, A. (1975) *Models and Projections of Demand in Post-War Britain*, London: Chapman & Hall.

(1981) 'NLFIML – A program for the estimation of the parameters of non-linear relationships', University of Bristol, mimeo.

Deaton, A. and J. Muellbauer (1980) 'An Almost Ideal Demand System', *American Economic Review*, **70**, pp. 312–26.

Hickman, B.G. and L.J. Lau (1973) 'Elasticities of substitution and export demands in a world trade model', *European Economic Review*, **4**, pp. 347–80.

Krugman, P. (1989) 'Differences in income elasticities and trends in real exchange rates', *European Economic Review*, **33**, pp. 1031–54.

Lachler, U. (1985) 'The elasticity of substitution between imported and domestically produced goods in Germany', *Weltwirtschaftliches Archiv*, **121**, pp. 74–96.

Oliveira-Martins, J. and J. Toujas-Bernate (1992) 'Macroeconomic import functions with imperfect competition: an application to EC trade', Chapter 9 in this volume.

Orcutt, G.H. (1950) 'Measurement of price elasticities in international trade', *Review of Economics and Statistics*, **32**, pp. 117–32.

Pelkmans, J. and L.A. Winters (1988) *Europe's Domestic Market, Chatham House Paper*, **43**, London: Royal Institute for International Affairs.

Reinert, K.A. and C.R. Sheills (1991) 'Trade substitution elasticities for analysis of a North American free trade area', US International Trade Commission, Research Division, *Working Paper*, **91–01–B**.

Stern, R.M., J. Francis and B. Schumacher (1976) *Price Elasticities in International Trade: An Annotated Bibliography*, Toronto: Macmillan.

Winters, L.A. (1984) 'Separability and the specification of foreign trade functions', *Journal of International Economics*, **17**, pp. 239–63.

Winters, L.A. and P.A. Brenton (1991) 'Quantifying the economic effects of non-tariff barriers: the case of UK footwear', *Kyklos*, **44**, pp. 71–92.

Discussion

RICCARDO FAINI

Much of the (static) effects of the completion of the European internal market will depend on the pattern and size of price responses of trade flows. Unfortunately, until now, researchers endeavouring to build computable general equilibrium models have found little econometric evidence on which to rely to select the parameter values to be used in their models. Most often, they had to resort to unappealing guesses. Chapter 10 provides much needed guidance to those applied economists in search of reliable estimates of price and income elasticities of trade flows at a disaggregated level. It is a useful and stimulating chapter; not only does it fill a gap in the empirical trade literature but, in doing so, it also endows future research with a valuable set of comprehensive and consistent data. Most crucially, it relies throughout on a well-defined choice-theoretic framework, which facilitates interpretation of the results. Finally, it advances existing contributions by not making the standard assumption of separability between home goods and imports. Winters himself, in (1984), found little support for this assumption at an aggregate level.[1] The chapter's main results can be summarised as follows. First, price elasticities are lower than generally assumed. As a result, existing estimates may exaggerate the impact of the completion of the internal market. Second, expenditure elasticities for imported goods are typically lower than 1 and substantially smaller than the corresponding elasticities for home goods.

Most of the chapter's discussion focuses on the first result; in what follows, we shall draw at length on some possible, and somewhat surprising, explanations of the second.

Let us first consider, however, the finding about price elasticities. The chapter here revives a long-standing controversy in the empirical trade literature by arguing, albeit with some reservations, that price elasticities are lower than traditionally assumed and, in the authors' results, clustered around 1. There are of course several reasons why estimates of price elasticities may be subject to a downward bias. Suppose, for instance, that the import price is measured with error and therefore correlated with the stochastic term (recall that, in the chapter, import prices are proxied by unit values, a notoriously unreliable measure of trade prices). This would by itself bias the price elasticity estimate toward 0. Furthermore, if an error-ridden price measure is used both as an explanatory variable and as a deflator of the dependent variable (which is indeed the case in the chapter), then the price coefficient would be biased toward -1 (Goldstein and Khan, 1985). It would not be altogether surprising, therefore, to find that the price elasticities' estimates are not far away from 1. The authors argue, however, that controlling for the most obvious source of endogeneity (i.e. the prices of domestic and imported goods) does not affect the results.

The finding about expenditure elasticities is more puzzling. Taken literally, the result that such elasticities are lower than 1 for imported goods would imply declining import penetration. Does this reflect some actual trend in the data? Apparently not, as shown, for instance, in Table D10.1, where import penetration ratios for Italy (one of the two countries analysed in the chapter) are found to be steadily increasing. Similar trends for the major EC economies are found by Neven and Röller (1991). Neither can the result be predicated on some peculiar features of the model's specification. On the contrary, it is easy to show that in the AIDS model, income elasticities are negatively related to expenditure shares. We would then expect that the commodities with the relatively larger expenditure share (i.e. home goods) would display lower rather than higher expenditure elasticities. A more palatable hypothesis would attribute the result to the effect of trade policies. As a matter of fact, trade policies in the EC have been characterised by growing protectionism *vis-à-vis* the rest of the world. This by itself would imply that domestic prices of imported goods have risen faster than the corresponding import prices.[2] The authors, however, observe only import prices. Their estimates would therefore tend to attribute the effect of the faster growing domestic price of imports to lower expenditure elasticities. It would be interesting in this respect to check whether those commodities which have been subject to

Table D10.1. *Import penetration ratios in Italy*

	1980	1987
Foodstuffs	15.8	18.7
Textiles	12.8	20.3
Clothing	5.3	9.7
Footwear	2.8	13.7
Engineering	20.5	27.9
Chemicals	35.5	46.6

Source: ICE, *Rapporto sul Commercio Estero*, Rome (1991).

restrictive trade practices show lower import elasticities. But even protection may represent, at best, only a partial explanation. Indeed, it cannot account for the general pattern, including the fact that expenditure elasticities for EC imports, which have certainly not been subject to increasing protectionism in Germany and Italy, also appear to be lower. We are therefore left with one main explanation for the expenditure elasticities' puzzle, i.e. the econometric specification. The authors acknowledge that the statistical properties of their estimates were somewhat less than satisfactory and that they were forced, as a result, to introduce both a time trend and a (fairly restrictive) partial-adjustment mechanism in the equations. Unfortunately, both of these expedients are difficult to justify from a theoretical point of view and make the interpretation of the results particularly arduous. Yet, they may help to reconcile the pattern of expenditure elasticities with the stylised fact of rising import penetration. In particular, it would be natural to expect that the coefficient on the time trend would typically be positive for imported commodities and negative for home goods. Even so, the question would remain of why a time trend rather than expenditure captures the fact of rising import ratios. Overall, it seems fair to conclude that our understanding of both the pattern and the determinants of trade elasticities is still somewhat limited. This chapter advances, considerably, our knowledge of this issue, but also shows that there is much work left to be done.

NOTES

1 Notice, though, that rejecting (weak) separability at an aggregate level does not necessarily imply that separability will not hold at a disaggregated level. It is indeed possible that consumers follow a three-stage budgeting process where they first allocate total expenditure among different categories, then make a choice between imports and home goods and finally distribute imports of a given category among the various sources of foreign supply.

2 The only exception would be when the trade restrictions are administered by the exporting country and perfectly competitive conditions prevail. Notice, though, that existing evidence shows that, even for VERs, the exporting country is able to retain only a part of the quota's rent (Erzan, Krishna and Tan, 1991), with the remaining part being reflected in the gap between domestic and landed price of imports.

REFERENCES

Erzan, R., K. Krishna and L.H. Tan (1991) 'Rent sharing in the Multi-Fibre Arrangement. Theory and evidence from U.S. apparel imports from Hong Kong', *PRE Working Papers*, **597**, Washington, D.C.: The World Bank.

Goldstein, M. and M. Khan (1985) 'Income and price effects in foreign trade', in R. Jones and P. Kenen (eds), *Handbook of International Economics*, Amsterdam: North-Holland.

Neven, D. and L.-H. Röller (1991) 'European integration and trade flows', *European Economic Review*, **35**, pp. 1295–1309.

Winters, L.A. (1984) 'Separability and the specification of foreign trade functions', *Journal of International Economics*, **17**, pp. 239–63.

Index